THE GUN DIGEST
BOOK OF KNIFEMAKING

**By Jack Lewis
and Roger Combs**

DBI BOOKS, INC.

About Our Cover
The four knives pictured represent the spectrum of knifemaking; from a quickly assembled folder to a professionally scrimshawed boot knife. From the left: a small boot knife by Chuck Stapel with ivory Micarta handle scrimshawed by Georgia Davenport (Gigi); a knife made by Editor Roger Combs from a House of Muzzleloading stainless steel blade blank, handle is bubinga wood; the little folder, also by Roger Combs, is from an Atlanta Cutlery kit; the Jody Samson skinning knife features fancy file work on the back of the blade and stainless steel decorative pins in the Micarta handle. **Photo by John Hanusin.**

Publisher
Sheldon Factor

Editorial Director
Jack Lewis

Production Director
Sonya Kaiser

Art Director
Gary Duck

Artists
Denise Comiskey
Kristen Bunn

Copy Editor
David Rodriguez

Production Coordinator
Pepper Federici

Photo Service
Sylvie St. Denis

Lithographic Service
Gallant Graphics

Technical Advisors
Wayne Clay
Bob Engnath
Chuck Stapel

Produced by

GALLANT CHARGER

OUTDOOR GROUP

ISBN: 0-87349-035-5   **Library of Congress Catalog Card Number: 88-51673**

CONTENTS

INTRODUCTION

When we first talked about making this book, we asked ourselves one pointed question: "Why would someone want to make a knife or read about how to do it?"

We had our own thoughts, of course, but since both of us have a long-term interest in cutlery, custom knives and the makers, we felt that our views were somewhat prejudicial. So, at a knife show, we asked a number of custom knife-makers why they had started making knives. The expanded answers by some are contained in this book's first chapter. The majority agreed that they had made their first knives on a hobby basis, because, "I had need for a good knife and I couldn't find what I wanted commercially. I made my own." From that beginning, hundreds of careers in full-time custom knifemaking have originated.

Most of these makers, now professionals, had little in the way of information relative to steels, grinding, shapes, ad infinitum, when they started. A few found professionals who were able to put them on the right path and criticize their first efforts. The majority, however, learned by doing.

In our own case, there was learning by doing, too, in preparing the material for this book. And again there were helping hands. Had it not been for sterling gents as Bob Engnath, Chuck Stapel and Wayne Clay, this book probably never would have been completed. Their help and advice is impossible to value. Let it simply be reflected in the fact that this tome was completed and we sincerely hope that you will learn as much from its pages as we did in assembling the information.

Jack Lewis   Roger Combs

Capistrano Beach, California

Above: Pat Crawford has found success as a custom knifemaker. More than money, Crawford says he gets plenty of personal satisfaction from his production.

Arkansas knifemaker Jimmy Lile, above, is often credited with influencing and guiding several of the best knifemakers, including Pat Crawford, at left.

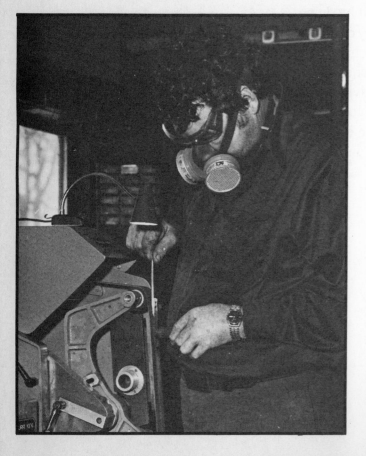

Left: Wayne Clay is another knifemaker who says he derives great personal pleasure from his art. He also earns a fair income from his work, turning out several hundred knives a year. He is a believer in safety precautions, wearing respirator and goggles.

Chapter 1

WHY MAKE YOUR OWN?

Here Is How And Why Some Of The Pros Started — Your Reasons May Match!

OKAY, SO you're looking at the first page of a book on knifemaking. Some of you probably are asking yourselves, "So why would I want to make a knife?"

For those who are either mechanically or artistically inclined, the answer probably has to do with pride of craftsmanship; you feel you may be able to make a better knife than some you've seen, selling for respectable amounts of money. Then there is the matter of challenge, as was the case with the mountain climber who was asked why he wanted to scale Mount Everest. His reply was simple: "Because it's there."

There probably are a few who have heard of the big prices that some of the recognized custom knifemakers get for their products, and they'd like to join the ranks.

Whatever the reason, the fact is that you've read this far. That means you must be interested.

But let's take a look at the thinking and a bit of the respective backgrounds of some of the leading professional custom knifemakers. You may see definite similarities between yourself and these individuals.

For example, Pat Crawford, who operates as Crawford Knives, was with a firm of certified public accountants. He read an article in the *Gun Digest* about custom knifemakers and decided to try his hand.

Today, Crawford makes knives full-time and credits the old pro, Jimmy Lile, with giving him a lot of help, maintaining his interest and inspiring him to constantly improve his work.

Crawford is not hung up on his own designs. As he puts it, "I make all kinds of knives: folders, boots, fighters, hunters, Bowies, penknives and an ever-growing number of concealment knives. I also take special customer designs on a limited basis."

The Arkansas craftsman makes from ten to twenty knives a month and some of his designs have a waiting period of up to a year. That, in custom knifemaking, is a sign of success.

"Why am I a knifemaker?" he ponders. "For the personal satisfaction I receive in being my own boss and producing the thing of beauty that I feel will stand the test of time.

"What do I like best about knifemaking? Financial reward is close to the top," the former accountant is quick to admit, but, "personal satisfaction of a customer reorder means more than the money."

Crawford responds to all custom requests, but reserves the right to accept or reject the order. "Some designs are so far off the wall," he explains, "that the price would be out of this world. I don't feel right about charging a price that, in my opinion, is out of line. My customers would resent it and I would, too. When I get orders like that, I try to get the customer to check out my standard models. Most can be modified to suit an individual need.

The craftsman also has some thoughts on the business

Texas knifemaker, Jim Pugh, realizes a comfortable income from his work, but he got started in the craft because of a layoff which forced him to change jobs.

Pugh's workshop is a model of neatness and order. He utilizes the latest in modern technology, while relying on his artistic skills to produce knives.

end of knifemaking that should be of interest to the would-be knifemaker.

"I've learned that I have to disassociate knifemaking and money," Crawford says. "One has to get far enough ahead that the knife he's working on at the moment doesn't get viewed as the family's groceries, the car payment or the mortgage. Making a knife for money that one has already spent can be a trap; that trap tends to snap closed if, for some reason, you don't sell the knife you're working on at the time!

"When I started making knives, I realized there was the possibility of going broke, no matter how much I loved the work. So I had to make certain I had enough orders to keep me busy and enough financial padding for a year. That way, I didn't have any immediate funding worries. Since then, I've found that, if my knives are good, the money situation just takes care of itself!"

Wayne Clay of Pelham, Tennessee, is a farmer, although he describes himself now as "a hobby farmer." Actually, he's a full-time knifemaker with a backlog of about six months' work.

"I came off the farm and went to the Detroit area, where I spent a couple of years in metal-finishing. I spent most of that time polishing the bumpers for Chrysler Imperials so they could be chromed." Needless to say, this polishing experience has come in handy in his custom knifemaking endeavors.

"I decided I'd had enough of the big city," he recalls, "and came back home. As a farmer, I'd learned a good deal about making do; having to make my own tools for a certain job or else repair tools and machinery on my own.

"I'd bought a couple of knives and wasn't very happy with either one of them, so I decided to make my own. I'd no sooner finished it than an old boy saw it and wanted to buy it. I sold it to him at just about the cost of materials, because I had learned enough in that first trial, building that knife with nothing but files, that I knew I could do better."

That was in 1978 and the first seventy-five knives that Clay made were fashioned with files. "After that, I discovered power equipment," he jokes.

Clay joined the Knifemakers Guild in 1982 and has never been without orders for his work since. At the moment, he has a backlog of about six months despite the fact that he estimates he completes about 350 knives a year.

"If you think making knives is a fun, romantic business, you may be overlooking an important point," Pat Crawford advises. "Making knives is enjoyable, but making them full-time is hard work. There is a big difference between hobby knifemaking and full-time knifemaking. What used to be something you liked to do in your spare time has suddenly become something you have to do to exist."

Wayne Clay agrees wholeheartedly, thinking back to his own beginning. "By the time you've turned out a knife blade of 154CM steel with nothing but a batch of files, you know you've been through a day's work."

Jim Pugh, who has built a wide-spread reputation for artistic perfection with his knives, claims he got into knifemaking through necessity.

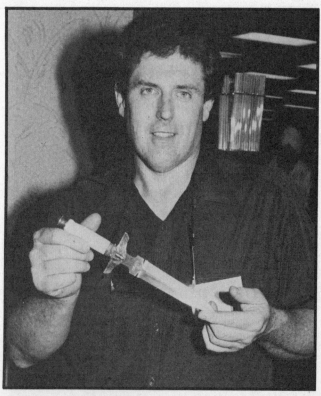

A serious auto accident injury forced Jack Crain out of his job. He approaches knifemaking as a business.

Pat Crawford's fighting knives and daggers have found a following among knife buyers. He finds he can maintain a one-year backlog to his knife orders.

"The year was 1969," he recalls, "and it was somewhat bleak." He had just been laid-off as a machinist at the Bell Helicopter Corporation. His $8000 a year paycheck—big by standards of the day — was gone and there was "no place to go, except into my twenty-foot square tin garage. With no heat or air-conditioning, that was the beginning of a nightmare as far as comfort was concerned."

But, grasping the proverbial bull by the horns, Jim Pugh began to build custom knives. Today, that garage has been replaced by a highly insulated building with central air-conditioning and heating in what he believes to be "the finest pollution-control system ever used in a custom knife-maker's shop."

Many of Pugh's originals feature an animal's head created through the lost wax means of casting. His wife, co-owner of the business located near their Azle, Texas, home, does much of the hand engraving on his knives.

"As in most new businesses," he recalls, "I had to start at the bottom. In fact, I had to look up to see the bottom. There was no one to turn to for a simple answer. I just kept working and trying not to make the same mistake twice."

Jim Pugh has made his reputation with what he terms "investor knives." These are true works of art. Today, he is making a series of miniature knives that measure only five inches in overall length. A set of four of these miniatures, featuring an eagle, an elephant, a sheep and a buffalo — one to a knife — is priced at $7500.

By his own admission, the best thing that ever happened to Jim Pugh was being laid off by Bell Helicopters.

Bob Loveless, the gent who has been credited with starting much of the current interest in custom-crafted knives, got into the business through an admitted fluke.

"At the time, I was working on a tanker for the Sun Oil Company," he recalls. "I was living on the East Coast and, one day, went into Abercrombie & Fitch in New York to buy a Randall knife.

"A rather prissy sales clerk informed me that they didn't have any Randalls in stock. Sold out. I asked how long it would take for them to special order one. I was told it would be a minimum of ninety days.

"I said to hell with that," the outspoken Loveless says, "and went back to the ship, stopping in a junk yard on the way to buy a leaf out of an old automobile spring.

"I got into the ship's machine shop and, in my spare time, turned out my first knife. A few weeks later, I was back in New York and took the knife to Abercrombie, where I showed it to the buyer. He liked it enough that he ordered three of them. It was agreed that I'd be paid $14 each for them!"

Loveless heard no more from Abercromie & Fitch. Meantime, he was sailing about the world on his oil tanker. Several months later, he stopped in at the New York City store and walked into the buyers office.

"I'm Loveless. Remember me?" was the greeting.

"I've been looking for you," the buyer declared. "I need some more knives."

"How many do you want?" Loveless asked, thinking in terms of three or four.

"I need at least a gross," was the reply.

Loveless, who admits to a ninth grade education, did some mental calculations. "That's a dozen dozen, right?"

"Right."

"How about half a gross."

The price also was adjusted upward; clear up to $20.70 per knife. Abercrombie & Fitch sold them over the counter at that time for $42. Those same knives today, are collector items. If one were lucky enough to find one, he could plan on paying $1000 to $1200 for it, according to Loveless.

"That's when I started making knives full-time," he recalls. "The business has been good to me."

Jack Crain of Dallas, Texas, was in the formica installation business, when he was badly injured in an auto accident in the early Seventies. He was told that he probably never would walk again and would be confined to a wheelchair.

"I'd been making knives all my life," he recalls. "My grandfather had taught me how to make blades out of old files. I turned out knives all through my high school days, but I could hardly give them away."

He continued to make knives as a hobby and attended a few knife and gun shows in the Dallas-Fort Worth area, selling them. But it was not until the accident that he became serious.

"Confined as I was, gave me more time to work on knives, to think about them and attempt to make them better. I wasn't going anywhere and there was no rush."

Crain, as his health improved, looked around for new business opportunities. It wasn't until his wife counted his orders one day and announced he had enough orders to keep him busy for a year that he realized he *had* a business: full-time knifemaking.

"Since then, I've taken a business approach to it," he adds. Through contacts, he has designed knives for such motion pictures as *Predator, Commando* and *War of the Worlds.* Such exposure, of course, has been an aid to his custom business.

More recently, he has joined with W.E. (Bill) Smith, a well-known knife collector, to form Crain Classic Blades, Incorporated. This company plans to introduce production versions of some of Jack Crain's more popular styles.

That should give the reader an idea of how some of the leading knifemakers got into the business — and why they began to make knives.

Each knifemaker has his own story and can give you his own reasons as to why knifemaking intrigues him. For every professional, there are dozens of custom makers who turn out a few finished blades, selling them among friends or at local knife or gun shows.

But they have their stories, too, as to how they became interested. Just as you may have your own tale to tell after you've completed that first knife.

Every knifemaker or hobbyist needs a large selection of various kinds of files. They have hundreds of uses.

As the maker scribes a line of the blade, the ever-present vise is seen bolted down to the work bench, ready for any task.

Chapter 2

BASIC HAND TOOLS

Primary and Secondary Shop Tools That Every Beginning Knifemaker Should Have

MANY OF THE BASIC tools the amateur knifemaker needs are already on hand in the shop or in the kitchen drawer. Some other essential tools probably will have to be purchased, new or used. There is a certain basic minimum number of tools with which it is possible to complete a simple knife; others might be considered more specialized and therefore put on the convenience list.

The first thing needed might be termed a bench tool, rather than a hand tool. A bench vise, either a carpenter's model or a mechanic's type may be used. If you do not already have one or the other, we recommend the purchase of the mechanic's vise as the more useful for knifemakers. To a point, when it comes to vises, bigger is better. The vise should be bolted solidly to the workbench, but there is something to be said for the heavy mass of metal with which to work.

The vise jaws must open enough to accommodate the largest blade or handle meterial with which you are likely to work; you also will be using the vise for other bench work over the years, so jaws with at least a four-inch opening would be the minimum.

An optional anvil surface at the rear will be mighty useful later and provision for a 360-degree swivel base will speed your work.

A good vise is not cheap to buy, but it almost never wears out, at least not in a single lifetime. Therefore, swap meets and garage sales are good places to look for used vises. They can be found at rummage sales and surplus outlets, too. As long as the jaws are not sprung out of line nor the jaw faces too badly scarred, a big used vise should last for years after a minor financial investment.

A much lighter-weight model which is screw-clamped temporarily to the bench or table is almost too light, but if that is all you have, it can be put to use. However, such lightweights are apt to slip or rotate under stress; your work can be ruined.

Whether or not your vise has an anvil back, the anvil tool on the bench will be used frequently. Small bench-size anvils are to be found in the same places as the vises. A short section of railroad track is an excellent anvil and can be found on the work benches of many professional custom knifemakers. A small section has enough mass to provide a solid surface for pounding, but is light enough to be moved around the work surface.

We learned a slick trick from Bob Engnath, who does beautiful scrimshaw work, as well as makes his own knives. On top of the vise jaws, Engnath drills three holes; two on the far side and one on the near side, centered between the other two. The three holes are drilled at slightly

Bob Engnath, who has ground thousands of knife blades, maintains a full shop of hand tools, all in neat order.

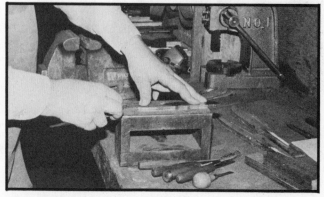

Engnath's workshop boasts at least two large bench vises, firmly bolted down. They get plenty of use!

For some work, Engnath uses a pair of smooth metal parallel jaws in shop vise to protect delicate work.

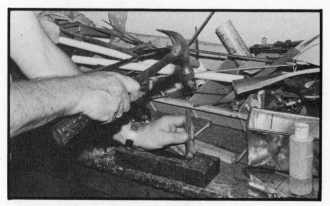

A short section steel channel serves as a special work surface and lightweight anvil during profiling.

A two-inch-deep channel may be clamped in vise jaws to provide a loose hold when straightening blades.

Three common hand tools in action: a claw hammer, a metal punch and a section of steel/anvil.

less than ninety degrees with the metal surface so that, when three short metal rods are placed in them, they will angle inward, toward each other. The rod sections should protrude from the jaw surface about three-eighths-inch and be cut or filed off parallel with the vise surface.

These three rods or buttons on the vise have several useful purposes, especially that of holding a knife blade firmly, without slippage, as the jaws are tightened. Angling them slightly inward keeps the metal component from slipping out, as pressure is applied with a drill, file or sandpaper. If you wish, the holes may be drilled slightly oversized so

the rods may be removed at any time. Drilling the holes, Engnath says, does not weaken a heavy vise.

A ball peen hammer or two must be on your essential tool list. This tool has many uses for knifemakers and handymen, but its primary function is to carry out its name: peening down pins or rivets. We have found that one small model is adequate for most tasks by knifemakers, but a second large one might be in order. Most of us have at least one such hammer in the workshop. A claw hammer can be useful in the knifemaker's shop.

To put together a standard knife kit with all the parts cut

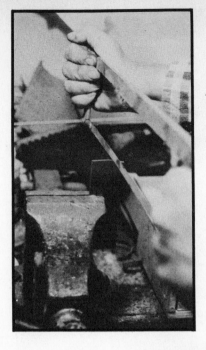

A good hacksaw will find many uses in the knifemaker's workshop. At left, a blade blank is carefully profiled.

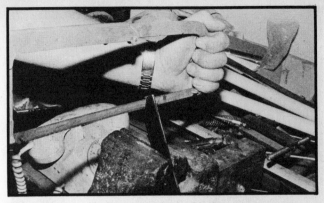

One who is skilled in the use of a hacksaw may even cut steel along a curved line, shown above.

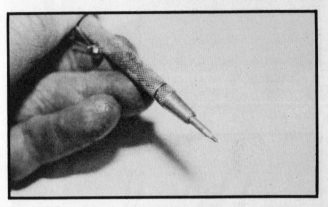

A close-up view of a metal scribe, shows a pencil-like retractable point, tipped with extremely hard carbide.

Construction is underway on a Japanese-style wood knife sheath as Bob Engnath marks the outline.

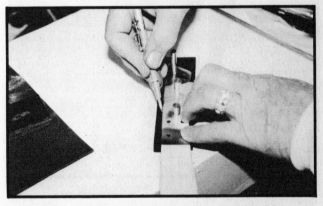

Knifemakers will use a scribe for many things. Here, we outline the tang shape on a pakkawood handle slab.

to shape will not require a saw, but as you become more advanced and wish to cut your own handle from rough stock, you will need a hacksaw. A hacksaw will also cut through softer metal, heavy pins and rivets when the need arises. If the handle shape becomes more complicated, a simple coping saw will also come in handy.

You will need several files. We suggest three mill or flat files: a small, medium and large size. A small and a medium round file, both with fine-cut teeth, will find plenty of work on hilts and when smoothing handles. For rough-shaping wood or Micarta handles, a rougher-cut rasp will be faster.

Two or three needle files will help you reach some of the tighter places you will be working. Files are tools which eventually wear out and are frequently abused in use. They may be found at garage sales and the like, but you will be money ahead in the long run, if you buy them new for your projects. They are not that expensive and, if taken care of, will last a long time. Care means keeping the file teeth clean at all times. One trick you may already know is to coat the teeth with chalk dust before using. The metal filings will stick less and those that do will clean out easier with a file brush. Always clean file teeth before and after

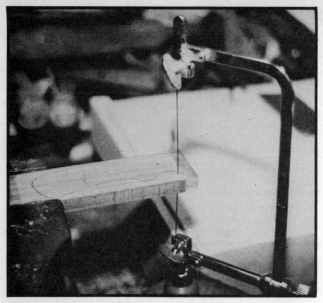
A variation of the simple coping saw is the jewelers' saw, a precision-made and more expensive hand tool.

Above: A drill press and a small file combine to reduce the diameter of a solid brass handle bolt.

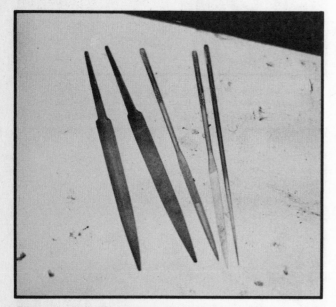
Files are available in many sizes, shapes, pitches, teeth, coarseness. These five will have special uses.

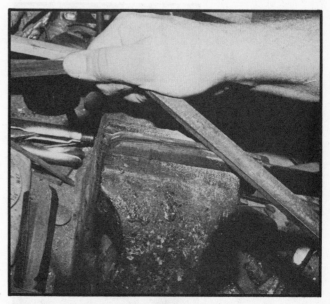
The knife handle is locked in the vise jaws as the knifemaker files down excess material around tang.

each use and do not allow them to rust.

The next indispensible-tool group includes pliers and vise grips. You will have several kinds of pliers, including those commonly called channel locks. Perhaps the most versatile are the vise grips, available in several sizes and qualities. Get the best you can afford; used specimens are serviceable as long as the jaws are not sprung. You will find use for at least two pair of them and four is not too many. Many times, the vise grips will serve in place of small clamps when clamps are not available. New vise grips and plier jaws are sharply serrated to hold the work firmly, but they will also damage soft metal and wood. Be prepared to

tape the jaws when holding tender goods.

As for wire cutters, tin snips and parallel cutters, if you have one, it may not be necessary to buy the other, but you will need something to trim off excess pin lengths while assembling handles. High-quality steel that holds the cutting edge is important when selecting any of these tools.

We mentioned clamps earlier. Most knifemakers will have more than a few of various types. Metal C-clamps, for instance, are made in many sizes, ranging from one-inch openings up to the large heavy-duty clamps with jaw openings of eight, ten or more inches. For knifemaking, four or five clamps with openings of two or three inches should be ade-

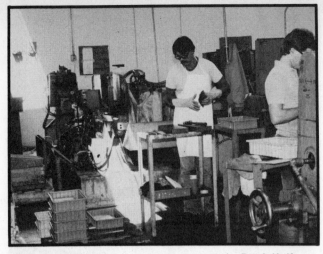
Surrounded by sophisticated power tools, Buck Knife production worker has ample use for ball peen hammer.

Camillus factory workers rely on non-marring hammers to tap dozens of folders into multiple tooling jigs.

Wood sheath block is held in vise as Bob Engnath makes a first cut with a small, sharp wood chisel.

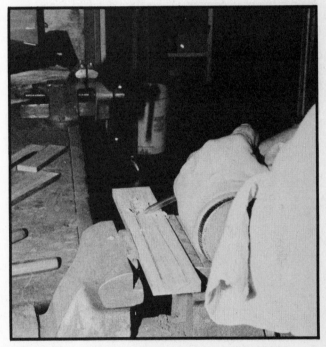
With the outline in the wood, a heavier chisel makes cross cuts. Note three pins atop vise in background.

quate for most of your work. For small, lightweight knives, simple spring clips will hold handle slabs to the tang while your epoxy cement cures overnight. If you already have the spring clamps on hand, you may use them, but we would not recommend running out to buy them for your first few projects.

You will need several screwdrivers of various types and widths. Large, medium and small screwdrivers usually are found in most households and workbenches. As you get into knifemaking, you soon will identify several more you will wish to have. We recommend you buy them as you go, rather than purchasing one of each before starting. Kit

knives and first non-kit projects need only a basic blade screwdriver to tighten the cutler's screws which will hold the handle slabs to the tang. There may be a few knife parts somewhere that require the use of a Phillips head or hex head driver, but we seldom encounter them; they will not pop up in our projects.

In the next chapter, we will be discussing power tools, but a hand drill fits our present category. Good quality hand drills may be found at swap meets or surplus outlets and they need not be prohibitively expensive. They are produced in many sizes and qualities, so look at several before buying. Most have hollow handles in which drills or

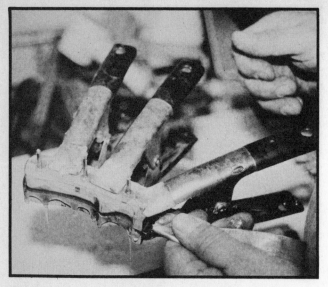

Spring clamps provide firm, but minimum pressure to handle slabs and knife tang which has just been filled with epoxy cement. Clamps are quick to apply.

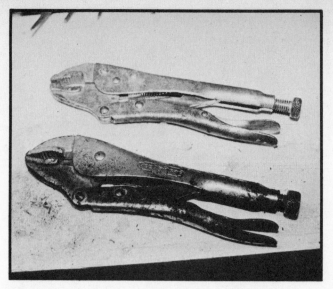

Vise-Grip is brand name which has become almost generic for adjustable, locking/unlocking jaw pliers.

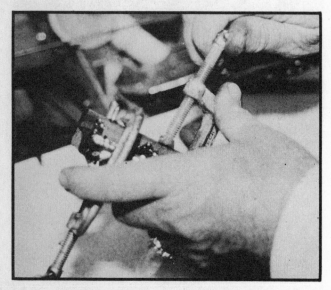

When more pressure is needed, C-clamps with their threaded bolt handles, are used on handles. Note that clamps are placed in opposite directions, above.

Graduated, direct-read calipers are used to check steel uniformity, thickness before cutting, grinding.

reams are carried, although such a procedure is sure to dull the cutting surfaces. A good hand drill will be heavy enough not to bounce around in use and the main power wheel should have enough mass to produce some centrifugal force. For extra-heavy work, a power drill often is required, but there are some operations which are done best with a hand drill.

For the hand drill, you will, of course, need a set of metal drill bits. These should be purchased new and of the best quality you can find. Cheap drill bits are a waste of money. Most hardware stores or tool supply outlets will have several selections, usually in sets carried in plastic boxes with sepa-

rators to hold and identify the drill bit sizes. You should not need bits larger than three-eighths-inch diameter.

You will find use for a small micrometer, a metal straight-edge, a metal scribe and set of punches, if you continue beyond putting together simple knife kits. You are usually safe in buying these tools used, as they seldom wear out and any minor damage is easy to detect. Micrometer jaws can be sprung out of line, but that is rare. You may wish to take something of known thickness along with you to check out the accuracy of the tool before you buy.

A small propane torch is used for heavy-duty soldering and brazing; you may also heat-temper some blades with

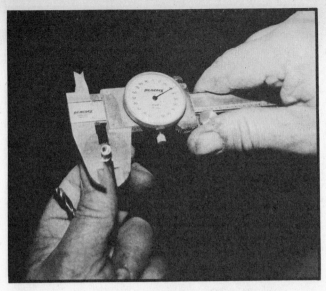

Here, the calipers are reading the outside diameter of a handle bolt before drilling tang holes in blade.

An adjustable square will have many uses in the shop, including finding accurate 90- and 45-degree angles.

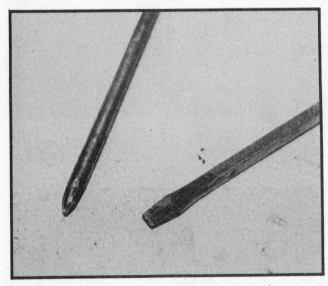

Every workshop will have several screwdrivers in various sizes to fit Phillips and regular screw heads.

A small propane tank is easily screwed into a burner attachment to form a portable shop blowtorch.

the open flame. The torch is simply a small tank of propane gas with a tube and burner attached. Buy a set at your local hardware store.

The final non-power tool every knifemaker has is a sharpening stone. We will go into these essential items in greater detail in a later chapter, because sharpening knives is a skill or talent which must be learned and developed. These are, as we shall see, literally dozens of knife sharpening devices available, but you will want to have at least one good oil stone of bench size in your shop. It will be put to use honing down the burred screwdrivers, drill tips and knife parts, as well as putting a good edge on your home-

made knives. Sharp kitchen knives also help maintain domestic tranquility. New large stones are not that expensive and it is difficult to judge the quality of the seldom-seen used ones.

High-quality hand tools are always a good investment and can last for generations. Cheap tools will break under stress and could cause the builder to ruin a blade which has already had several work hours put into it. Whether you buy all new, used or a combination of both, get the best hand tools available. They will pay dividends all during your knifemaking career.

A major knife producer, such as Buck, above will have hundreds of power tools from the simplest to the most sophisticated. The beginning knifemaker must not invest in too many. Custom knifemaker, Chuck Stapel, below, works on his buffing wheel.

Chapter 3

POWER TOOLS

Don't Go Overboard, But A Few Basic Power Tools Can Ease And Speed Your Knifemaking Career

IT IS POSSIBLE to build knives without the use of power tools. The little folding knife kits we shall look at are assembled with only hand tools. There are some purist knifemakers who take justified pride in making all their knives without the use of any power tools. But most of us have — or soon will want to have — a basic bench supplied with electrically powered tools to make the task of producing knives considerably easier, faster and more efficient.

Many of you already have some of the power tools useful to knifemakers. Some probably have them all. Some tools will be available at less than $50 while others will cost several thousands. Those professional power tools will be most useful only to those of us who decide to go on to serious knifemaking or who eventually move into the ranks of the professionals. As with hand tools, we must keep in mind that there are power tools of good quality that are worth their cost and others that are virtual junk which will have to be replaced in only a few months. Beware of being carried away. There are some machines that even the successful professionals cannot justify for their shops.

Probably the first power tool that comes to mind, one that many of us already have in the shop, is the electric drill. Such drills have so many uses for so many projects that they are almost essential to most of us. Drilling holes is only one of the many jobs that can be done with an electric drill. And these days, we are no longer limited to the length of the electric power cord as to where we can drill. New developments in rechargeable battery-powered drills make it simple to take them anywhere at any time.

Electric drills are available in several grades and price ranges. A cheap model may be purchased for only a few dollars and may last for a year or so. Those little lightweights are not satisfactory for the basic knifemaker. Get one powerful enough to do all the jobs required of it without too much strain. It should last a lifetime.

The electric drill you decide upon should be powerful and rugged enough to accomplish all your tasks. Get one that will take a drill bit of at least one-quarter inch; three-eighths or half-inch would be even better. Often, it is possible to find good buys on new or used power tools at swap meets and garage sales. One must look closely at such tools to make sure they have not been damaged or worn out, but there are some bargains around. Be sure to demand an opportunity to try the tool or, at least, turn it on at an electrical outlet before laying down your money. Listen to it run and avoid those which sound too loose, noisy or just plain worn out.

Above: This ¾-horsepower electric grinder was found at a local swap meet and purchased new for less than $50. Made in Taiwan, it seems to be of high quality.

This is one of the homemade buffer/grinders discussed in text. Electric motor with step-down belt pulleys is located beneath tool stand and was not expensive.

A variable-speed drill lets you drive screws the easy way, too. This probably is not what you will use the drill for in making knives, but it is something nice to have around the house. You will appreciate the variable speed for other reasons while at the workbench.

There are any number of attachments that you might buy for electric drills which convert it into a drill press, a buffing wheel or a disc sander. A low fractional horsepower rating won't do the job for you and that is another reason to get as much power as you can find. These attachments also are found sometimes at swap meets at bargain prices, so it is a good idea to check them out. Mail-order houses are other sources for these accessories. We have seen several metal and plastic bench mounts to hold the drill down firmly without marring the bench's finish.

It is a simple matter to rig your electric drill with a homemade bench mount and use it as a buffer or disc sander. Essentially, the drill is mounted upside down on the edge of the bench, so the chuck faces toward you. The simplest arrangement we have seen consists of a couple of pieces of wood, half-inch plywood works well, wide enough to accommodate the width of the drill and cut with vees to accept the drill body. These two pieces are glued and screwed to a base, such as a two-by-six, cut to a length shorter than the drill body.

The two Vee pieces are attached to the ends of the heavier base and the base is attached to the bench. The base needs to be solidly attached, permitting no movement while you are working, so screwing or bolting it to the bench is best.

The Vee openings should be padded with felt or foam rubber strips into which the drill body fits. Window weather stripping works well. Simple metal straps held down by wing nuts, or even fitted, inverted wood Vee cuts are used to hold down the drill. We have seen large circular hose clamps, with padding, successfully used for this task. Whatever the method used, it must hold the drill without movement. Remember that you will want to remove the drill from time to time to use it for other jobs.

A bench-mounted drill is converted easily to a buffer by chucking in a small quarter-inch shaft buffing wheel. Grinder wheels also are available to fit electric drills. Having

Chuck Stapel saves valuable bench space by mounting his power buffer on a floor stand. He constructed plywood boxes for each wheel for safety, shelf space.

Final polishing and buffing at the Camillus factory. Note the use of taped thumbs, fingers on safety gloves.

the drill firmly mounted is almost like having a third hand when it comes to precision hole drilling. It is usually easier to move the piece to the drill when drilling knife tangs and the like.

Another highly versatile power tool is the Dremel. There are, no doubt, other brand names for the same type of tool, but Dremel is probably the best known. It is a small electric drill motor, highly portable, with dozens of grinders, cutters, polishers and sander attachments which fit into the chuck. The Dremel can save a lot of time and effort when working in small places on metal, plastic or wood. Dremel makes a flexible shaft which can be added, allowing the worker to reach into the tightest spots. Most knifemakers and gunsmiths have one of these useful tools in their shops; they use it all the time.

Here is a trick to be used with a Dremel tool that we learned from Bob Engnath of the House of Muzzleloading (1019 East Palmer, Glendale, CA 91205). Engnath is a blade grinder as well as a supplier of everything any knifemaker might wish to have. He and other knifemakers have discovered that hard blade steel, such as 440C and ATS-34, is tough on hacksaw blades, as well as arm muscles. So he has little seven-eighths-inch abrasive cutoff discs that are fitted to the Dremel machine and used to score the steel about halfway through. One disc usually lasts through one line of the blade pattern. The excess steel then is snapped off. Engnath sells them by the hundreds

With attachments, a drill press will do many things, but its primary function is to drill holes at precise angles. The holes are being drilled in the tang area to accept pins or bolts. Blade is taped for safety.

Rows of belt sanders occupy the Buck factory floor as production is underway. Eye and ear protection is required and all machines are vented to outside.

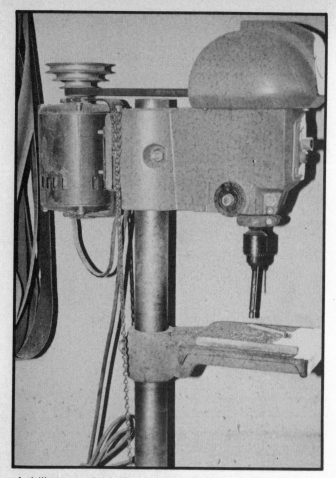

A drill press of this size will accomplish most any task required by the beginning or advanced knifemaker. To change drill speeds, move the belt to another pulley.

A professional knifemaker will find use for this milling machine, but it is too much machine for most of us.

and says that most hobby shops also carry them to fit the Dremel tool.

The next power tool which we probably should consider is a buffer and grinding wheel. There are always hundreds of uses for one of these. We have seen them for sale at most swap meets and plenty of garage sales. Many seem almost new at used prices. As long as the motor is in good shape, it can be a bargain. You will be buying your own new buffers and grinding wheels anyway. Again, you need to see and hear it run before buying.

Power grinders are rated according to their motor horsepower. Most home workshops will have motors rated at a horse and a half or two horses. These are adequately powerful for most knifemaking needs. Professional knifemakers may have two or three grinders set up in their shops, one for grinding and two more for different kinds of buffing and polishing. Those that aren't mounted on the bench will be on shop stands, not taking up bench space.

Power grinders are sold with several safety shields attached. Usually, the wheels will be partially enclosed with a transparent plastic eye protector over the grinding wheel. You can see the work in progress while the shield catches most of the particles of metal or other material being thrown off the spinning wheel. We know most home craftsmen remove most of the safety panels and shields on grinders, but they put themselves at greater risk by doing so. True, those panels and shields will vibrate and make a lot of noise while the wheels are running, but they should be left on.

We know of some knifemakers and home craftsmen who have made their own bench grinders from readily available components at reasonable cost. It is a rather simple task, works well and you may have some of the components around the place already.

You will need a small table or stand on which to mount an arbor and step-down belt pulleys for variable speeds, a belt and a good electric motor to run it all.

The arbor, shaft and pulley wheels are mounted on the stand or small table with an opening through which to run the belt. The motor can be mounted below or behind the shaft and pulleys. Beneath is usually better, because of the considerable space saved.

Buffing wheels of various sizes and compositions can be mounted on the ends of the shaft. Grinding wheels may be mounted in the same manner. To change wheel speeds, move the power belt from one pulley to the other. The sys-

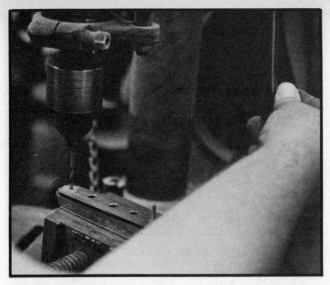

Using the tang as a guide, the handle slab is drilled through. Lever at right raises or lowers drill bit to work. A drill press vise holds work securely, above.

If the work to be drilled is fairly soft and hole location is not that critical, the bit may be lowered directly down, holding only with fingers, above.

tem works well and it is possible to mount a powerful electric motor this way.

Most makers will use eight-, ten- or twelve-inch wheels on their power grinder; the eight-inch is the most common. Buffing wheels are made of sisal, or stitched or loose muslin cloth. Each has a use in the knifemaker's shop.

The buffing wheels must be used with an edge coating from grease sticks. These grease sticks are available in several grits; all color coded. Black grease stick will cut into blade metal and will leave a faintly satin finish. Green stick leaves a polished mirror gloss, similar to a white stick, but the green has a higher concentration of abrasives in it. Cloth and sisal must be kept well loaded with the grease compound or the cloth will grab uneven abrasives and tend to leave streaks on the work.

Few power tools are as versatile and useful as the drill press. It is, we admit, rather expensive and not the sort of tool everyone will want or can afford to have. But a drill press will do almost everything for you, including shining your shoes. It will drill straight, accurate, exact holes in almost any material, of course. It will also sand, plane, rout, carve and polish any material you can pick up and place upon its table.

In its most simplest form, a drill press is an electric drill permanently mounted to a shaft or tube, which allows it to move up and down onto the work. Actually, the drill press is much more than that. It is a precision tool for boring holes at precise angles at various drill speeds.

The drill press head, mounted on the shaft, contains the electric motor, step pulleys which are used to change the drill speeds and the spindle which has the drill chuck on the end. The whole thing is mounted on a base with a swiveling work table in between. When maximum depth is required, the table may be swung around on the mounting tube out of the way. The table will move up and down to accommodate the work to be drilled; better drill presses have

When drilling in steel and when more precision is required, a drill press vise should be used. Jaws are smooth and will not damage edges of your knife blade.

The Baldor industrial motor is a rugged, long-lasting power source for some power tools. This might be too much for the average beginner, but will serve well.

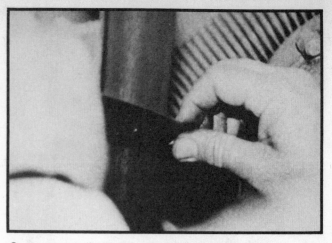

On some sanding jobs, a platen is in place behind the sanding belt. Metal will soon become hot, above.

This smaller, hobby-level belt sander uses a 48-inch belt. The platen and metal safety guards have been removed to show the unit's configuration. The sander is mounted on a heavy, rubber-dampened foundation.

methods of tilting the table and locking it at specified angles for precise hole drilling. Most have provision for mounting a small clamp or vise on the table or base to hold the work as it is drilled; otherwise the part may suddenly grab the drill bit and spin out of one's grasp. Sometimes, the work is simply bolted down on to the table.

A drill press will accept several accessories in its head to allow it to do many more tasks than simply bore holes. We can attach a drum sander with its shaft in the chuck. It is ideal for sanding curved surfaces, especially finger grooves on a knife handle. The drum is brought down close to the table on which the blade or handle material is held. The work is moved across the table and against the drum. These drums, incidentally, are available in several different grits.

A disc sanding attachment is chucked in and the work to be sanded is brought along the table beneath the disc. This can work quite well on knife handles, if nothing else is available.

A router bit can be mounted in place of the drill bit and perform the same function. The drill press should be rotating at least 3400 rpm, with speeds of 5000 rpm better for the task. There probably is little application for knifemaking for the router attachment, but it is something else that can be done with the machine.

A grinding wheel may be chucked in, providing the drill press is not operated faster than is safe for the wheel. Top speeds are labled on grinding wheels and should not be exceeded. The grinder may be used to sharpen knives or other tools, just as the standard bench grinder is used.

In a similar manner, a buffing wheel is another possibility

Chuck Stapel, above, uses push stick against the knife blade as he works on hollow grind. A bucket of water is placed to catch falling hot metal sparks.

Bob Engnath, left, claims to have ground thousands of blades. He keeps in mind safety measures as he wears safety glasses, leather welding apron, gloves.

for the drill press. It has the advantage of adjustable speeds, which a regular buffing wheel machine may not have. Slow buffing is necessary for some felt-back wheels and grits.

Drill presses are made in many sizes up to huge industrial machines. But you will not need one that large. A medium-size drill press, massive enough to provide all the power and adjustments needed for knifemaking, will do you well. Take a look at several in stores, catalogs and surplus stores and swap meets before investing in one. Talk it over with other knifemakers or experienced home handymen to get their ideas on size and brands. You can make plenty of knives without ever using or needing a drill press, but a good one will simplify and speed up many of the steps if you plan to make more than a few knives.

The last power machine we shall discuss is the belt grinder. This is a machine not found in many home workshops, but is one with dozens of uses, especially for the knifemaker. We know of several professional knifemakers who, if asked to name one power tool they could not do without, would name the belt grinder.

As with all things, belt grinders come in several sizes and qualities. The best do not come cheap; the most sophisticated can cost upwards of $2500. That is a lot of money,

The 72-inch belt sander with knifemaker's attachment may be used in horizontal or vertical position. If you are serious about getting into knifemaking, a good belt sander is almost essential. Get the best you can.

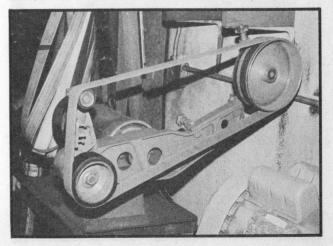

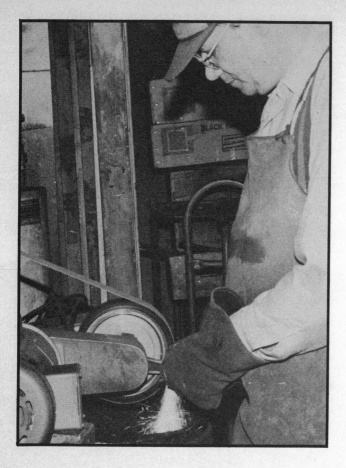

Engnath establishes his belt grinder in the horizontal mode while working on a blade, left. He also has a water bucket placed to prevent blade from overheating.

Chuck Stapel is a custom knifemaker who finds use for more than one belt sander. This one is solidly floor-mounted to save space and reduce vibration.

but there are those who contend the ease with which you might keep all your kitchen knives sharp using a belt grinder is justification enough to get one.

A used belt grinder is seldom found for sale. There are some cheap, fall-apart models being imported from the Far East, but we would advise you not to waste your money on them. They are not likely to last long.

Bob Engnath recommends two brands. One is the Coote, which goes for slightly under $500 and is considered ideal for the hobby knifemaker. Engnath says it is sturdy and basic and should handle a full one-horsepower motor easily to grind blades from any bar stock. The Coote, he notes, does not come with a motor.

The Burr King is the belt grinder recognized for its quality and utility by knifemakers. It probably is found in more professional knifemakers' workshops than any other power tool. With the addition of what is called a knifemaker's attachment, it can be used to make a complete knife from start to finish. The basic machine has a flat grinding platen and, with a one-horsepower motor, will operate at 1750 rpm.

The knifemaker's attachment has a platen measuring two-by-six inches, with a two-inch wheel above and five-inch wheel below. Both wheels may be used for hollow grinding by tilting the entire head into the correct position. The platen is removed quickly and easily for slack belt grinding while shaping handles and other such work. The basic machine may be ordered with either eight- or ten-inch diameter contact wheels, but most makers prefer the eight-inch. Some makers will have two or three Burr Kings in the shop, one with each size contact wheel to save time when moving from one task to the next. At this writing, the basic Burr King — with knifemaker attachment — is selling for slightly more than $1200.

The Burr King and other brands similar to it, can do so many things so well that the potential buyer should seek out a dealer or a knifemaker who uses one to see it in action. Once you have tried one, you may wonder how you ever got along without it. If you are going to make knives, eventually you'll get a belt sander.

There are many more power tools which the home workshop might have, but none that might be heavily used by the knifemaker. In some shops, you may find a band saw, a radial saw, table saw, lathe, router, power sander or a sabre saw. If you have one or more of these, each can be used to make knives, substituting for some of the other tools discussed.

If you have none of the above and are determined to set up a shop for knifemaking, you should consider the drill press and the belt sander as basic equipment. With a good set of hand tools and those two machines, you should be able to make knives at reasonable speed with all the skill you have.

They are sure to save you a lot of work.

It takes skilled hands to sharpen a blade with the belt slackened, above. This is not a job for beginners.

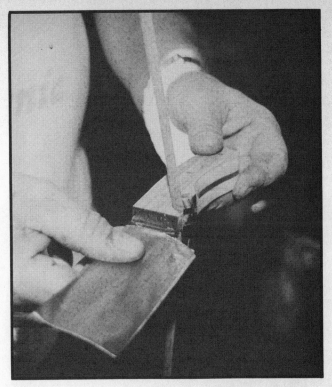

Here is a method of sanding finger grooves and other curved surfaces. A standard 72-inch belt is split to an inch width, placed in a vertical position and left slack. Finished blade is protected with tape.

Before mounting on the tang, a pair of handle slabs is clamped together and the ends carefully shaped on the belt sander using the ten-inch power wheel.

The short platen behind the belt permits the maker to use maximum pressure while sanding the tang area.

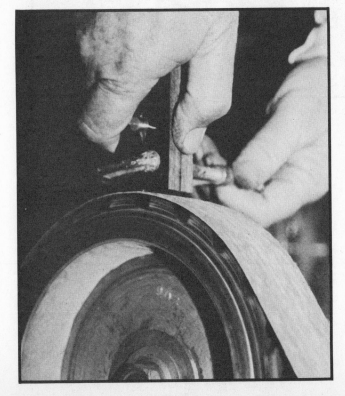

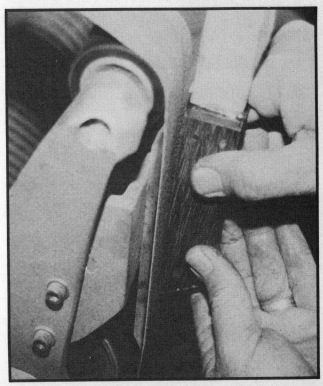

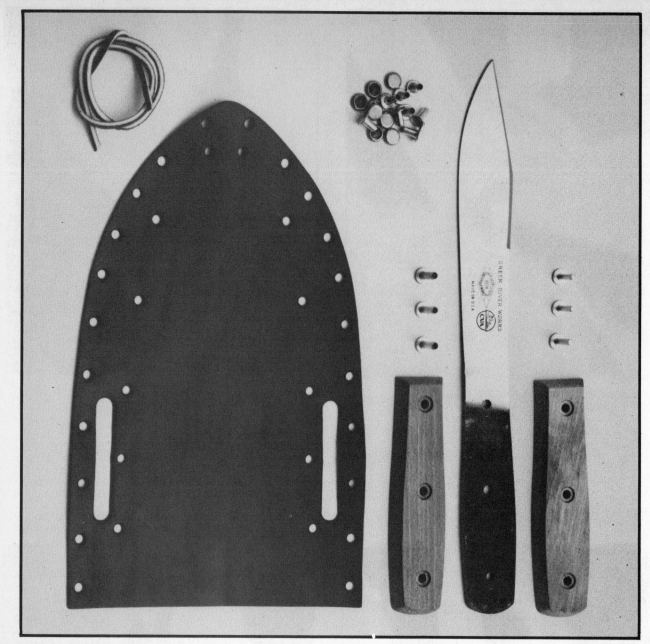

Perhaps one of the most basic and simple knife kits is this one for a CVA Green River knife. If any more were done, it would be a complete knife rather than a kit to build. All holes are drilled. Components need only quick basic assembly.

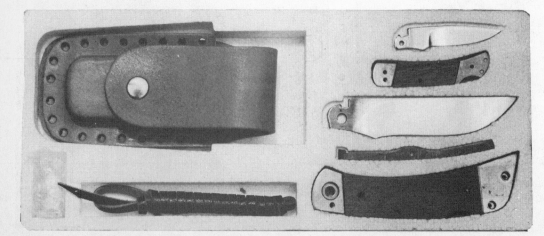

Folding knife kit contains enough to assemble two knives; a small pocket model and a larger folder for belt pouch carry.

Chapter 4

BASIC KIT KNIVES

With Several Simple Knife Kits Available, This is One Of The Easiest Ways To Start

NIFE BUILDING KITS of varying degrees of difficulty may be found at knife specialty shops or listed in mail-order catalogs throughout most of the country. True, many small towns do not have knife specialty shops, but most shopping malls have at least one cutlery store and mail-order catalogs are everywhere.

There are literally dozens of such kits available, the simplest to the most difficult listed among them. Some kits are comprised of a set of components with finished parts ready for assembly to complete a knife. Others require a great deal of time and effort to create a true, custom-made knife of high quality.

The simplest kit we have encountered contained a finished blade, two finished-to-shape handle slabs, two rivets and a small amount of two-part epoxy cement. Once finished, about all that was left to do was to put a fine edge on the blade and put it to work. Such a kit is hardly a builder's knife at all, as there is virtually nothing unusual or individualistic that the maker can do to the knife. But such a simple kit is a good place to start for those with limited mechanical skills or who wish to increase their knowledge of knives with hands-on experience.

The simplest type of knife has a single, non-folding blade with a small or self-handle. But that would not be a knife-making kit at all; it would be a store-bought knife without a handle. There would be little to build or do, except sharpen the edge.

There are some boot knives and throwing styles available which are little more than as described. To customize one of these, one might choose to wrap the handle tang, perhaps with the nylon cord used on some survival knives. If the cord is not treated or permanently affixed to the tang, it could act as an emergency line in a survival situation should the need arises. This is a technique used by one of the more successful custom knifemakers, Phil Hartsfield. Much of his knife production features simple handles of handsomely wrapped cord. The heavy line will not unwrap accidentally, but it may be removed from the tang should the need occur.

Finished blade blanks are available from several catalog suppliers and specialty shops, ready for handles to be installed. The choice of handle material is almost unlimited. We will discuss these aspects of knifemaking in more detail in later chapters.

Matching finished blade blank and ready-made handle halves is quite simple. The handle slabs may be bolted, riveted, pinned, cemented or held by some combination of two or more of the choices. For most rugged outdoor work or for a knife that will have to go through the dishwasher, a

The simplest sheath knife kit assembled and ready for use, includes a rudimentary thong-sewn belt sheath.

combination is recommended. There will be more on this subject in Chapter Ten, but for now, keep in mind that most automatic dishwashers use water quite hot in the final cycles and feature heated air to dry the items. Some cements, including the two-solution-mix type, tend to soften under such heat. Check the label and do not use a substance which will fall apart when heated.

In any case, the best bet is to combine pins, rivets or cutler's bolts with a good two-part epoxy cement. If the handle slabs are not pre-drilled, that must be done at this point. The blade blanks should be pre-drilled with a minimum of two holes through the tang area. Metal fasteners, braising rod, rivets, cutler's bolts or something similar are usually included with the kit. The fit through the metal handle tang should be snug with little or no play. The hole in the handle slabs may be a bit looser.

Test the fit and match of all parts before mixing up the two-part epoxy. The holes may have to be re-drilled or reamed out if too far off. Assembling the components before cementing also gives the builder a bit of a psychological boost, because the knife may appear almost as it will when finished.

If all is well, mix the epoxy according to directions. As we shall see in later chapters, there are several kinds of cement which may be used and the choice — unless included in the kit — depends upon ultimate use of the knife. Follow the mixing directions carefully to avoid problems later. Use plenty of cement to obtain a complete seal between steel and handle material. Excess cement will seep out of the joint, but may be cleaned up later.

Most epoxy directions call for clamping the parts together for a selected period of time, usually at room temperature. The time may range from a few minutes up to twenty-four hours. C-clamps or alligator clamps or, in an emergency, even heavy rubber bands which may be cut away later can be utilized. The drying period should not be rushed; follow the directions on the package. Heavy excess is wiped away before it dries.

The pins or rivets should be inserted through the two handle sides and the tang after applying the cement. Most makers prefer to apply the wet cement first, then insert the pins. In this way, the pins, too, are coated with epoxy, effecting a better bond for the handle slabs.

Remove the clamps after the prescribed period of time

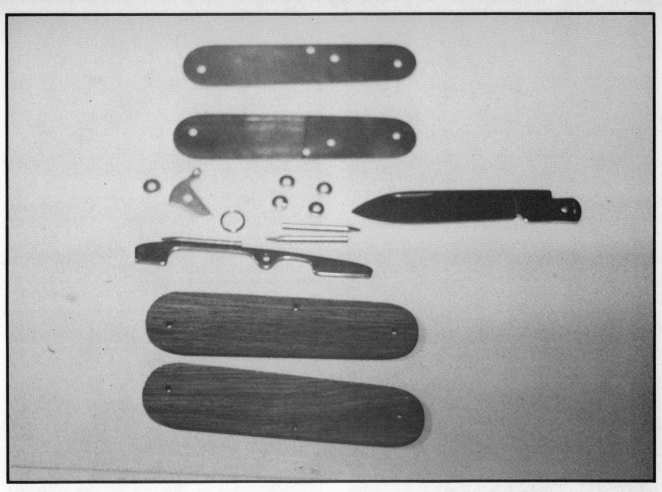

The Atlanta Cutlery folding knife kit is a bit more complex containing several moving parts, as well as several components, easy to misplace. Check the content of the kit package before beginning work.

— usually overnight. At this time, the bolts are tightened or the pins peened. Do this work carefully, as the handle material may split if too much pressure is applied by the hammer or screwdriver. Excess pin or bolt length can be snipped and filed off for an attractive fit and appearance.

If filing or sanding is required, do so carefully. It is too easy to scar or cut the handle material, leaving unsightly marks. Wood and plastic handles can be filled with wood filler or more epoxy, but the knots will still be there. File down the pin ends just to the level of the handle.

The fitted handle now needs only to have the excess epoxy, which was squeezed out by the clamping action, removed. This can be done with more file work, although the file teeth will fill up and have to be cleaned frequently. Coarse to fine grits of sandpaper also may be used to rid the handle area of excess epoxy and to remove any overlap of the handle slabs. There probably will be no more than a sixteenth of an inch at any one location. An experienced knifemaker or home workshop enthusiast might use a belt sander or other power tool for this step, but it is easy to remove too much handle material with power tools.

If sandpaper is used, be sure to back it with a sanding block. As with power tools, it is easy to take off too much handle material along the metal tang without a block.

Another technique many makers favor is to place a full sheet of sandpaper on the work surface for the paper backing and as much pressure as necessary may be applied to the handle, as work progresses.

As a safety measure, be sure to tape over the entire knife edge while working. In addition to avoiding a nasty cut, the tape will protect the blade edge from damage which otherwise would have to be polished out later.

With the handle cleaned up, the fixed-blade knife is finished. Except for final sharpening, it is ready to use. The knife may need a sheath, construction of which will be examined in later chapters.

Making a sheath or kitchen knife from a kit should take only a couple of hours, discounting cement drying time. It is easy, requiring only a basic knowledge of simple hand-tools.

The next simple project involves the construction of a folding knife. This is a bit more complicated, but with detailed instructions and plenty of illustrations, it should be another short, easy job.

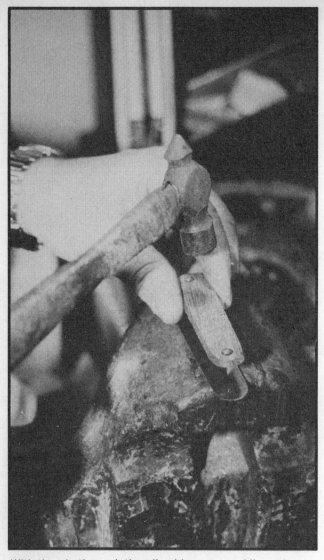

With the pin through the pile side cover and liner, the backspring is followed by the mark side liner. The mark side cover will be next. The backspring fits but one way.

The first pin, in the center, is inserted through the pile side cover and liner. If the fit is tight — and it should be — the side may be flipped and the pin tapped down.

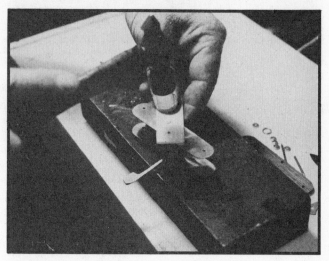

A section of solid steel is used as an anvil as the tight-fitting mark side cover is tapped onto the pin.

The easiest folding knife kit we know of — actually there are three different models — is from Atlanta Cutlery of Georgia. Only basic hand tools are required for its completion. One evening is all we needed to complete this single-blade folder.

Atlanta Cutlery also offers a two-blade knife and a locking-blade kit, but they are slightly advanced from our current project. Complete the single blade knife first and the others will be easier to construct.

The basic tools needed to complete this knife are: a ball peen hammer for the pins, a second cut flat file, wire cutters or diagonal cutters, a sturdy bench vise and a couple of sheets of 400-grit wet or dry sandpaper. A pair of vise grips may be substituted if a bench vise is not available, but we recommend the vise if at all possible.

For this and other projects, if a good vise is not available, some sort of steel surface will be required on which to peen the pins and provide a sturdy, impenetrable flat area on which to work. Some craftsmen use short sections of railroad track as a sort of anvil. The large bench vise with an anvil-like projection on the back is ideal. Review Chapter Two for some possible sources for these tools. A buffing wheel or belt sander will speed some of the work, but are not necessary for this knife kit.

The Atlanta Cutlery folding knife kits are mailed in small padded paper envelopes, inside of which the parts are sealed within a clear plastic bag. Everything normally comes through in good order, but if anything turns up missing, a call to Atlanta will rectify the situation right away.

Before beginning construction, the first thing to do is to take inventory. The knife kit includes detailed written instructions with illustrations of each part and where it goes. It is easy to compare the contents of the kit with the instructions to ensure everything fits where it should.

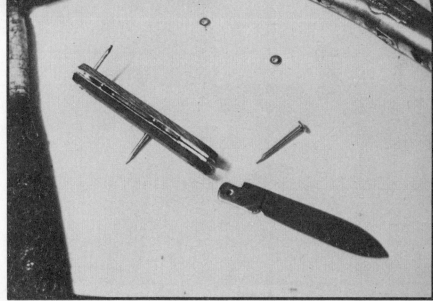

The components are beginning to look like a knife as both covers, or sides, are assembled with the backspring. The protruding center pin will be trimmed off later, with the other pins, before finishing.

The catch disc has been installed at the wider end using a second pin and birdseye. The spear point blade awaits assembly via the third pin through smaller end.

Open the envelope carefully and slide the components onto the workbench. Some of the parts are tiny, so take care that nothing rolls or bounces out of sight. The kit should contain fifteen parts, plus one bag carrying split ring and an assembly aid called a slackner. The slackner is simply a small rectangle of thin aluminum that performs an important spacing function during pin peening. The carry ring may or may not be attached after the knife is built.

With the parts on the workbench, we should have a set of written instructions, a spear-point knife blade, two brass liners, two jacaranda wood handle covers with pre-drilled matching holes, one backspring of heavier metal, three nickel-silver pins which are easily cut and peened, one aluminum washer and four nickel-silver birdseyes. The birdseyes may be distinguished from the single washer by not only the metal cover, but also because the birdseyes are not flat in profile. The four birdseyes, yellowish in color,

are slightly smaller than the washer and are convex and flat on opposite sides. If the shape seems odd, it all becomes clear as construction commences.

Altogether, there are a dozen assembly steps and fifteen parts to the knife. The wood slabs are called covers, because they cover the internal parts of the folding knife; simple enough. One side is called the pile side cover, because it is the side onto which the rest of the parts are piled during assembly. The other is the mark side cover, because on a production knife, the maker will place a shield, nameplate or other mark on the handle piece. You may notice that one end of the cover is wider than the other. Keep in mind that the blade is pivoted from the narrower end. The two covers are pre-drilled for the three pins used in assembly. You can identify the outer surface of the covers, due to the two countersunk holes around the two end pinholes. The four birdseyes will be set in these countersinks.

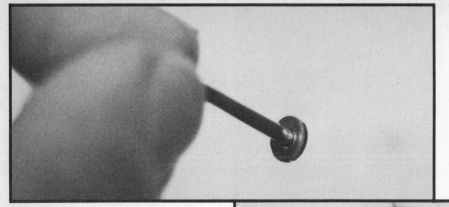

Four birdseyes and three pins are included in the Atlanta Cutlery knife kit. It is important to place the birdseye so that the flat side faces into the wood covers.

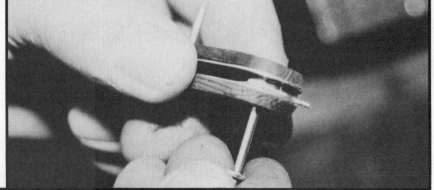

When properly inserted, the catch disc works against the backspring and balances out width of blade.

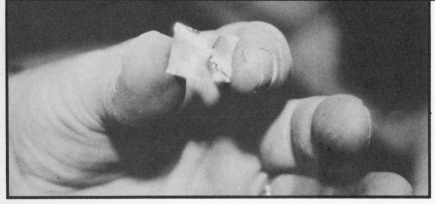

The small rectangle of aluminum sheeting is called the slackener. A small V-section is cut out with a pair of scissors so the blade pin will fit through. The slackener is a spacer to prevent binding while peening at the blade end.

To identify the pile side cover and get started correctly, first place both wood covers on the work surface in front of you. Put the wider end to your left with the smooth surface upward. Now place the cover with the middle pin hole closest to you. That is the pile side cover and the part with which construction begins. Push the mark side cover some distance away, as it will be placed in the unit last. Note that the brass liners are cut and drilled to match the two wood covers; they are called pile side and mark side liners. It is a good idea to put the matching liners and covers near each other.

With the pile side cover in front as described, insert one of the pins up through the center hole only. It should fit snugly, but should slide through the hole without undue force. The pile side liner is next; it should be a tighter fit around the pin, requiring some careful hammer work.

Turning the cover and liner over, you can hammer the pin home by placing the work over the edge of the workbench.

A better method is to use your metal vise with the jaws almost closed. Let the pin point hang down between the jaws, resting the liner on the vise jaws and lightly tap the pin down until it is nearly flush with the outer side of the pile cover. At this point, insert only the center pin; the others come later.

The next part to go onto the pin is the backspring. It is not symmetrical and will fit into the knife in only one direction, but that will be obvious. The mark side liner and cover may be assembled on the center pin at this time. Making sure the narrow ends of the brass and wood parts all face in the same direction, then press the sides gently together. Your knife is beginning to take shape!

Our third step involves the other two pins and the birdseyes. At this point, it seems a good idea to assemble the pins and birdseyes, one on the blunt end of each. As mentioned, the birdseyes are convex on one side, flat on the other. You will want to end up with the curved or convex surfaces facing

The backspring must be compressed enough from the back end to line up all the pin holes of the blade. The easiest way to do this is with your handy-dandy bench vise, left.

After the final two birdseyes have been tapped onto the two end pins — well nestled into their countersinks — the pin ends are cut off with wire cutters. The pin metal is rather soft, but some force is needed to snip evenly.

outward; the flat surfaces must be flush against the wood covers in their countersinks. The metal vise works well for this task.

Start the pointed end of the pin into the convex side of the birdseye. With the vise jaws nearly closed, carefully hammer the pin down through the little ring. Hammer it down until the end of the pin is nearly flush with the convex surface. It is a good idea to do both sets of pins and birdseyes at this time.

The first pin and birdseye assembly is placed through the wider end of the knife and will hold the nickel-silver catch disc. The wide end is called the cap end, incidentally. The pin starts into the pile side cover and liner, through the catch disc and through the mark side liner and cover. The fit will be snug, but do not hammer so hard that you damage any parts. The sharp end of the pin will extend some distance through the mark side, but ignore it for now.

Remember that when the birdseye and pin are fully inserted, the rounded or convex side must face out from the wood. One edge of the catch disc is straight and that must meet the bearing surface of the backspring.

The last pin and birdseye will go through the narrower end of the handle along with the blade and small washer. The washer offsets the width of the catch disc. For this step, the bench vise is invaluable, but the work can be done using vise grips, if nothing else is available.

To line up the holes for the pin, the backspring must be squeezed at the cap end of the handle. Carefully squeeze the assembled covers, liners and backspring at the wider end until the backspring is clear of the pin hole and you can sight down through everything. Start the pin with the birdseye facing the right direction and carefully tap it into position through the blade tang and the small aluminum washer.

You should still have two birdseyes yet unused. They are installed on the protruding sharp ends of your two outer pins. Remember to place them so the the flat side will nes-

Vise jaws may be used as an anvil to peen down the cut pins. Use care to not hammer too hard as cover wood may split if pins are expanded too far or wood is struck.

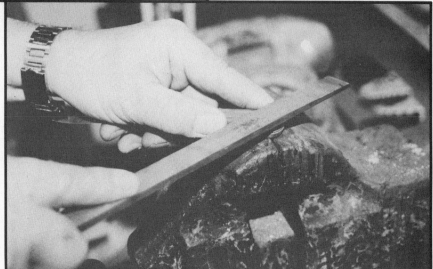

A flat file will remove excess pin metal after peening. Take short, brisk strokes to control the file. Careless work at this point will ruin you entire knife project.

tle down into the countersunk holes in the wood covers. The easy way is to start birdseyes by hand, then turn the pins down, protruding into the slot between your vise jaws, about a quarter-inch or less apart. Tap the pin and knife assembly down on to the pin until the third and fourth birdseyes are seated in their recesses. It now will be obvious why we did not trim off the excess pin length before. Do not pound too hard nor try to work too fast, as a careless move can bend the pin before it is trimmed and peened. Proceed in the same manner for both end pins.

Using a pair of wire cutters or diagonal snips, now is the time to trim off the excess pins projecting from the mark side of the knife. The nickel-silver of the pins is quite soft and can be cut with no trouble. Leave about one-sixteenth-inch protruding for later peening and finishing.

Before peening, the little slackner must be prepared and inserted. The slackener, you remember, is the rectangle of thin aluminum supplied with the kit. Its function is to separate the blade tang from the liner as you peen, so that a slight amount of space is left between the two. Not much space is required, but it must be enough so the blade will

not bind as it is being opened and closed. The thin slackner material is easily cut with a pair of scissors. A small V must be cut in the rectangle, about half-way through the little sheet. The opening of the V must be large enough to take the pin.

The slackner is used only on the blade end of the knife. Nothing extra is needed when peening the other pin. Work carefully as you open both ends of the three pins, using the rounded end of the ball peen hammer. Tap a few on one side, then turn the knife over and tap a bit on the other side, but with great care. Striking too hard may cause the wood slabs to split as the pin mental expands. Use the slackner only on the blade pivoting end of the knife.

Except for finishing, you have a functioning folding knife at this point. It is not pretty, but it will function.

One or two files and some 400-grit sandpaper are needed for the finishing touches to the knife. The jacaranda wood panels may be waxed or oiled, but Atlanta Cutlery recommends leaving them as is, allowing the natural oils from handling to create a finish.

Use a flat file to remove the excess pin material, bringing

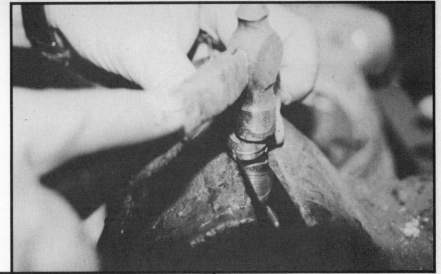

The pins may need more opening after filing if birdseyes come loose. Experience will teach you how much and how little to peen.

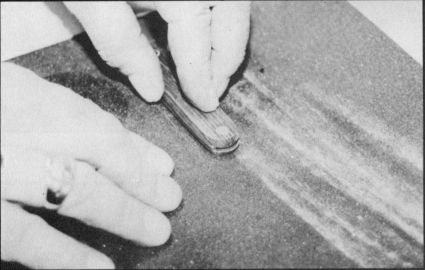

Our final construction step is to sand down the covers, pins and birdseyes smooth and flush. Easiest method is to slide the knife over the sandpaper while on a flat surface. Work down to fine grit paper. The jacaranda wood covers need no further work.

the pins down to the birdseyes' level. Use short, mild file strokes. Too heavy and you might put a gouge in the wood which may be impossible to remedy. The knife can be held in vise jaws or in the vise grips as you work or you may simply hold the knife in one hand and file with the other. In the same manner, file down the edges on the liners and wood covers until all are flush. You will have to work with the blade open for part of this, so use care around the sharp knife edge. Covering it would be the safest step.

Advanced amateurs and professionals probably will use a belt sander for the final shaping. It takes only a few seconds this way. If you have a belt sander in the shop, by all means use it, but be aware that the high-speed belt can take the handle cover or the metal down to almost nothing if too much time or pressure is used.

The easiest way to sand down the covers and the pins with birdseyes is to place a full sheet of 400-grit wet-or-dry sandpaper face up in the work surface. Hold the paper down and slide the knife across it, working with the wood grain. Not many strokes are needed for each side; examine the work frequently so you don't take it too far down.

When the knife is smooth and even over all, your project is finished. If you wish to customize the pocketknife further, you may do so at this point. Some will want to file finger grooves or a canoe pattern into the handle. Some have managed a bit of fancy filework on the back, but this is tricky because of the location of the backspring. It harms nothing to file the wood cover near the backspring, but if you should cut into the spring metal, you could ruin the knife.

If the knife is to be attached to a key chain, go ahead and run the little split ring through the eyelet on the end of catch disc. If it seems to be in the way, you can always take it off.

Atlanta Cutlery also offers a two-blade folder of similar design, as well as a locking-blade knife in kit form. Both are slightly more difficult to assemble, but the construction principles and procedures are the same. You end up with a tough, lightweight little folder for minimum cost, plus a genuine sense of accomplishment. Knife construction discussed in the next chapter will be a bit more difficult, but more rewarding.

The selection of knife design, shape and steel depends, in part, on the anticipated use. This is a pilot knife.

A boot knife or fighting knife will have a different shape, steel and handle. The factory-made Gerber is a versatile design.

Chapter 5

FROM STEEL TO KNIFE

Build Your Own Genuine Custom Knife To Your Own Specifications

WE ARE ready to move onto more difficult knife building, using components which are not contained in a kit. This chore can be a bit tougher to do, but with the skill and experience gained in our earlier projects, we should be able to produce an attractive, functional custom knife we can show and use with pride.

As usual, before starting construction, we must make a few decisions. We need to determine the type of steel to use, the shape of the blade desired, the type of handle material best-suited to the knife, and we need to determine whether we will work from a finished blade, a heat-treated but unfinished blade blank, or cut out our own rough blade from a piece of bar stock.

There are dozens of knife supply companies, large and small, that carry all the equipment and components with which to make knives of all styles and uses. Three we have dealt with throughout the writing of this book are Bob Engnath's House of Muzzleloading, Atlanta Cutlery and the Matthews Company. Each has been generous with advice and each has a warehouse full of blade blanks, steel and handle materials.

Most of the finished blades available from suppliers are of stainless steel. Most beginners should consider that route and not have to become involved in doing your own heat-treating. The chapter on that subject explains why.

Some of the tool steels used by knifemakers — 0-1, 0-6 and the W series — are popular because they are easy to cut and grind and are rather straightforward when it comes to heat-treating. Some of these steels are used in car and truck springs, files and road grader blades. They are tough! Many beginning knifemakers pick up used files or automobile springs at junkyards as raw materials for blade making. This is a cheap source of steel and will produce excellent working blades, although not for the art knife category.

The stainless steels most commonly used by professional custom makers are 440C, 154CM and Japanese-made ATS-34. These three probably account for ninety percent or more of all the custom knives made in this country.

Part of your decision probably will depend upon the size and shape of the knife you plan to make. If it is to be a hunter, skinner or a backpacking utility knife to be carried into the mountains in any type of weather, these call for one of the stainless steels. A shop knife or a small kitchen knife which will be used every day could easily be made of one of the tool steels. They will corrode if neglected, but that should not be a problem, if you use the knife every day and care for it properly. A kitchen knife need not be made of stainless steel.

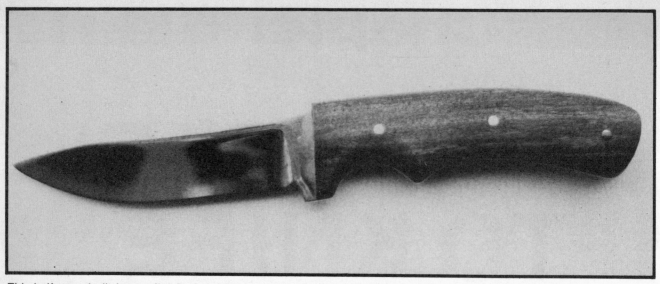

This knife was built from a finished stainless steel blade from Atlanta Cutlery. The handle shape was somewhat dictated by the pre-formed tang shape. Natural wood and brass pins were selected to construct the handle.

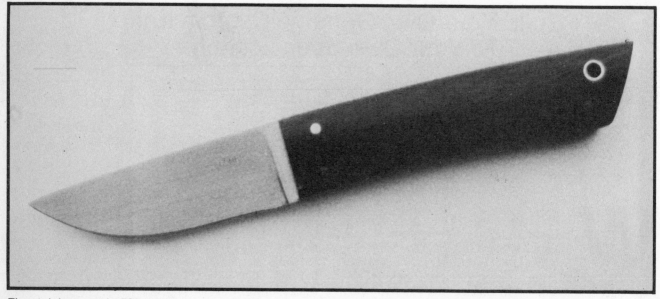

The stainless steel ATS34, full tapered tang blade is from Bob Engnath's House of Muzzleloading. The knife was hand finished to a 220-grit sandpaper finish. Pins and thong hole liner are brass; handle slabs are bubinga wood.

Knife supply companies usually keep blade stock on hand. It is sold in strips, already precision ground on the sides to eliminate any manufacturing variations in thickness. A four-foot strip should be enough for three or four large or medium-size knives, with a bit left over for a couple of small capers or paring knives.

Thickness will probably the be three-sixteenths or one-quarter inch. Sheets of eighth-inch stock are available, but they usually are used for folding knife blades. Most of us will prefer the three-sixteenths thickness, if we are not going to use a finished blade blank.

If you want to go the Damascus blade route, Rob Charlton of Damascus USA has a wide selection of blade shapes and

sizes forged to shape. You can produce a most unusual and high-quality knife, using these forged Damascus blades.

The blade shape may be rough cut, using a band saw or even a hacksaw, if the pattern is not too tight or small. A knife six to eight inches long overall will be easier to make for this project. Larger or smaller knives can present additional difficulties.

Most experienced makers recommend coating the steel with Dykem layout fluid so as to provide a dark surface on which to scribe the pattern. The deep blue Dykem will not stain the steel permanently and the lines will be much easier to see while you are cutting and grinding.

Use either a knife pattern you already have or construct

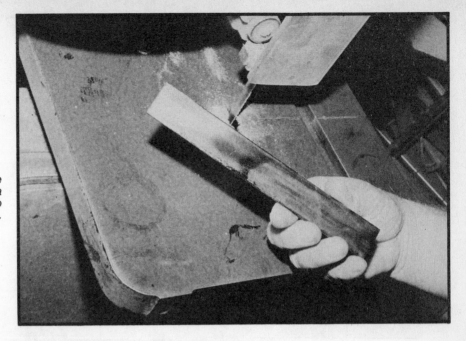

The basic blade pattern can be cut from a steel blank using a band saw. Care is exercised so rough cuts do not ruin the design.

Bob Engnath, who has formed and ground thousands of knife blades, uses a circular cut-off saw to rough out blade lengths.

the pattern from light cardboard and trace it onto the steel stock. Makers who produce several knives of the same design often make the blade pattern out of clear, hard fiberglass and save it for use again.

Use a hand scribe and trace around the pattern onto the steel. If you make a couple of slips or runs, they will not be a problem when cutting out the metal. Cut out the pattern, remembering to stay outside of the scribed lines; "save the lines," is the term. If you plan to, use only hand files and no power grinders, cut as close to the lines as possible. A belt grinder will make quick work of the excess metal, but remember to keep the steel cool by plunging it into a bucket of water as you work.

At this point, the blade should be formed, using a simple taper, rather than a complicated hollow grind or other fancy configuration. This work is done best on the belt sander, using the contact wheel. Grind carefully and don't try to rush it. Always grind with the blade edge down for less chance of the blade flying out of your hand if it catches.

For such grinding, Bob Engnath recommends a simple technique. To pass the blade across the face of the belt and get an absolutely uniform grind is nearly impossible. Streaks will show up. He suggests holding the blade firmly in both hands, both elbows locked at your sides. From the hips, move the entire body back and forth across the wheel. This helps maintain constant, uniform contact between the belt

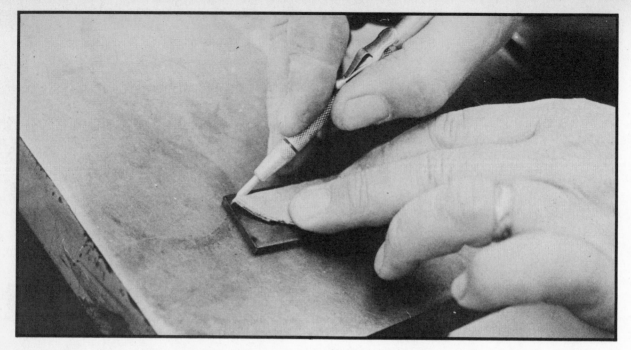

Using a cardboard or plastic template, the knife pattern is scratched, using a scribe, on the steel.

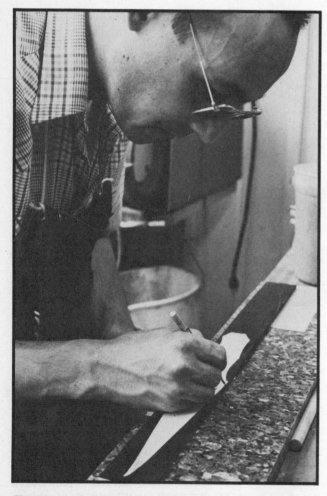

The blade steel is darkened with a coating of Dykem dye before the pattern is scribed. The dye produces a background against which the scribed lines stand out.

and the blade metal. A stranger entering your shop while you're doing this might misunderstand your action, but the technique does what it is supposed to do.

A full, untapered tang is the easiest for installing handle slabs, but for most knives, such a tang looks kind of chunky. On a really big knife — like a Bowie or a survival knife — a full tang will look fine, but most hunters and capers look better with the taper.

If you decide to not use pre-finished blade blanks and wish to cut and grind your own from steel stock, the task of producing a clean tapered tang arises. Look at a professional's tapered tang knife and you will realize that the best have a perfectly symmetrical taper on both sides with no waves and no warp. They look so good when finished that the work involved is never apparent. If you try it yourself, you will come to realize there is a lot of practice and skill involved in such a tang.

Wayne Clay of Tennessee, mentioned before in these pages, uses a technique he learned from Bob Loveless back in 1981. A generous man, Clay offers a few insights and shortcuts to the perfect tapered tang.

There are, says Clay, more than a couple of methods which the knifemaker may use. Some knifemakers who have the equipment will use a milling machine. Some prefer a surface grinder, others use a nine-inch disc sander, while still more utilize a 6x48-inch flat sander. No matter which method you choose, Clay is the first to state that producing smooth tapers for the tang is a bit more difficult than actually grinding out the blades in the first place.

Clay starts by marking the tang along the edge of the steel blade blank. He uses a machine called a height gauge,

Bob Engnath uses special vise jaw inserts of a softer metal to hold knife blanks without damage. The jaws may be adjusted to be exactly parallel and are kept free of grit.

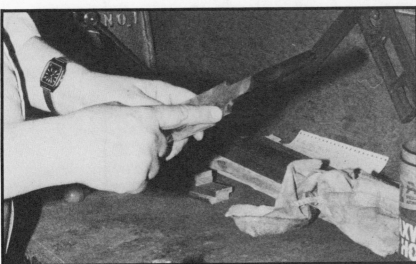

The area where the tang will join the blade and hand guard must be perfectly shaped before assembly.

but most of us do not have one of those. Any device that will mark a line along the edge a uniform distance from the side will do. Clay leaves a sixteenth-of-an-inch space in the center of the tang on his knives. He grinds to those lines only, so the tang does not get too thin. The next step for Clay is to grind down a slight hollow in the center of the tang using a worn 60-grit belt over his six-inch contact wheel. Caution is required to stay in the center of the tang as you are grinding.

Hollowing out the tang slightly on the contact wheel saves wear and tear on the belt grinding platen, which is used in the next step. Clay installs a fresh 60-grit ceramic oxide belt on his grinder and starts his grind, using a push stick against the work. The platen is extended above the two rubber wheels where the flat work area is.

Carefully start the grind at the rear of the tang and let the belt curl upward as you grind. Make sure the tang remains flat against the platen. Watch the sparks flying off the sides of the tang to gauge how well you are doing. The amount of sparks off each side should be about equal if you are grinding straight. If the grind runs higher on one side than the other, says Clay, you will have to go back and start the grind over, while holding a gentle side pressure in the opposite direction.

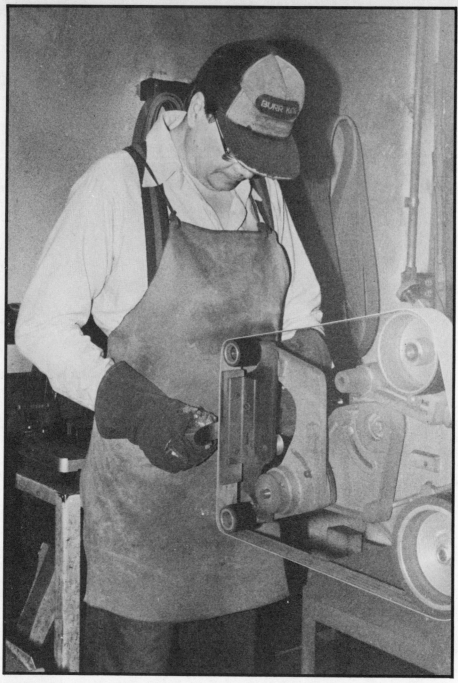

A belt sander is ideal for shaping and grinding blades which have been cut from stock. Note safety equipment.

The tapered portion should end on the scribed line on the edge of the tang where you left the sixteenth of an inch marked.

Clay now moves to his flat grinder on which he has installed a flat disc set up with a 220-grit plate. Using this, he cleans up all the flats on the knife.

Wayne Clay is able to taper a knife tang in only three or four minutes using his Loveless method. The Clay knives we have inspected prove the validity of the method.

Leave about a sixty-fourth of an inch unsharpened along the blade edge. You can do some real damage to yourself throughout the polishing and finishing phase if the edge is sharpened too soon. Furthermore, grinding it down now will leave too little metal on the blade for the most efficient heat-treating that comes later.

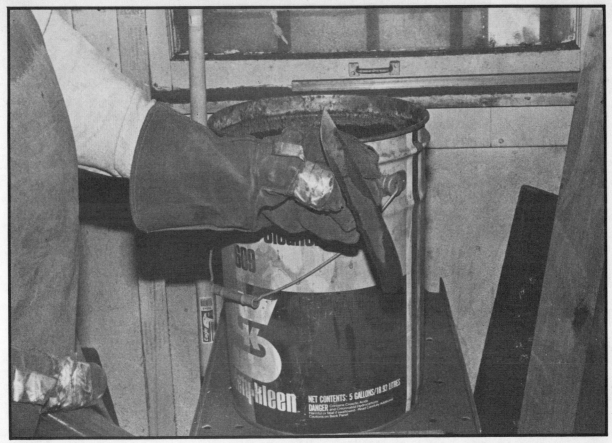

During any grinding operation, a bucket of water is kept at hand to frequently cool the blade steel.

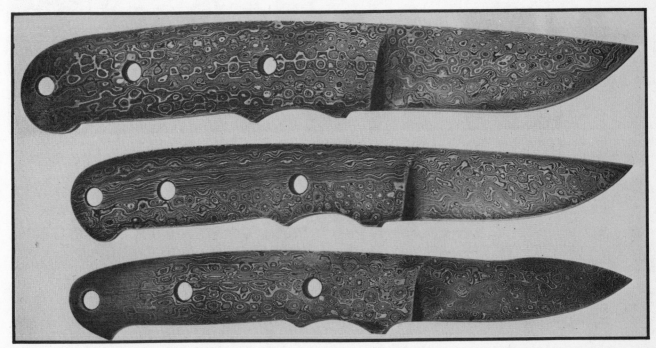

Plenty of work can be saved and unusual knives may be produced using Damascus USA forged-to-shape blades. The blades are already formed and ground; they must be finished and handle materials assembled.

Professional custom knifemaker Wayne Clay has devised an easier way to taper tangs, a method he says he learned from Bob Loveless in 1981. Clay has fashioned a height gauge to scribe center lines a sixteenth-of-an-inch apart.

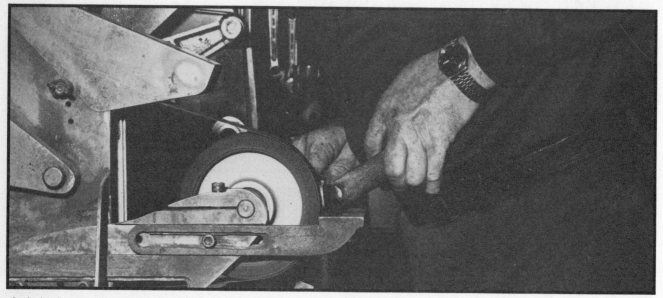

A six-inch contact wheel is set up with a worn 60-grit belt to hollow out the center of the tang. This must be done carefully, using a push stick, to hollow out only the center of the tang. The method takes only a few minutes.

With the blade profiled and the tang tapered, we are ready to drill the pin or bolt holes in the tang. You may use your own artistic eye to determine how many pins should be used and where they are to be placed. Some makers use dozens of pins as decorations, outlining the handle shape with contrasting pins. But two, three or four are enough for good alignment and strength when used with epoxy cement. Simple pins made of welding rod or soft stainless steel are what most advanced knifemakers use, although there is a wide selection of bolts and rivets that also may be used. If your knife is to feature a metal bolster, the bolster will have to be pinned and soldered onto the knife blade, as epoxy will not hold it well enough.

You may wish to include a thong hole in the handle, depending upon the size and style of the knife. If so, it should be drilled out at one-quarter inch, the standard size. Later, it can be lined with a section of brass tubing for a more attractive appearance. The thong hole will be near the butt end of the handle toward the spine.

Pin holes in the tang should be spaced evenly to provide maximum strength. If a bolster or guard is to be used, one or two holes should be drilled in the tang near the blade section. Some makers also drill out lightening holes in the tang at this time. They will be filled with epoxy when the time comes, giving added strength to the tang/handle bond.

The tang holes will have to be slightly larger than the

This is the result of the first hollowing cuts to the tang. The technique saves time and wear on the platen.

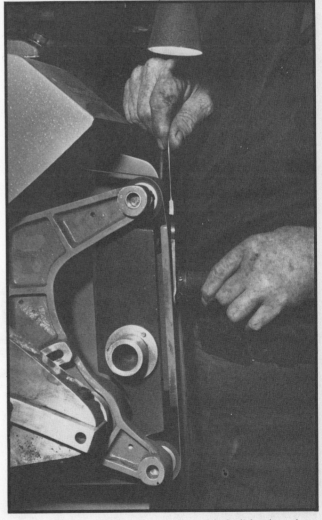

A fresh 60-grit 3M Regal ceramic oxide belt is placed on the sander in front of the platen. Start the grind at the rear of the tang and let the belt cut upward.

pins or bolt shafts you will be using, so select the correct drill bit for the job. Engnath, for one, has standard brass stock for pins in several diameters ranging from one-sixteenth up to one-quarter inch. One-eighth inch is a standard size for most knives.

Select the hole locations and mark them with a punch. If you have a drill press, this is the time to put it to use. You will have holes drilled at perfect ninety-degree angles through the tang, which will be important when drilling the matching holes in the handle slabs. Remember to chamfer each hole slightly after drilling.

With the holes drilled, your blade blank is ready to be heat-treated. If using pre-finished blades or blade blanks, we can begin our knife construction without waiting for anything to come back from the heat-treater. The pre-finished blades and unfinished blanks already will have the holes drilled. Often, they will come with extra holes drilled out so the maker can use any of several choices of hole locations and sizes for joining. The unused holes will be filled with epoxy.

No doubt, you have chosen the handle material for your knife. If you use a man-made Micarta or resin-impregnated wood, such as the commercial Pakkawood, there will be no problem with the two halves matching in grain, color or texture. The man-made materials are uniform throughout, so matching is not a consideration.

If using wood, bone, antler or some other natural material which has color and grain, the halves should match up. Check the end grains in particular to see that you have a match. Once you have it, mark the insides, left and right sides. As you pick them up later, you will not have to guess which is which.

If the knife design does not call for a bolster or guard,

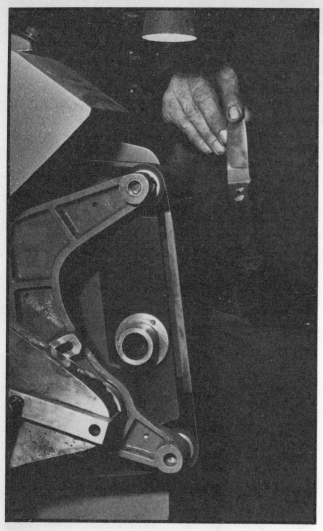

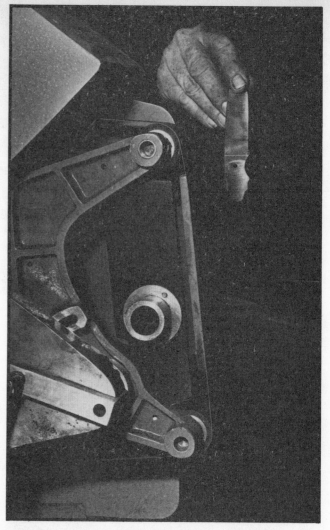

With the taper almost completely ground to the scribed lines, only a trace of the hollowing out process is still visible. The taper must be even.

As the tang is ground, it must be frequently checked for straight lines. The platen holds the grinding belt out slightly from the line of the rubber wheels.

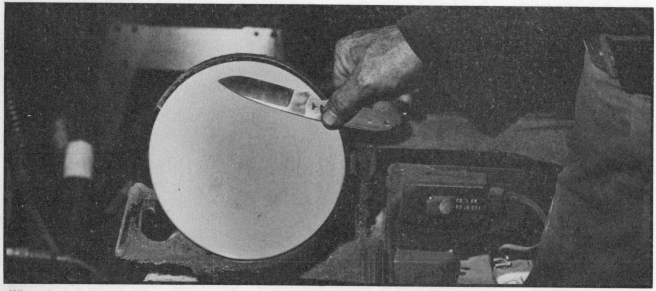

When the tang has been gound down to the scribed lines. Clay moves to his disc grinder with 220-grit paper to clean up the flats on the blade. These final grinding steps make or break the design.

The final step before the knife is sent to be heat treated, is to chamfer each pin and thong hole with a 45-degree countersink drill, left. Chamfering makes later assembly easier and also relieves some of the stress during the treatment. Clay's push stick and height gauge are shown above. Total time required to taper a knife tang is but three or four minutes.

portions of the handle halves which would be nearest the blade must be finished completely at this point. You will not be able to touch up the area after the blade has been finished without the risk of unwanted marks and scratches on either the blade or the handle. Sand and buff that area to its final finish, whether it is to be slightly curved or absolutely flat.

Before drilling, tape all the blade metal to protect both your hands and the finish. If using one of the finished blades, you may proceed with the handle drilling. If one of the unfinished but heat-treated blades is being used, here is where you will want to finish it.

Blade finishing is the most tedious, time-consuming part of a knifemaker's job. Hand-finishing will produce the most satisfying and attractive appearance, although it takes many hours, especially for the beginner. Once you have done it, later knives will not take as long nor seem as difficult. Best advice is to hand-finish your knife, rather than attempt a buffing wheel finish. Buffers will do the job much more rapidly and easily and many professional custom makers do it that way; but you should know how hand-finishing is done.

The tang area is not smooth finished, of course, but any residual discoloration left over from heat-treating needs to be removed. The epoxy will adhere better to the clean metal, but is should be slightly roughened for best results.

With the tang cleaned up, clamp the knife in the vise, blade toward you. A safety note is in order here. When doing this sort of work and you take a break or walk away from the vise for any reason, remove the blade and place it on the bench. A sharp blade left in the vise is an invitation to an accident. You are almost guaranteed to run into the point eventually and sustain a serious injury. It takes no more than a second to remove and replace the blade each time.

Tighten the blade in the vise enough so the pressure you use while rubbing will not cause the blade to move. You are not likely to bend or warp a normal blade by too much pressure in the vise.

Assemble your supply of wet-and-dry paper in various grits. Most custom knives will be finished at least to 220 grit. Many makers take theirs down to 400 or 600 grit. The finer you wish to go, the longer the job. Paper at 220 is a

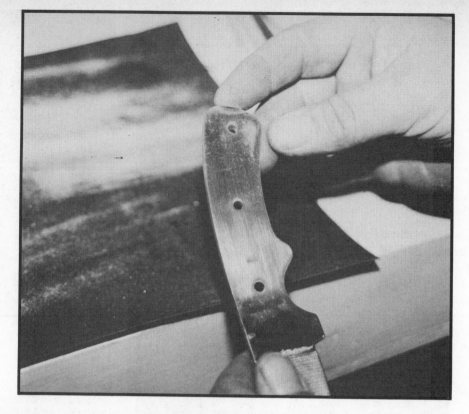

After the treatment, it is a good idea to roughen the tang area a bit to facilitate a good epoxy bond.

The knife held in the bench vise for hand finishing. A portion of the tang will be visible on the finished knife and must be sanded to the finish of the blade itself. Always use a sanding block behind the paper.

good place to start on the House of Muzzleloading finished blade blanks. When he grinds them, Bob Engnath has semi-finished the blades to a 220-grit wheel before heat-treating. It may not be obvious at first, but there still are plenty of grinding marks to remove, even with that fine a finish.

Fold the sheet of sandpaper into thirds and tear or cut it into strips. This trick makes the paper easier to use and also means less waste as you work.

You will need some sort of solid sanding block. A piece of aluminum, steel, wood or Micarta works well. It needs to be only about three or four inches long and about a half an inch across the sanding surfaces. The corners should be rounded slightly so as not to cut through your paper too fast. The paper is folded carefully around the block, starting at one end, with enough up the side to hold onto. As the paper becomes smooth, the paper is moved up to the next clean section and the blade rubbed some more. At first, the grit will last only a few strokes, until it is worn out.

Use short strokes lengthwise along the blade. Start at the back of the blade and work toward the tip as it faces you. Use enough pressure to get a small bite of grit with each

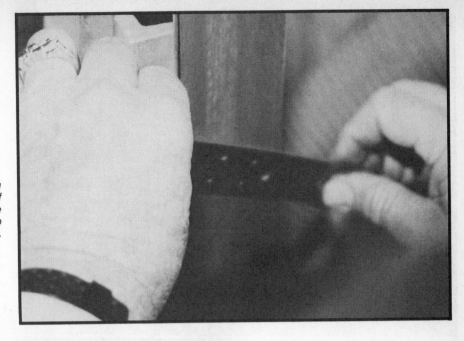

A quick way to rough up the tang area is to use a belt sander, if you have one in the shop. Take care that the metal does not heat up so much as to damage the temper.

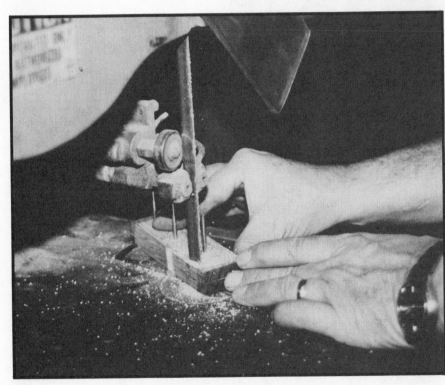

Handle slabs should be matched for grain and appearance, cut together. A band saw may be used to cut the handle pattern, left. The maker should be using a safety push stick.

stroke. Progess should be slow, but steady. You soon will begin to see where the old grind marks are showing up beneath the paper. Every one of those marks must be polished out before moving to the next finer grit paper.

Use care as you reach the blade tip. Moving too rapidly or too soon is liable to put the tip into your finger or hand. We sustained several light stabs at first, but learned how to avoid that painful and unwanted step within a few minutes.

Stroke with a section of paper until it has been ground down and filed smooth, then move to another section. For a change of pace, rub the back of the blade, too. Pay a lot of attention to the area just in front of the bolster or guard. Once the knife is finished and the handle is affixed, you cannot go back and touch up any flaws you leave now.

Work on one side for a while, then turn the knife over and work on the other. Thus, boredom is reduced and you are less likely to become careless. Speaking of carelessness, if you start to get tired while buffing, take a break. You do not have to set any speed records; consider this a learning process. The better job you do now, the better looking the final product will be.

Examine the blade area from different angles under the

Black Pakkawood is cut with a band saw, this time using a push stick. Final shaping may be done on belt sander or grinder.

Pin holes are drilled through both handle halves at once for uniform fitting. Copper tubing protruding from material will become the thong hole liner when completed.

brightest shop lights you have. Just when you think you have rubbed enough, you probably will find a few more scratches that have to be worked on. When you think you've done enough, do some more.

A hand-rubbed finish will require several sheets of paper. Hang on to the used paper as it can be used for some final rubbing after it is worn out.

If you want to go no further than the 220-grit finish, as we did on our own project, you may quit when no more scratches are visible. However, many makers carry the finish of their knives on to finer grits. To do this, cut the paper into strips as done earlier, but make the next grit — the 320 — strokes at an angle to what was used on the 220 paper. Engnath suggests stroking with the finer grits at a

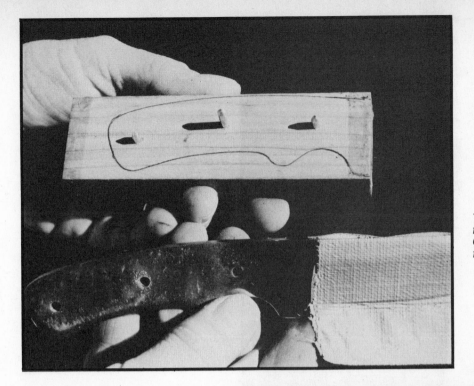

This knife is the completely finished blade from Atlanta Cutlery. Pins are placed through first side and matched to tang.

Three brass welding rod pins are placed for a test fit through the tang and handle slab. The blade portion of the knife is taped for safety, as well as to protect the finish. Both sides of handle are cut to shape after both have been drilled.

forty-five-degree angle with the first paper. Bear down hard enough to clean off the lines left from the 220-grit paper with the 320, then 400-grit to remove the 320 marks and so on. The 220-grit is the hardest work and should use up the most paper.

Some will want to add water to the wet-or-dry paper for faster cutting. If so, use enough water to keep the grit clear and cutting, but not so much as to build up a muddy layer on the blade. Try to maintain the strokes even and parallel.

Engnath advises doing the final rub three times, using 600-grit paper. The first rub is a forty-five-degree angle, the second is along the length of the blade. Stop at that point, rub the guard and grip area, then come back for a

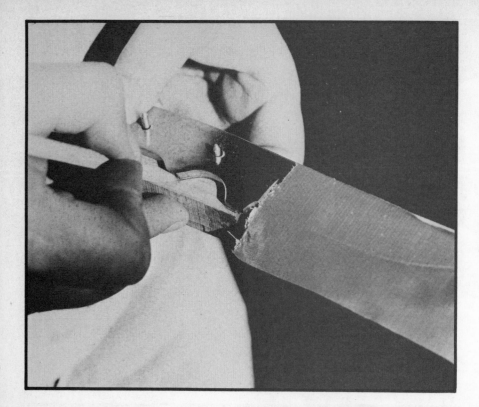

Pins temporarily hold the handle half in place as the tang shape is outlined with a pencil, left.

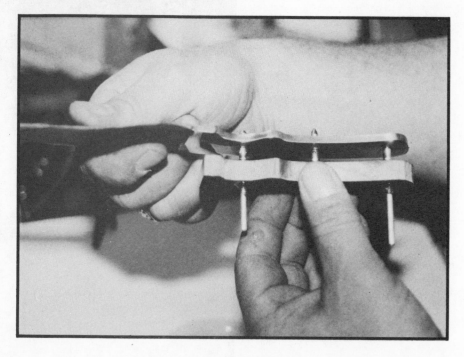

On this model, using the finished Atlanta Cutlery blade, the tang is left full thickness, not tapered.

final 600-grit rub. On this final rub, use oil instead of water and rub along the length of the blade.

As each progressively finer grit is rubbed, the knife should start to take on a mirror effect. It should become noticeable with the 400-grit and really show up with the second 600-grit paper. If there are any residual scratches at this time, they will show and haunt you forever, unless they are taken out. The slightest scratch will show up too well against the 600-grit finish. You will have to go back to

a more coarse paper and work back down to get the marks out.

Never sharpen the blade edge, until all rubbing and polishing is complete. Rubbing knives with grind lines along their lengths requires more care than a simple, full flat-blade style. The flat surfaces on each side should be treated as separate areas and must be sanded with extra care or the junction of bevel and body will round off and begin to disappear. These lines must be kept clean and

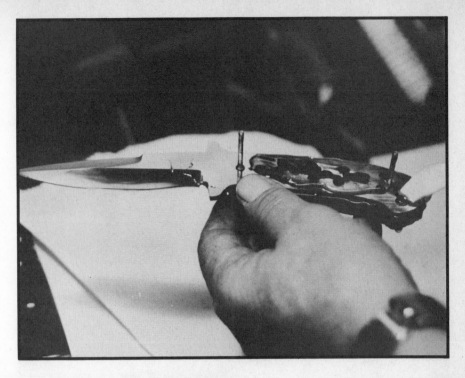

The tang on this fighting knife has been drilled out in several places to reduce the weight and to provide better contact for the mixture of two-part epoxy cement.

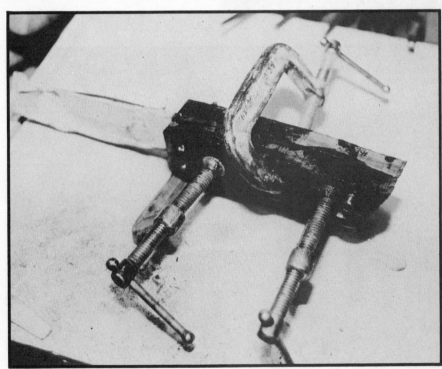

This is a construction technique gone bad. Threaded bolt and nut fasteners were tried, but the female ends filled with epoxy and prevented the slabs from contacting the tang. The cement hardened too rapidly and the side and bolts had to be sawed off and begun again.

crisp for the maximum custom knife effect.

The same thing applies to knives with a false edge at the tip. Although the area is small, it should be kept crisp and well finished, adding a great deal to your finished knife. If you find yourself rocking the sanding block across the flats, try rubbing at a diagonal to get the feel of more surface. Most makers learn to hate false-edge designs after doing a few.

Blades with fancy choil designs or filed backs present extra finishing problems. They require more patience to achieve a good finish. The rubbing paper should be wrapped on dowels or V-shaped sanding blocks to get the paper down into those little spaces. You will have to rub in one direction only. The filed areas cannot be cleaned up on a belt grinder, leaving a rougher surface to start with.

If hand-rubbing your knife seems like too much work or you are running out of time, Bob Engnath offers a quick and dirty finish using four buffing wheels in sequence.

If screwdriver-slotted handle bolts are used, left, slower-acting epoxy should be used so the bolts can be tightened before the cement sets up.

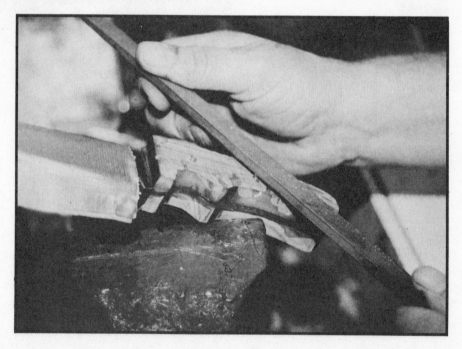

Using a wood handle, final shaping and smoothing can be done with only hand tools. The work is a bit slower, but results can be the same.

The first wheel is loaded with 220 to 240-grit greaseless buffing compound, the second is loaded with 300-plus greaseless compound, the third contains black grease stick and the last, green grease stick. Plain hardware store wheels may be used so long as they are well stitched for a rather firm surface.

Begin with the 220-240 grit wheel, holding the blade with the cutting edge downward at about a forty-five-degree angle across the wheel. The 240 grit will heat up rapidly and you will see sparks as the belt grinding marks are taken off. Have your bucket of water at hand and quench the blade often enough to keep it cool.

When you have an even finish from the first wheel, move to the 300-grit wheel, holding the blade at a slightly different angle. Then move on to the black and finally the green wheel.

Engnath says the transition from the 300-grit to the black compound will take the longest and probably will

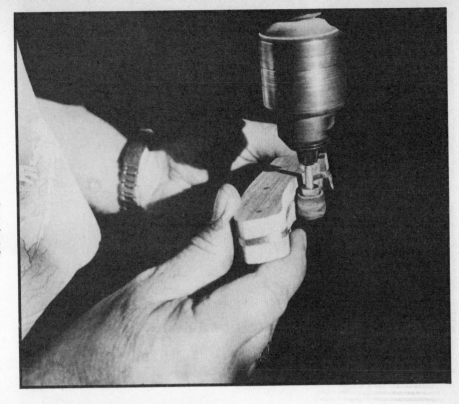

A fast and easy way to shape and sand contoured handles is using a drill press. A small diameter drum sander is chucked in the drill head and the knife is held firmly against the rough grit.

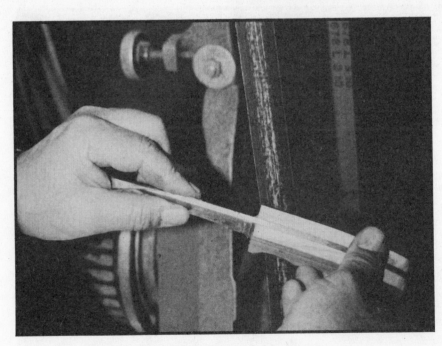

Here, the sanding belt has been split to provide a thinner cutting surface. The platen is removed, leaving slack to sand the contours.

show up some scratches which you will have to take out before going on with the buffing process. Final buffing with either green or white compound is more of a burnishing process, not really removing any material. Ripples and scratches seem to be pushed along without actually being removed. You cannot remove scratches made by 320- or 400-grit paper with the green or white buffing compounds. You should do that before you reach this point.

The buffing wheel finish is fast, but if it's used, don't expect to get top dollar or top judging in a knife show. It tends to round off the sharp grind lines and corners, if one is not careful and skillful. For fully flat blades such as kitchen knives, it is ideal. Knives with fancy file work or complicated blade designs should be hand-finished, no matter how long it takes.

At some point, you will reach a stopping point for either the hand-rubbed or the buffing-wheel finish. When you think you're done, take another close look to make sure

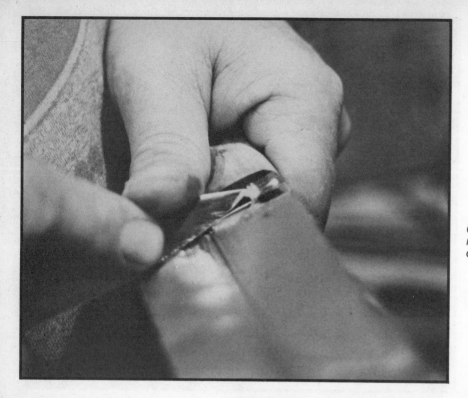

Carefully used, a sharp knife will remove excess epoxy that has oozed out from the tang onto the blade.

A half-round file will begin to form the finger groove in this handle design. The blade is held in the vise jaws with a protective piece of soft folded leather.

there are no almost-hidden flaws which you can clean up with a few more minutes of work. If satisfied, it is time to mount the handles and finish the knife.

Correct and precise placement of the pin or bolt holes in the handle slabs is important for the best final fit. Start with one slab lightly clamped to the tang in its approximate final position. Using a drill press or a hand or power drill, carefully drill through the tang into the handle material. Drill all the necessary holes before removing the clamps. Some material will tend to splinter at the far side of the drill as it exits. Even some Micartas will tend to split or splinter, so take care. New or sharp drill bits help eliminate this problem before it starts.

Place a pin or bolt in the first hole after you have it drilled out to help maintain the position of the handle. Move each pin in its turn as you clamp and drill the second side of the

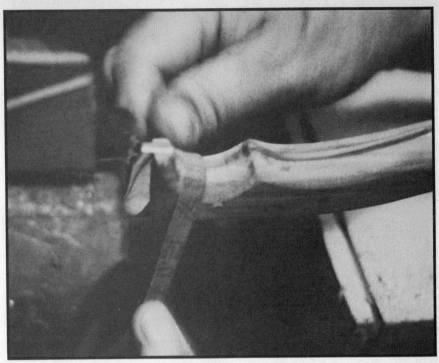

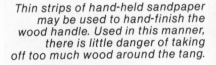
Thin strips of hand-held sandpaper may be used to hand-finish the wood handle. Used in this manner, there is little danger of taking off too much wood around the tang.

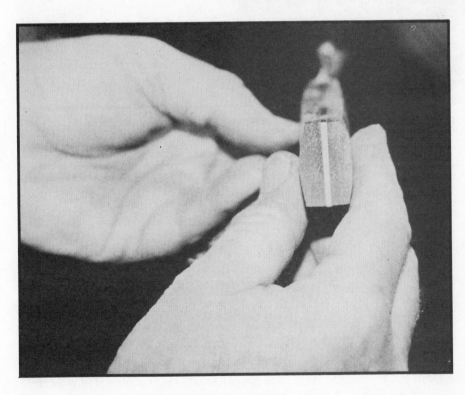

The end of a tapered tang knife shows matched grain handle halves and tight epoxy cement bonding.

handle material. Leave the pins or bolts in for a trial fit before mixing the epoxy. You might wish to notch the underside of the bolt heads slightly to provide better anchoring in the epoxy.

As mentioned elsewhere, the best epoxy is the slower setting type; one that takes overnight to harden. The five-minute epoxy will set up too fast. Mix the cement carefully and according to directions.

Lay on plenty of the cement. Get into all the holes and on the pins and bolts. If you are using bolts or rivets with non-outlet cavities, do not get the epoxy in those cavities. The cement will not force out and will prevent the male ends from bottoming out and locking in the female ends.

No epoxy can do its job properly on a perfectly smooth surface or one which has bench or finger grease on it. Always rough up the surfaces to be glued and make certain

It is all too easy to take too much wood away in the tang area, leaving metal protruding beyond the handle material. Final finishing of the back spine might be better done by hand, rather than using a belt sander.

all are clean and free of oil or grease.

If you use threaded bolts to join the sides and tang, slowly tighten them down while the cement is still soft. You may use clamps while the epoxy sets, but do not use too much pressure. You will be in danger of cracking or otherwise damaging the handle; or you may set up unwanted stresses which will cause trouble later. Too much stress and even the best epoxy could let go after the clamps are removed. The fit should be good enough that excess clamping is not necessary.

If your design includes bolsters or a guard, be sure to snug the handle up against the metal before the epoxy sets and locks in place. It must not slide later. Epoxy will fill the

crack, but it will be unsightly for the life of the knife.

When the epoxy has set — wait overnight, if you can — saw the bolt heads or snip the pins off as close to the handle material as possible. Shape the pins or bolts as you shape and smooth the handle. Wood grips can be power-sanded or filed with a coarse file, using a half-round for the curves.

Micarta can be rather hard and almost requires a power belt sander to shape. Use the platen behind the belt to act as a sanding block so the handle material is not sanded down farther than the pins or bolts. If the handle will have finger grooves or some other contour, slack-belt sanding without the platen is a quick way to clean things up. Sand a little on each side, working slowly so as not to take too

Another critical area which critics and potential buyers will always examine, is the area where the bolster might be, if there is one. The visible junction of handle and blade is almost too difficult to repair if the finish is damaged. It is also an area where excess epoxy must be removed for the cleanest final appearance.

much down and end up with a lopsided handle. If using bolts, don't take so much handle material down that you also sand away all the bolt heads.

When sanding the rear of the handle along the tang, it is very easy to take off too much handle material, leaving the metal tang extending too far. This can happen when using the belt sander without the platen. Use a sanding block and finish off that area without power tools.

Wood grips should be sealed to prevent later staining. Tung oil or Danish oil will do the job, although any oil will tend to darken the wood. Urethane-type sealers should be avoided for knife handles. Micarta or other man-made handles need nothing on them.

Another good way to work on contoured handles after gluing is to chuck a small drum sander in the drill press. The variable-speed drill press will operate slowly enough for you to be in complete control, as you sand along any tricky curves.

Well, your first really custom knife is finished, except for sharpening. We have included a later chapter on that subject. Sharpen it, use it or display it with pride. If making your own knife does nothing else, the process should offer some idea of just how hard and long the professionals must work to produce the kind of knives they make. We now can appreciate their work all the more.

Buck Knives, Too, Has Its Own Custom Knife Making Capability

The man who bears the name of the company, Chuck Buck, examines examples of Buck custom knives, turned out in one portion of the Buck Knife factory, above. With the knife pattern etched into the steel, a band saw is used to cut out the shape. A dark coating on the steel lets the etched pattern stand out, below.

NOT ALL the better custom knife makers are solitary artists living high in the Idaho mountains, visiting the city only when they have to buy beans, flour and knife steel.

The new Buck Knife factory in California maintains a facility within its walls for the production of handmade custom and one-of-a-kind knives.

We asked author C.R. Learn to give us a report on the custom shop and here is what he found!

THE FIRST BUCK knives were made by Hoyt H. Buck back around 1906-1910. He made them from good metal for friends and soon started to sell a few now and then. These would be classified today as custom knives, made by hand by one person, all the way through the process. When World War I broke out, H.H. Buck started getting orders from servicemen, which led to a great future for Buck Knives.

The Buck family moved to San Diego, California, in the early 1930s and made knives under the name of H.H. Buck & Son, Lifetime Knives. The now much larger company moved to El Cajon, just east of the San Diego, in 1968. They were then still making a few Buck custom knives on order only. The full line of Buck knives was being made in

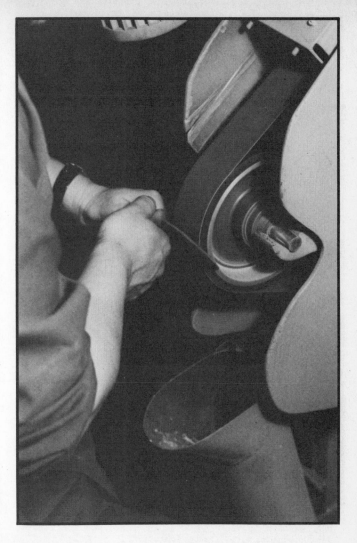

The Buck custom knives are made one at a time, just as we beginners do it. After patterning, the blank is cleaned up and hollow ground on the big belt grinder, right. The belt wheel provides just the right radius for the hollow grind. While the steel is still soft, pin holes are drilled for handle and bolster.

the plant and the custom work was a small part of the total.

In 1980, Buck moved again to their present plant also in El Cajon. They once again had a custom knife shop at the new quarters. They had come full circle.

C.R. Learn has been interested in the Buck line of knives, as a writer and photographer, for more than twenty years. He has used and carried many Buck knives over the years and has had a few laughs with Buck while discussing some of the ways people can find to abuse knives.

The Buck Custom Department started with a few top craftsmen from the plant who used their years of knifemaking knowledge to produce knives for those who had ideas, but not the equipment or the training.

One of the first things to determine is the price of a custom knife made by Buck. This is a difficult question to answer, because the cost varies with the amount of work, the type of steel, the handle material and many more variables. Mark DeFelice, production manager of the Buck Custom Department, estimated a low $100 to a possible high of $3000 in 1989 dollars.

The first step toward a Buck custom knife is a sketch of the blade style and the handle. This should be done on quarter-inch graph paper, but DeFelice has received designs drawn on almost all types of paper, from detailed ones to rough sketches.

The designer calls for some fancy file work on the back of the blade and tang, left. This, too, is done before the steel is heat tempered and hardened. Tools are the same as might be found in any home workshop. Bolsters and handle slabs are installed after blade is hardened. Stainless steel pins hold bolsters in place.

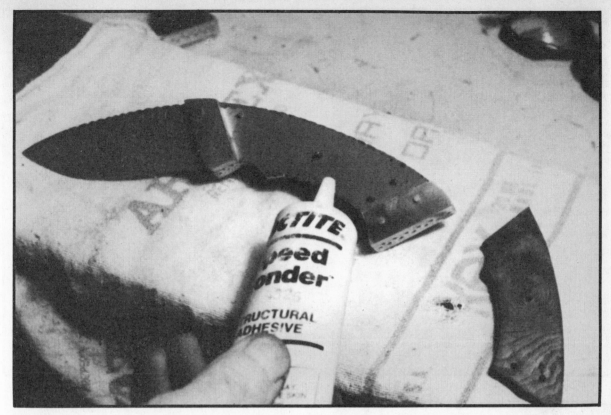

In a previous step, the handle slabs were profiled and formed of Arizona mesquite wood which shows interesting grain patterns. Fit must be exact before industrial strength glue is applied to tang, above.

Below: The custom maker uses the butt of a second knife to tap the stainless steel pins in place while the cement is still fluid. Excess pin length will be snipped off just as in the kit knife project.

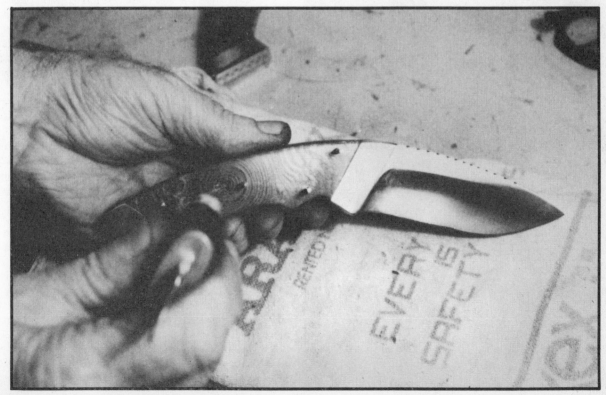

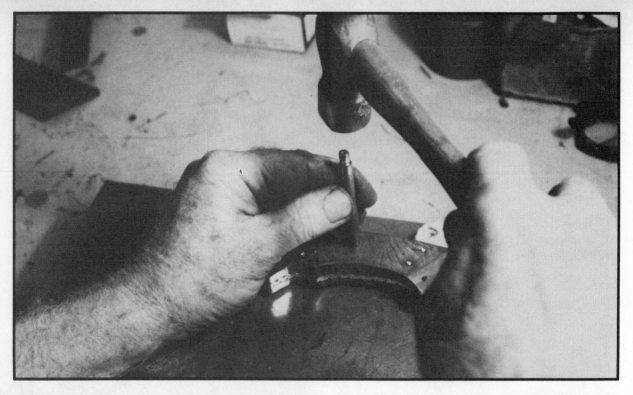

Above: The handle pins have been clipped off almost flush with the wood slabs before they are slightly peened to set them in place. Because they are professionals with years of knifemaking behind them, the Buck craftsmen are able to grind a keen blade edge on a large belt. We might use a stone.

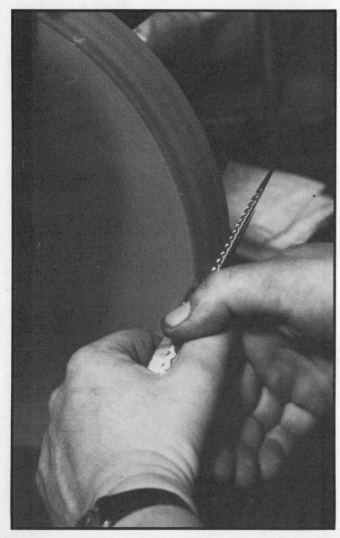

DeFelice then transfers your sketch to graph paper. He determines the specifications of steel thickness and handle material. A price estimate is agreed upon by customer and the maker. Once in agreement, the customer is asked to submit fifty percent of the price and the work will start. It will take from eight to ten weeks for completion of a custom knife. The balance is due on completion.

The more the customer adds to the knife in the way of weird shape and exotic handle materials, the more it will cost. DeFelice has received several of what he terms "fantasy" design sketches. These have exotic blade shapes with many cuts and circles and exotic handles that would take more time to make than the knifemaker can justify without an increase in price. Some of these designs go far beyond what any science fiction buff might dream up; they are just not practical to make.

Many of us have ideas of what we would like to see in a knife. Learn's knife didn't fit into the far-out realm, but was different. Learn submitted patterns for two knifes: a solid full-tang fixed-blade hunter and a long-bladed fishing knife. They had a bit different design; there are no others like them on the market. When a customer receives a custom knife made by Buck, the design remains the property of the customer.

The hunting knife has a cutting edge of four inches, a favorite length. The blade and handle have a decidedly curved shape. Learn designed his blade as a drop point, but

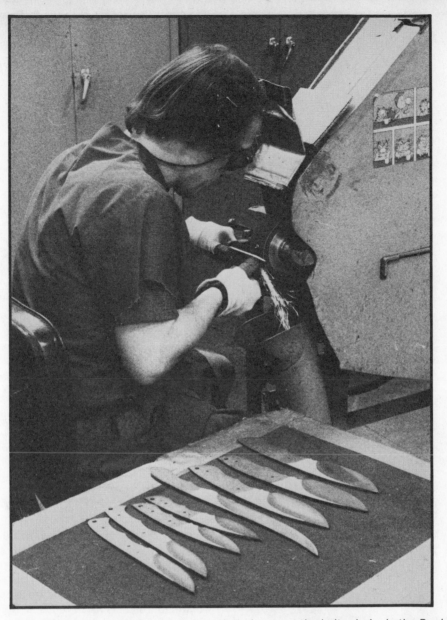

A number of semi-finished blades await their turn at the belt grinder in the Buck custom shop section of the factory. Leroy Remer is a man with more than fifteen years of experience with Buck Knives. Note the use of safety eye goggles by Remer.

extended the idea a bit and radiused the entire knife in a pleasing curved configuration.

The total length of the knife is 9¼ inches, leaving more than half the length to the handle for a good grip. Learn supplied his own handle material. He had picked some swirl-grained knotty mesquite wood years ago and was waiting for the right time to use it.

The fishing knife has a blade length of 6½ inches, big enough for most any freshwater and many of the saltwater fish varieties. It also had a radius to the handle area, but the radius is reversed. It is upswept at the end to give it a double curve. The handle material was of the same slab of mesquite, so the pair of knives matched in shape and handle material. They work even better than designer Learn had anticipated.

The steel was selected from a stock of 440C, but the cus-

tomer may choose from many others. The 440C is rust-resistant steel which has proven itself as a good knife steel. The tang section was to be file marked, a popular option.

With design and price established, the first step is to transfer the blade pattern onto the 440C steel plate for cutting. That slight radius design is one reason this knife will not be a popular one for production. The radius requires more steel than a standard straight blade. The cost of extra steel isn't practical for a production line knife.

The pattern is scribed onto the steel and the two pieces are cut apart to allow easier sawing. The Buck Custom Department uses band saws to form the basic shape. This technique has proven itself, because it doesn't heat up the steel and maintains the molecular structure better than a heat or plasma cut.

The basic blade shape is cut by stock removal on a sand-

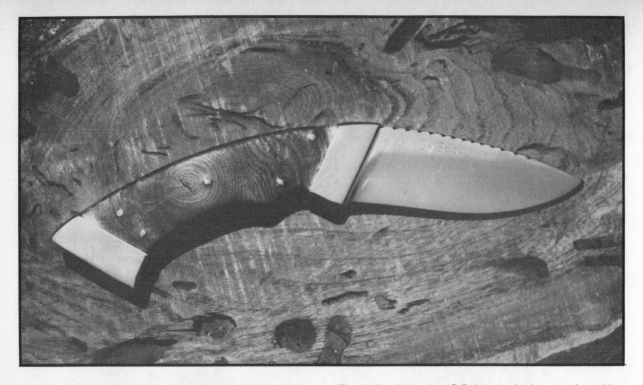

The knife above is a C.R. Learn design, produced in the Buck custom shop. It features a blade of four inches and measures 9¼-inches long overall. The Arizona mesquite handle slabs complement the curved blade shape. The fancy file work on Learn's knives extends the full length of the tang and blade back.

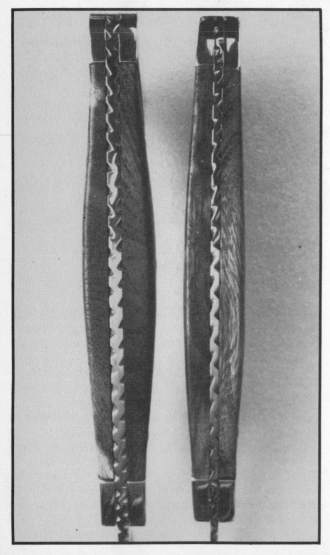

ing belt. Again, this doesn't generate damaging heat. The blades are hollow ground, not a good style for a production knife, as it is too delicate. A slight twist when working and a nice half-moon section is taken out of the blade.

The file art is the next feature to be added to the knives before the steel is hardened. The Buck knifemakers got a bit carried away with the file work with full handle, top, bottom and butt plus the top of the blade filed.

From the pattern, holes are drilled for the bolsters and finger guard. These are filled with stainless steel rod sections to match the bolsters. That done, the blades go for heat treating at the Buck plant by Paul Boss, a master craftsman in this field. When cooled, the blades were tested on the Rockwell machine at an even 59C.

The blade is lightly buffed, the stainless steel bolsters are added and the pins cut off flush. The mesquite handles are cut and fitted for a tight wood and metal fit. The handle slabs are drilled to match the pin holes in the tang. Stainless pins are inserted through them and clipped off before grinding the basic shape on the slabs and bolsters.

Learn had an opportunity to see the semi-finished knives at this point and thought his choice of swirled mesquite handles was a good one. There were some small cracks in the wood, but these were left unfilled. Mesquite is a tough wood, but it is almost impossible to find a section that doesn't have some flaws.

The final phase was a good polish on the buffing wheels

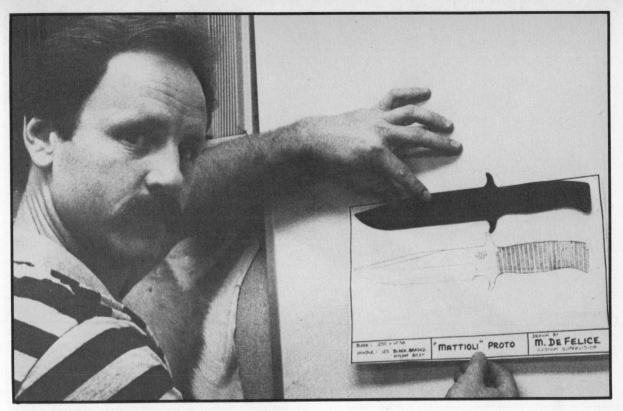

Mark DeFelice is the production manager of the Buck custom shop. He works from the customer's idea sketch, makes a final paper design and submits it, with a cost estimate to customer for approval.

to bring out a mirror finish on the blades and the bolsters, while accenting the figure in the wood slabs.

The only thing left to add was a quality sheath which is furnished with all Buck custom knives. They are made by a true craftsman in leather, Wes Chapman. He will make a sheath of heavy leather that will fit the knife in style.

The fish knife followed the same procedure as the hunter, although it is longer, thinner and more flexible. Learn says he never carries a fish knife in a belt sheath. It stays in the tackle box, so the leather sheath acts to keep the ultra-

sharp blade from cutting lures and other fishing gear in the tackle box. Learn reports one stint of four solid hours using his knife to fillet bass and crappie with no sharpening and no problems.

The customer who sends his deposit for a Buck custom knife won't know exactly who will make the knife, but the craftsmen there have a collective seventy-five years experience in the knife business. The three senior men are John Knapp, Leroy Remer and Bob Miller. The two new members of the group, each having only sixteen years experi-

The custom design below shows some complicated exotic curves and sweeps in front of the hilt. Such special touches are attractive, but add to the cost.

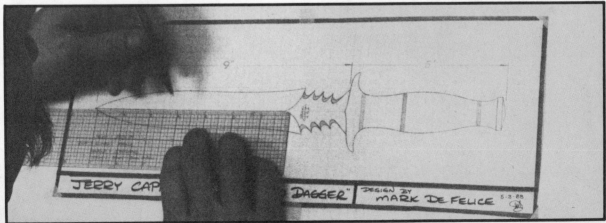

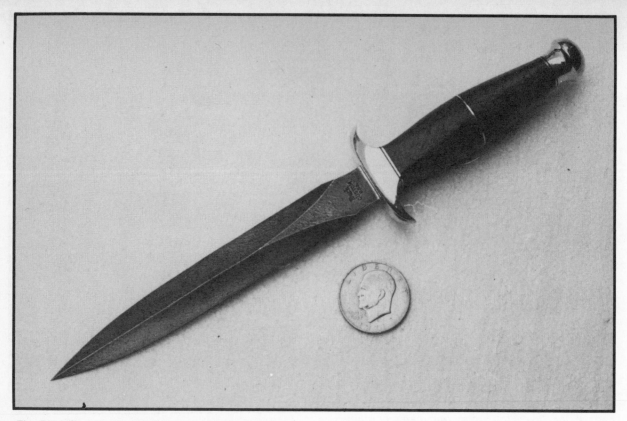

The Eisenhower silver dollar gives scale to the Buck custom shop dagger, crafted from Damascus steel.

ence at this point, are Juan Yuriart and Dave Pestcoe. They do finish and handle work as they move up to final custom knifemaking.

Buck has a beautifully illustrated brochure that shows what they have done for customers as well as some of the knives made for display. They require eight to ten weeks for a custom knife and four to six weeks for a customized production knife. The steel materials offered include 440C ATS-34, D-2 tool steel and Damascus. The Damascus is really something different, says Learn; so is the cost on some of it.

The guard material choices include brass, nickel silver,

In this case, the Buck custom knives shown below have been decorated with scrimshaw on the handles.

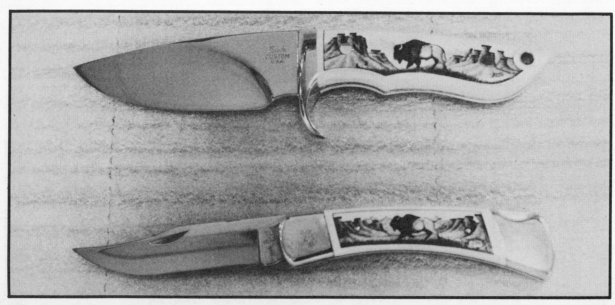

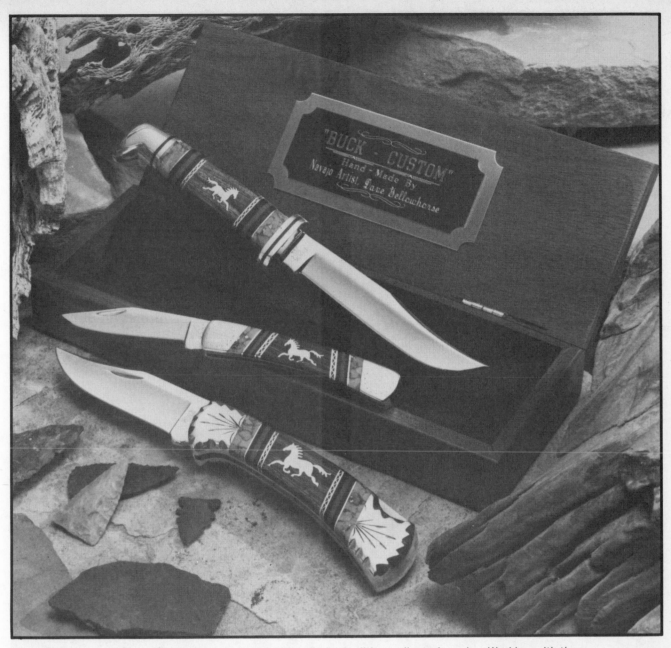

David Yellowhorse, a noted Navajo artist, created this limited edition collector's series. Working with three standard Buck knife models, he applies his distinctive channel inlay process, blending turquoise and other native Southwest stones with brass and wood to create unique designs. Bolsters are hand-tooled by Yellowhorse.

stainless steel and aluminum alloy. Buck Custom has even put handles on knives that came from rafters of grandpa's barn and fossil mastodon ivory more than 10,000 years old.

They also offer handles from animal horns, including water buffalo, American elk, Sambar stag, stag crown and sun-bleached elk horn. Natural woods include bocota, cocobolo, Gaboon ebony, lignum vitae, rosewood, mesquite, wenge or a choice of others they may have on hand.

Man-made materials include Micarta, available layered or colored in several texture variations. This popular handle material is tough and does not shrink as natural materials might. Laminated wood and polyester pearl are also available.

For blade finishes one might select satin, mirror polish, bead blasted, black oxide, titanium nitride and etched Damascus. If you want the knife etched, engraved, or scrimshawed, Buck can have it done. Be aware, however, that the more exotic items put on a knife, the more it costs.

Learn had an opportunity to test out his Buck custom hunter when his hunting buddy downed his first bow-killed mule deer. The radius blade on the knife performed as expected. The blade tip is held away from the innards of the deer and the edge sliced along like nothing was there. From one side of the sternum, all the ribs were cut in one clean motion. The custom knife did a clean, neat job, which is what it was designed to do.

B.R. Hughes takes a turn with the hammer and anvil. He is wearing the mandatory heavy leather gloves and apron, while the necktie is optional. Any heavy-head hammer works. A section of railroad track will replace an anvil.

Chapter 6

FOCUS ON FORGING

This Aspect Of Knifemaking Has Made A Mammoth Comeback In The Past Two Decades

FIFTEEN YEARS ago, the future of the forged blade in America was far from bright. Once, virtually all fine blades were forged; by 1970, knives made by the stock-removal procedure were the rage and let it be said clearly and distinctly, such knives were truly good by any standard!

Several factors contributed to this state of affairs. One of the more obvious was the availability of such steels as 440C, D2, 154CN, etc., all containing sufficient chromium to make them stain-resistant, but none reacting particularly well to forging. It must be admitted, though, that a skilled smith can obtain satisfactory results with these metals.

Forging was and is a hot, dirty, time-consuming method of producing a knife blade and the average would-be cutler of 1972 generally observed the situation, took note of the excellent knives made by Bob Loveless, Ted Dowell, Lloyd Hale, George Herron, Corbet Sigman, et al, and said, in effect, "Why bother?"

The result of this was that, by the early 1970s, there were less than a dozen practicing bladesmiths in the United States, compared with a couple of hundred stock removal knifemakers; and the number of smiths was declining. Two major factors occurred to turn this state of affairs around.

First, at the 1972 Knifemakers Guild show in Kansas City, Bill Moran — at that time the chief executive officer of the guild — unveiled without preamble a number of knives featuring blades made of Damascus steel of his own manufacture. He thus became the first smith in this country to produce this material absent so many years that it had almost become a lost art!

Damascus is a beautiful and efficient blade material, but it is much more time-consuming to make than a standard forged blade. Also, the difficulty of producing this material perhaps can be grasped best by the fact that as late as 1975

A good forged blade will shave forearm hair even after it was used to cut through a four-inch log. The arm and the forged blade are James Crowell's.

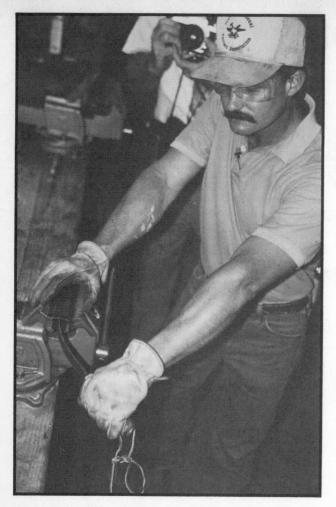

Wearing the obligatory safety glasses, Jerry Hancock shows how far a forge blade can bend without breaking.

After heat treating, the forge bladed edge is submerged in water while the metal is heated using a welding torch. Frank Gunn keeps heat off the blade edge tip.

— two full years after Moran displayed the material at KC — only two other American smiths were offering it! They were Bill Bagwell, who is still an active bladesmith, and the late Don Hastings.

The American Bladesmiths Society was founded in 1976 with Moran as chairman — a post he still holds — with the avowed purpose of preserving the art of the forged blade. The ABS has used a program of education to help achieve this goal and has sponsored seminars at Rochester Institute of Technology, Texarkana College, and the University of Wyoming. In 1988, the first school of blade-smithing in the history of this country was established in Washington, Arkansas, under the co-sponsorship of the ABS and Texarkana College.

Essentially, forging consists of taking a piece of suitable steel, heating it in a forge, then hammering the heated metal, until it achieves the desired size and shape. The proponents of forging have no hesitation in assuring all who will listen that a properly forged blade will outperform a comparable stock-removal blade, all things being equal. In support of this stance, consider that there are three levels of bladesmiths in the ABS: apprentice, journeyman and master. In order to gain the journeyman's rating, a smith must

James Crowell has already mastered the use of a hand-held hammer and moves on to the power hammer. To understand the process, the student forger must spend time at the anvil with a hammer and steel.

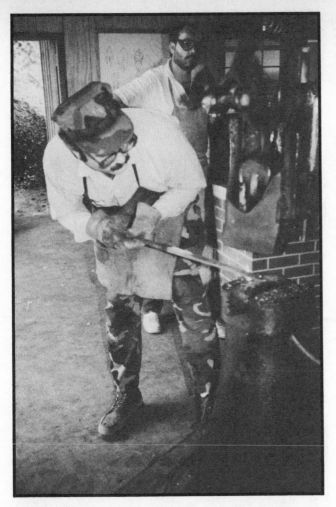

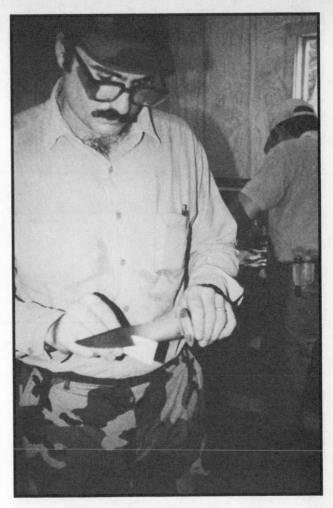

James Crowell and Timothy Hancock are carefully examining the edges of blades they have completed. Carefully drawn across a fingernail, a smooth knife edge will not produce any snags or drags as it goes.

Crowell demonstrates the cutting ability of the Bowie blade he has made by slicing through paper.

put in a minimum of two years as an apprentice, then pass a test that includes chopping up a number of 2x4s without damage to the blade he has made, cleanly cutting at least one free-hanging one-inch manila rope and, finally, putting the blade into a vise and bending it a minimum of ninety degrees without breaking it!

Bladesmiths will attest that at least part of the credit for this type of performance can be attributed to the fact that the grain of the steel in a forged blade is unbroken. The molecules of the material are compressed or "packed" into the cutting edge, since virtually no material is removed in the process of forming the blade.

Perhaps a decade ago, one of the better-known stock-removal makers of that period told me that, when he set out to make a knife, he simply took a piece of steel and using his belt-sander removed all the material that didn't look like a knife. Precious little metal is lost in the making of a forged blade.

All right, you're convinced there is something to forging, so how does one get started?

To begin with, you're going to need a few pieces of equipment that aren't found in stock-removal knifemaking shops. You will need either a coal or a gas forge. It really

It may not show up so well in black and white, but the tang and ricasso areas have been heat tempered, showing darker color. Back and edge remain harder.

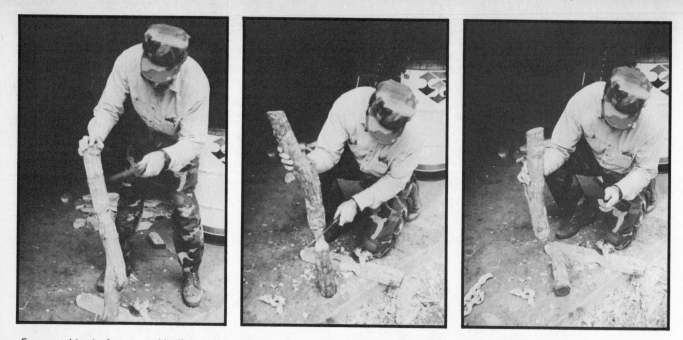

For a real test of man and knife, try this at home for fun and profit. The four-inch log is seasoned oak; plenty hard. At left, the forged Bowie knife that James Crowell made has started; halfway, center, through at right.

Held in a vise, this blade snapped after it was bent to forty-five degrees. It would not pass the test administered by the American Bladesmith Society.

Jerry Fisk is forging a blade with a hand-held hammer. The blade must be heated just right or it will be ruined.

doesn't matter a great deal which route you try; either can be used to create a superior blade.

A coal forge can be made from a variety of items. For example, Chuck Ochs, a well known Florida smith, made his current forge from an old kitchen sink — and it works fine! There must be some means of providing an air supply to the fire. A simple pipe into which a portable hair dryer or a vacuum cleaner can be installed will work in a satisfactory manner long enough for you to decide whether forging is for you. Charcoal is not recommended, although under certain conditions it can be used.

An anvil is a must. In the absence of a true anvil, a length of old railroad track can be used; I know a couple of smiths who use just that. Obviously, a hammer weighing two to three pounds is essential, but it doesn't matter much which type of hammer you select, so long as it has a smooth face. A common ball-peen hammer purchased at the corner discount hardware will suffice. You must have something with which to grasp the heated metal to keep from burning your hands. A set of blacksmith's tongs would be terrific, but a large set of vise grips can do just as well!

Don't get involved in forging without wearing a sturdy pair of boots or shoes, because a hot coal on exposed skin is no laughing matter. Heavy gloves and a leather apron also are required. Finally, never begin any knifemaking chore, including forging, without some type of eye protection.

Fisk removes a glowing piece of blade steel from the forge. If heated too high, steel cannot be used.

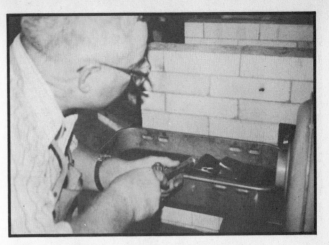

One of the key operations to producing a good forged blade is proper tempering. The blade edge is submerged to keep it from getting hot and soft.

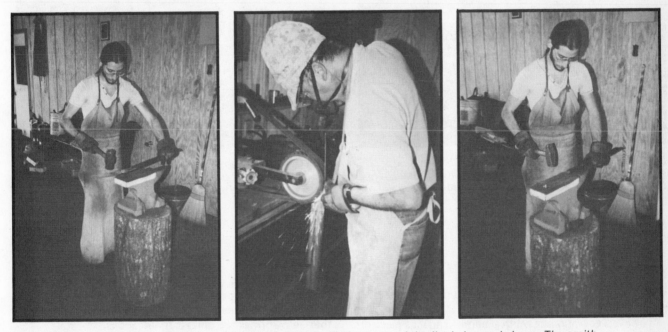

During the early hammer and forge operation, the steel will almost reach its final size and shape. The smith, left, must hammer both sides equally. At right, as forging continues, blade shape will be cut from steel blank with hammer. In the center photo, the bladesmith uses a belt grinder to touch up his blade. Beware of heat!

Start by building a small fire in your forge. Now you are ready to heat the steel from which you will form your blade. In my estimation, some of the better metals for forging include 5160, 1060 and 1095; do not select a high alloy tool steel or one that is air hardening. Don't fret about a supplier for steel. Just hike yourself down to the local automobile wrecking yard and buy some leaf springs. It is said that Rudy Ruana, the legendary Montana smith who died a few years ago, strongly preferred springs from Studebakers! If the wrecking yard will do it for a modest fee, you might have them cut your springs into blade-sized lengths.

If you leave your blade blank approximately two feet in length, it then will be long enough to handle, using only heavy gloves. After the blade has been hammer-formed, it can be cut off to its normal length prior to quenching, using either a hacksaw or a metal-cutting bandsaw. Otherwise, you'll have to use your tongs or vice grip when handling the heated metal.

Place the metal in the fire and allow it to heat until it reaches a forging temperature, which can vary more than the average person supposes. On the low side, it should be a dull cherry red and, on the high side, no more than tangerine orange. If in doubt, it is better to have the metal a trifle on the cool side rather than too hot. If it gets too hot, this fact will be known by the blade's "sparking" when removed from the forge. If this occurs, you've ruined it and

Bert Gaston is an experienced smith. He is forging a spear-point Bowie blade, considered too difficult for most beginning students. Other shapes are easier.

Under a power hammer, the blade has warped. The student smith will turn the glowing metal blade several times to straighten it as it is shaped.

nothing you can do will correct this sad state of affairs. You must start over.

The average beginning smith generally can hit a piece of heated metal eight to twelve times before having to reheat it. When striking the steel, hit it with the face of the hammer slightly angled, so as to deliver glancing blows. Remember that you are striving to "move" the material into the desired shape of the blade. It is not necessary to hit the hot metal unduly hard. Lighter hammer blows are easier to control and ultimately will result in a superior blade.

As the steel is struck repeatedly, the area being hit will become thinner and the metal will move away from the blows. This will result in an upswept point, which is an excellent blade shape for a skinning knife. If, however, you desire a dropped point, then the back of the blade near the point must be struck to bring about such a shape. Don't try to make a dagger or Bowie, until you have become more accomplished.

Both sides of the blade should be struck in alternate series, since the sides should be symmetrical. The beginner must be aware of the fact that, as the blade is hit, it will bend and curve. This must be corrected with hammer blows. There is an excellent chance you will ruin the first few blades you attempt. Comfort yourself with the thought that auto springs are amazingly inexpensive!

When a blade finally has been rough forged to the approximate size and shape wanted, it should be taken to your belt-sander or cone-lock wheel for grinding. The chore confronting the would-be smith at this stage is similar to that facing the stock-removal knifemaker when he approaches the grinder.

After the blade has been ground, it now is ready for hardening. The blade should be placed in a heated forge until it assumes that cherry red color. To gauge the correct temperature, check the heated metal with a magnet. When the steel becomes non-magnetic, it is ready for quenching.

You will need a large container holding a quenching medium to accomplish this task. Used motor oil will do a good job, although there are also commercial oils available. Do not use water.

The oil should be heated to approximately 100 degrees and, when the blade is cherry red, seize it with the tongs or vise grips so the back of the blade is parallel to the ground and lower it, back first, into the oil. Do not put it into the oil point first or with the blade down, as this can cause severe

A well-prepared fire is important to blade forging, as explained by Jerry Fisk. His student is W.R. von Bergen, at left. Forge may be coal or oil fired.

As Fisk lowers the heated blade into the quenching oil bath, bright flames are seen, not so unusual. The steel is left in the bath for about ninety seconds.

How to tell when the heated blade is ready to quench? Students learn that when the correct, temperature is reached, blade is not attracted to a magnet. It is time to quench.

warping. It probably will warp anyway, but this can be corrected at the forge.

The steel should be submerged into the oil with a moderately fast motion and, after it is submerged in the liquid, it should be moved forwards and backwards slowly — but not sideways.

After you have left the blade in the oil for perhaps ninety seconds, remove it and allow it to cool. The scale that has formed on the blade must be removed through the use of your grinder. Any additional grinding that is required should

be done at this stage of completion. As it now exists, the blade is too hard and brittle; to correct this, heat a kitchen oven to 400 degrees and place the knife in the oven for two hours. After that period of time, remove the blade and allow it to cool.

Next, the back of the blade must be drawn. This is a critical procedure and the goodness of the finished knife will depend in large measure on this operation. Make sure the metal is clean and, using a shallow container that is longer than the blade, pour between one-quarter and three-eighths of

Jerry Fisk steps up to the Bader belt sander to touch up the tip of his Bowie Knife blade. He should be wearing protective gloves!

A dull, flaky scale forms on the blade after it has been quenched. Before the next step, it must be re-polished with care.

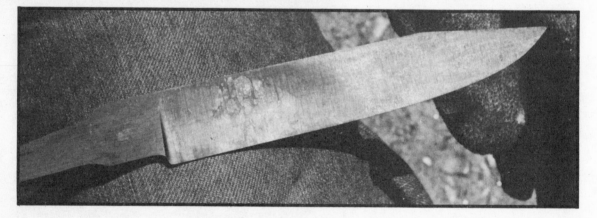

an inch of water into the container; no more and no less.

Holding the blade with your tongs or vise grip, place the blade in the water so the liquid extends up the cutting edge one-quarter of an inch. Now, using a hand-held butane torch or a welding torch with a rosebud tip, play the flame around the tang, the ricasso and the back of the blade until these areas turn blue. Do not allow them to turn red. If you do, you have incurred a setback which, fortunately, can be corrected.

If the blade gets too hot, set it aside to cool. Then clean it and begin the drawing operation again, this time making every effort to cause it to turn blue, not red. Obviously, the curved area of the edge nearing the point will not be covered by water, so take pains not to play the flame nearer than approximately one inch from the tip. The water will keep the cutting edge from becoming too hot, so this area will remain comparatively hard, while the back, the ricasso and the tang will become softer, thus providing strength and flexibility. When you have finished, there should be a readily apparent heat line approximately a quarter-inch above the water line.

Now you are ready for touch-up grinding and the polishing operation. This differs not a bit from what a stock removal knifemaker will do to his blade after heat-treating. After these operations have been completed, you are ready for the guard and handle.

Of course, you never will know just how good your blade is unless you test it. Granted, you may destroy the blade in the process, but if you have forged one good blade, you can forge another and, if the blade was not a good one, it wasn't worth saving. If the blade did not test up to your expectations, I would wager you over-heated it during forging.

The superlative blades made by such masters as Bill Bagwell, Michael Connor, James Crowell, Bob Hudson, Hanford Miller and Bill Moran are the products of forging, and you can rest assured that each of them experienced many failures before they learned their craft. By the time you have completed your fifth blade, you should begin noting definite improvement.

If you're interested in forging and would like to receive the benefit of formalized instruction, you might inquire about the series of courses, each of two-weeks' duration, taught at the bladesmithing school co-sponsored by the ABS and Texarkana College. Eighty hours of lectures and supervised laboratory work can probably save you years of mistakes! Inquiries should be directed to James Powell, Director of Non-Credit Programs, Texarkana College, 2500 North Robison Road, Texarkana, TX 75501.

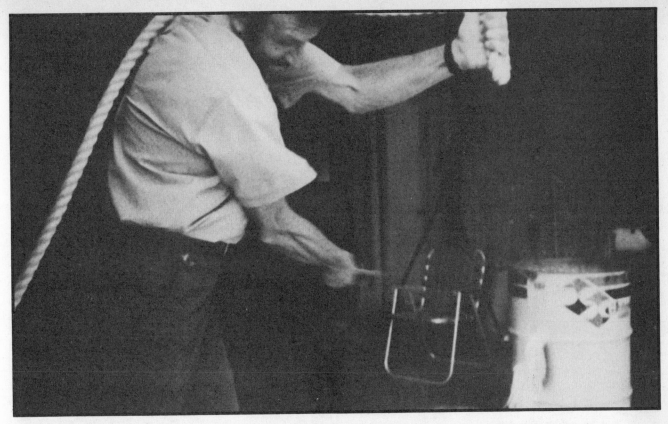

One of the traditional tests of a good blade, forged or otherwise, is to attempt to cut a one-inch free-hanging manila rope. Here, the maker holds the free end and slices rather close to his hand. A downward angle helps.

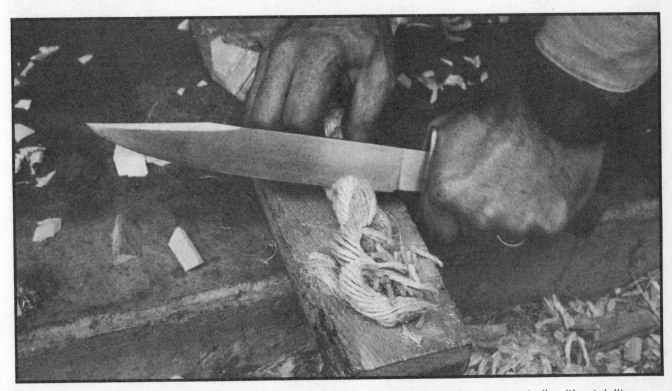

More rope cutting. A correctly forged and treated blade will cut through a one-inch rope repeatedly without dulling.

DAMASCUS FOR KNIVES —

Forge To Shape Or Remove Stock, But Know Your Quality!

The Custom Knifemakers Guild was founded in 1973 by artists interested in improving their skills and their service to customers. Among those instrumental in the Guild's formation were Bill Moran, left, and Robert W. Loveless, who was elected the first president. Moran was then and still is a proponent and artist in Damascus steel.

THE GUN DIGEST BOOK OF KNIFEMAKING

Wayne Valachovic's Damascus folder has a 3¾-inch blade. Note the star pattern blade and Damascus bolster. Handle is of impala horn.

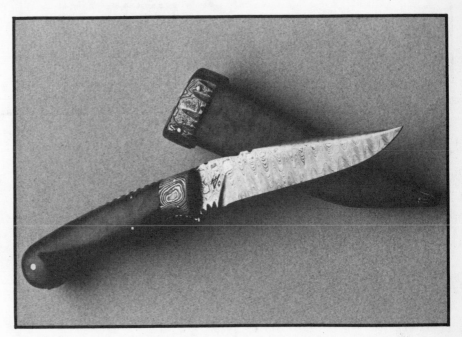

This Damascus Persian-style fighter is taken back to its roots by Wayne Valachovic. The blade is five inches long, made of high density ladder Damascus of more than 11,000 layers. Sheath fittings and bolster are also Damascus; knife handle and sheath are made of desert ironwood

I N THE past decade, there has been a renewed interest in Damascus, a type of steel which had become virtually a lost art. As the name suggests, it orignated in the Middle East centuries ago and it is alleged that the Turks introduced the process, trading sharpness of the blade for the strength that the Crusaders wanted in their battle swords.

It also is said that the knife — or knives — of Jim Bowie were fashioned from a type of Damascus steel that had been developed by blacksmith James Black. Years later, when Black had lapsed into senility, he attempted to recall and write down the formula he had developed, but never was able to do so.

Actually, the process involves welding two types of steel together, then heating, folding and pounding until you have countless layers, the two types of steel blending, but still retaining an unusual pattern. The proper treatment, according to Rob Charlton, who operates Damascus USA from his Colorado headquarters, is "a type of crucible process that produces an extremely dense crystalline structure in the steel."

Bill Moran, the founder of the American Bladesmith Society, must be given the major credit for returning Damascus steel to its current prominence. A long-time custom knifemaker, he developed the modern Damascus which he calls, "pattern-welded." The name has stuck and is the one generally applied to most of the Damascus steel made today.

Pattern-welded Damascus is produced by combining alternating lengths of high carbon steel with mild tool steel. As indicated earlier, this combination is heated to a specific shade of red, then hammered until the two steels are melded together. Then the resultant bar is folded, heated and hammered again. This hammering and folding process goes on until there may be several hundred layers of the alternating types of steel. It doesn't just happen, though. Even when Bill Moran, an experienced forger, began his experiments with modern Damascus, much of his work was experimental; trial-and-error, really.

The system described is a highly simplified account of what actually goes into making a billet of Damascus steel. It is a combination of the hot forge, the blacksmith's eye

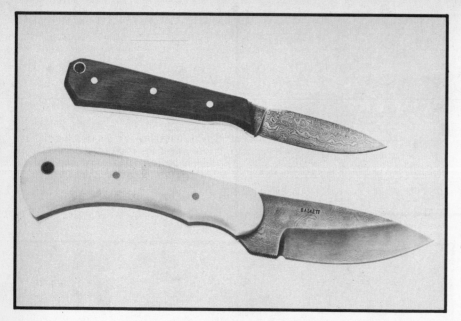

Gene Baskett uses Damascus blades from Rob Charlton's Damascus USA to make his hunting knife, below. Kevin Hoffman makes the smaller bird and trout knife, above.

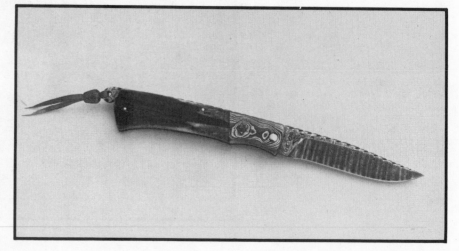

Certainly not a project for the beginner is Valachovic's ladder pattern Damascus steel blade of more than 11,000 high density layers. That is a lot of hammering!

and his hand with the hammer, all working in concert. The process comes down to a great deal of knowledge, experience and hard manual labor.

In making a Damascus blade for a custom knife, what has been explained is simply the first step in the process.

If one can't get into forging — and few of us have the facilities — there are a number of suppliers — including Rob Charlton — who can supply Damascus billets of specific length, width and thickness. A number of producers abroad also are making Damascus steel of a sort, but old pro Bob Loveless is quick to state that, when you are buying a Damascus billet that came from some of the Third World countries or the lesser developed nations, one never is totally certain exactly how good the blade will turn out to be. There are different grades of steel as well as different types. If quality products of the correct consistency are not used in forging the billet, one could end up with a

blade that is beautiful in appearance, but one that will not hold a decent edge.

A shortcut in preparing Damascus has been accepted by a host of enterprising knifemakers, who discovered that steel cable of the proper size and quality can be heated and turned into Damascus. The unusual but potentially beautiful pattern is incorporated in the twisted stands. Simply heating the metal and hammering it out can result in a blade with an unusual pattern. Folding and hammering a few more times can increase the thinness of the layers of steel, compacting them and often improving upon the Damascus pattern in the metal.

One type of Damascus steel was used in the last century for shotgun barrels that were loaded and fired with black powder. These barrels were sufficiently strong to withstand the pressure developed by the slow-burning charcoal-base powder. However, Damascus barrels do not have the

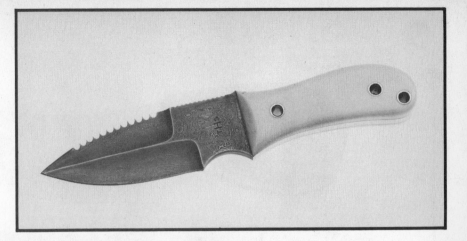

Thomas Hetmanski does some fine fancy file work atop his blade which is from Rob Charlton.

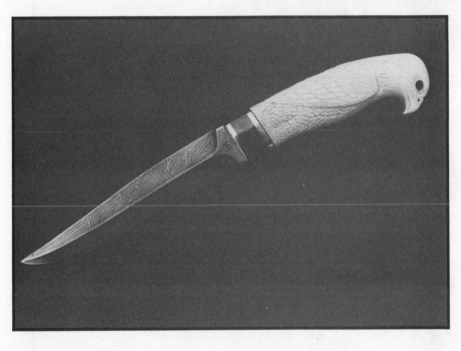

Damascus steel workers Don Fogg and Murad Sayen work under the name Kemal. They forge their own Damascus blades and their knives may sell in the thousands of dollars. At left is their Falcon dagger with a six-inch twist pattern blade and ivory handle.

strength to stand up under the pressures created by the fast-burning powders of today's modern shotshells.

This lack of strength is centered in the fact that the barrels were fashioned from a long strip of Damascus that was wound around a rod of the proper size, then the seam between the wraps welded. The steel itself is quite strong, but the same could not — and cannot — be said for the welding process that joined the various turns of Damascus. In instances wherein a modern shotshell has been fired in a Damascus barrel, the welds usually have given way and the strip of metal used to form the barrel has unrolled like a ball of string!

There are two schools of custom knifemakers today. There are those who forge their blades to shape and those who favor the stock-removal method. Bill Moran always had favored the forged blade, which led to his experiments with Damascus, but either of these techniques can be used

in making a blade from this type of steel. The billet can be shaped with hammer, forge and anvil or that same billet can be developed into a working knife with the stock removal method; this calls for cutting or grinding the blade to size and shape either by hand or machine.

"There is nothing inherently wrong with stock removal construction," Rob Charlton is quick to admit. "The result still retains the excellent qualities associated with Damascus steel. However, there are fewer layers of steel at the critical cutting edge and these tend to be somewhat more coarse than is the case with a blade that is forged to shape. The forging is used to pack the layers of steel tightly together." This, according to such experts as Moran, gives the knife a better cutting edge.

Comes the question of why bother with Damascus at all? Does it cut any better than modern stain-resistant steels or some of the higher qualities of tool steel? Will it

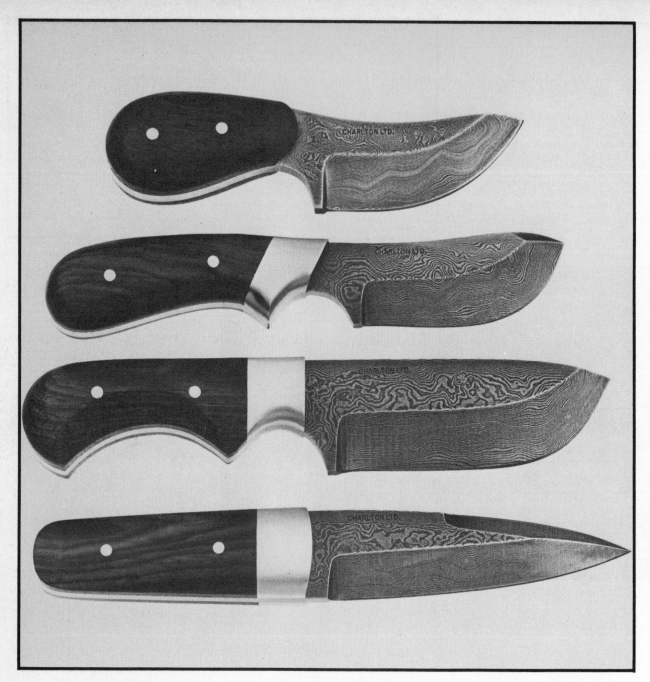

Ken Largin operates his knifemaking business under the name Kelgin and turns out an astounding number of knives per year, including some with Damascus USA (formerly Charlton Ltd.) blades. Series illustrates range of styles.

hold an edge longer? Again, we come to the subject of the materials that went into forming the Damscus billet in the beginning. They probably are little — if any — better than the steels available as standard products. However, there is an admitted romanticism about a Damascus blade that has been fashioned with long hours of dedicated labor, ultimately becoming an individual, one-of-a-kind work of art. That's one thing that obviously can be said about Damascus blades: No two of them are exactly alike.

Charlton, through his Damascus USA, has devloped a series of forged-to-shape blades that are more or less mass produced. That does not mean they come off of a machine production line, though. It means that he maintains several sets of size and shape specifications and a repeated number of Damascus blades are made from these specific patterns. For example, he offers a blade blank that is hand-forged to shape for a full-tang hunter measuring 8½ inches in length; this blank sells for about $90 per copy. He has

Commercial suppliers of Damascus blades can furnish a variety of shapes, patterns, such as these from Damascus USA.

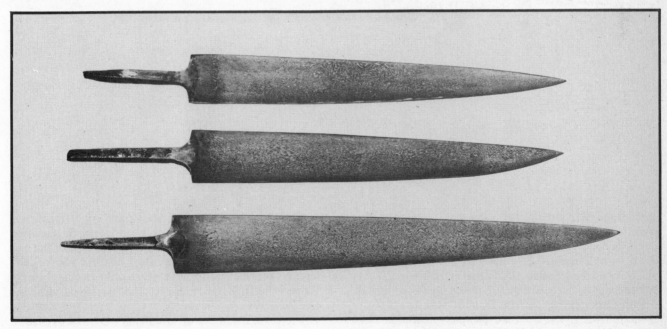

Rob Charlton proudly points out that he can supply real Wootz steel blade blanks to those makers who need them.

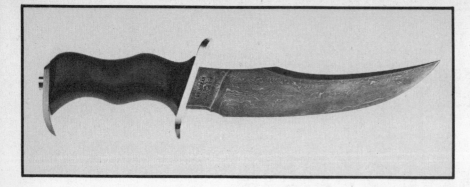

Bill Moran is one of the premier Damascus steel knifemakers. For his forty-fifth anniversary in knife making, he produced this interesting design, dated 1985.

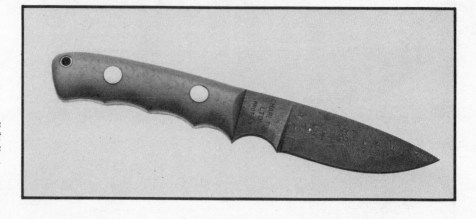

Another Tom Hetmanski design is this hunting knife at right. It is made using Damascus USA's steel which is forged to shape.

Gil Hibben is a well known and successful custom knifemaker who turned out this fascinating Manhattan boot knife.

another full-tang hunter-type blank that is a quarter of an inch shorter, but wider in blade width that sells for the same price. The individuality is still there; you can order half a dozen — or a hundred, if you like — and while the shape will be virtually the same, the pattern in the blade will vary considerably with each of these individually forged blanks.

Rob Charlton also markets Damascus knife blanks for several Bowie styles, one for a Tanto configuration and a 3½-inch blade meant for handmade pocketknives, if that's your thing. He also will accept special orders, shaping a blade to your own specifications, but he'll quote you a price that is considerably higher than his standard blanks.

Of the forged-to-shape blanks, Charlton will furnish you his standard patterns that have been totally finished and need only to be assembled with whatever type of hilt and handle material one desires. Most of these blanks even have holes drilled through them for handle rivets or screws. Each, being forged to shape, has the "packaged edge" described earlier.

There are a number of suppliers of Damascus blades. Damascus USA is headquartered at P.O. Box 220, Howard, CO 81233. Another source that offers a variety of forged-to-shape blanks is Bob Engnath's House of Muzzleloading, 1019 E. Palmer, Glendale, CA 91205.

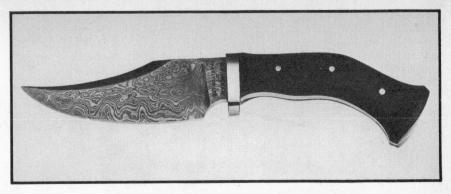

The knife at right is marked W.F. Moran by Charlton LTD. Charlton has since changed the company name to Damascus USA, moved to Colorado.

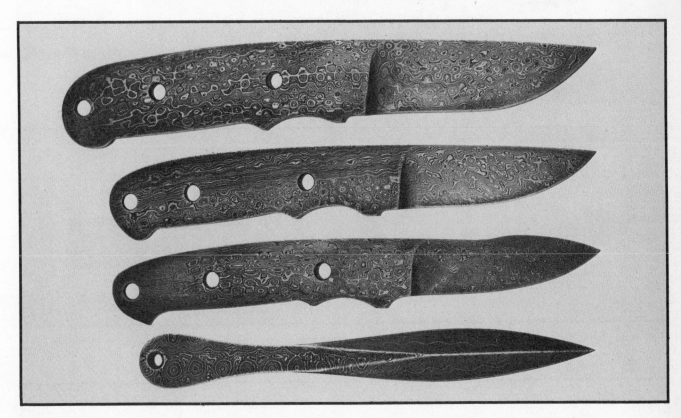

Of the four Damascus USA blade shapes above, the top three are completely finished and forged to shape. Bottom blade has some finishing to be done, but the amateur knifemaker need only attach handles to finish.

Even the major knife manufacturers seldom have the facilities for making their own Damascus and, for the greater number of custom makers, the process is too time-consuming to be profitable. As a result, most of the forged-to-shape blades are purchased from such sources as those listed above.

A number of importers also are supplying blades from low-cost labor countries such as Pakistan, where the quality tends to vary considerably unless the importer has the ability to maintain some sort of long-distance quality control. Damascus USA supplies forged-to-shape blades to a number of custom knifemakers. Others simply order billets

and utilize the stock removal method to create their own specific designs.

Which brings us back to you, the beginning knifemaker. The idea of standing over a hot forge *a la* Bill Moran and pounding out your own blade may seem romantic, but forget it, baby! Chances are, you have neither the talent at this point to create such a blade nor the loose funds to purchase all of the necessary forging equipment

If you're satisfied with one of the designs that Charlton, Bob Engnath of the House of Muzzleloading and a few others offer in their forged-to-shape blades, this might be the way to go in your initial efforts. As suggested earlier,

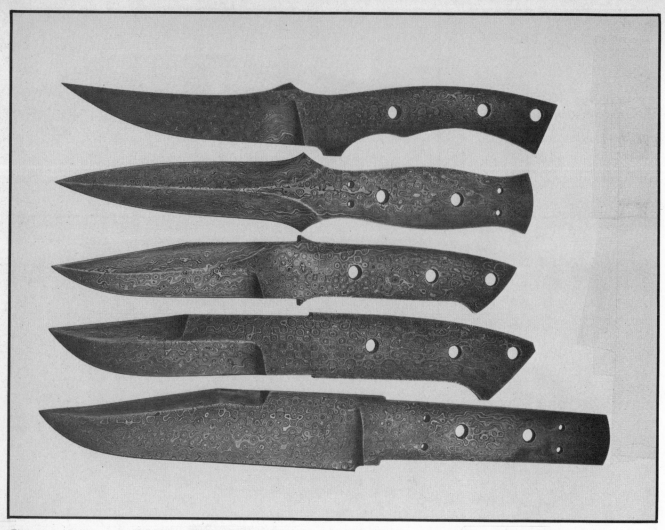

Five more Damascus USA blade blanks that are forged to shape and completely finished. Steel patterns may vary.

Damascus USA and others can furnish standard blade designs or special shapes on a custom basis. Ken Largin came up with the carving set idea and has produced a kitchen set of which a gourmet chef would be proud.

Here is a finished blade design available from Rob Charlton in the familiar USMC fighting knife pattern.

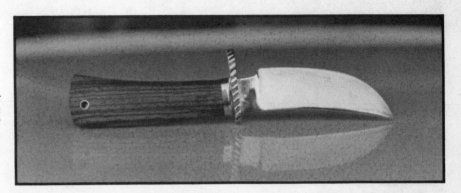

Bill Bagwell, too, is a pioneer Damascus steel worker who does his own blades. The knife at right is one of his favorites.

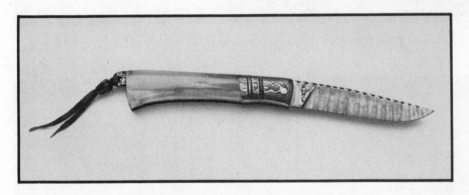

Another Wayne Valachovic folder which he has made of more than 11,000 layers of high density Damascus ladder pattern steel.

there isn't a great deal to completion, except deciding what type of hilt you want and selecting and finishing the handle material.

If you're feeling somewhat more adventurous and competent, you can order Damascus billets in varying lengths, thicknesses and widths from these sources. The billets can be used to create your own specific designs, utilizing the familiar stock removal method. Either method is going to give you a beautiful, serviceable knife.

It probably should be pointed out, though, that there are ripoff artists standing in the wings. All this harks back a decade or so, when the rage in costume jewelry was the turquoise pieces being created in the Southwest by our native American Indians. As this type of jewelry increased in popularity, so did the prices — often for pieces that really weren't that good.

This recalls two incidents that left an indelible impression. A friend was standing at a display of such jewelry during the so-called Flower Child Era, when all sorts of non-redskins were crafting and selling handmade goods, a lot of them copied from Indian designs. Also inspecting this display of quality Navajo and Zuni-made turquoise jewelry was a hippie who had been copying such jewelry, then selling it through a local shop that specialized in Indian goods.

The hippie looked down at the display with obvious displeasure, muttering, "Those damned Indians are trying to put me out of business!" Somewhere in that declaration one has to be able to segregate the height of irony.

On another occasion, this friend was in an elevator in New York City. He wore a turquoise-inlaid silver belt buckle and a matching bolo tie. He had purchased both from an Indian friend who had made them; they were authentic.

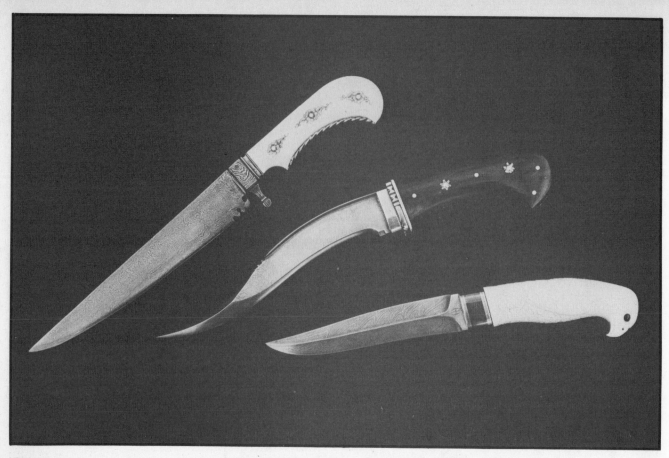

The Kemal team of Don Fogg and Murad Sayen have produced the three breath-taking Damascus knives above.

This is the appearance of forging your own Damascus steel using hand hammers and plenty of muscle.

Fogg and Sayen have established their Kemal team in Maine. They do it all, including heating and forging, even building their own forge, above.

Bladesmith Sean McWilliams forges a knife tang in his Colorado shop. He specializes in forging stainless steel, but works his own Damascus from tool steel.

A lady, a resident of the Big Apple to judge from her accent, spotted the buckle and bolo and gushed, "Oh, you're into turquoise, too!"

"I've got some of it," the buckled and booled gent ventured on a guarded note.

The woman reached up to open her mink coat to reveal a large squash blossom necklace that hung about her neck.

"How do you like my necklace?" she demanded to know. "I got a real deal on it."

"Oh?"

"I only paid $700 for it," she thrilled.

"I'm sure you'll be real happy with it," was the noncommital reply. He didn't have the guts to tell the necklace's owner the stones were plastic and the metalwork was zinc. It was worth $30 at most.

Those anecdotes may seem a bit far afield, but they're not. The same thing is going on these days in the sale of Damascus. Going back to the statement of Bob Loveless, "You don't really know what kind of steel went into Damascus," unless you know the source.

We've seen some blanks and billets at knife and gun shows that looked fine on the outside; all had the expected wavy two-steel Damascus pattern. But knowing the purveyors thereof, we'd not want to have to use the finished blades to cut our way through a jungle! Some of those same people, a decade or more ago, were selling genuine "Navajo-made." turquoise jewelry that came out of the local hippie commune!

In short, let the buyer beware!

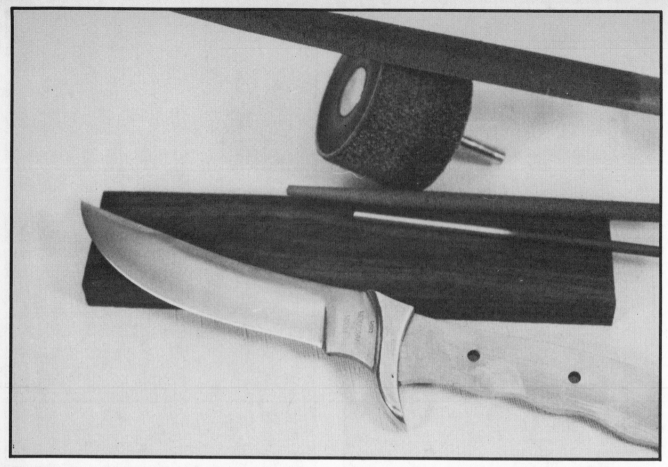

The Buck Akonua knife needed a new handle to make it look better than new. First step is to remove any handle material still adhering to the tang and clean down to bare metal. Brass hand guard is polished before other work.

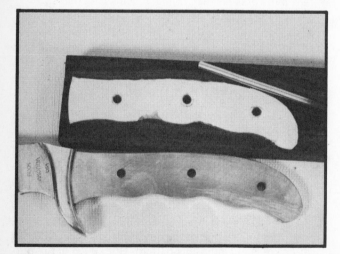

A paper pattern is traced from the knife tang and transferred to wood slab. Best wood and color should be found before cutting. Polished brass brazing rod will be used for pins.

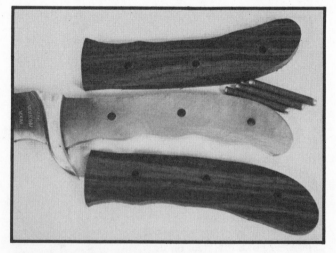

The handle slabs have been roughly cut to shape, the pin holes have been drilled through and the pins are cut. Pins are slightly long; they will be peened and filed down to exact length.

Chapter 7

A MATTER OF HANDLING

Any Number of Unlikely Materials Can Be Used To Make Your Knife A One-Of-A-Kind Cutter!

THERE ARE many types and styles of fixed-blade knives on today's market and among my favorites over the years have been those fixed- and folding-blade knives made by Buck Knives, Incorporated, right in my hometown, El Cajon, California. They are great people to work with and put out a good product, but they don't sell parts, pieces or kits for knives; the total knife only.

I find Buck knives to modify at garage sales and swap meets. It seems people just don't read any more, so when I see a brutalized handle on a piece of Buck steel I never bother to tell the owner he could send the knife back to the plant to be repaired or replaced, since each has a lifetime guarantee. If a person wants to sell me a good blade with a ruined handle, I buy it, rebuild the handle with available materials and put it in my collection or trade it off.

Browsing a recent garage sale, I noticed a familiarly shaped finger guard of bright, polished brass. It had a distinctive sweep just behind the blade on the bottom and I knew I had either the Kalinga or Akonua blade that Buck had marketed as one of their top knives for many years. I picked up the battered piece of excellent steel, complaining how badly the handle was damaged. I was told the youngest son had tied it on behind his bike and dragged it around the street for several days to see how much he could damage it

since it was his brother's and he hadn't gotten one like it.

Sibling jealousy gave me the opportunity to buy a $60 knife, the Buck *Akonua,* for a mere ten green ones.

The project now was to remove that battered handle from the full-tang blade and replace it with some exotic wood I had on hand.

The factory handle was of a tough black phenolic material. With my trusty belt sander system, I ground both sides of the full tang down to the steel, experiencing a real problem in the area around the brass finger guard due to the radius of the guard itself.

After final cleaning, I did some roughing on the wheel to leave some abrasion marks that would allow the epoxy to grip.

Coco bolo is a great wood to work with, since every time you cut a slab, you find a different figure in the grain. For color, I call it black and orange, but whether it is basically black with orange streaks or orange with black streaks I'm not certain. Maybe both.

The first step in making a full-tang handle is to make a pattern of paper or show card. This pattern is cut with scissors to give you something to move around on the slab of wood you are going to place on the metal handle area. I use this to get the best figure and color from a strip of wood

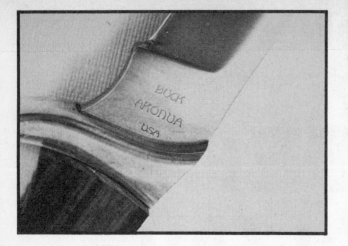

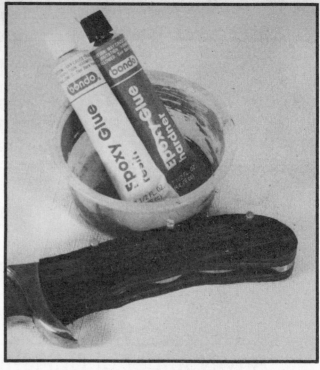

The curved area of the guard is the most critical for a precision fit with the wood. Take time to sand and form handle slabs to exact shape before mixing and using two-part epoxy cement, above right. Cement is liberally spread on wood and metal before clamping for at least 24 hours to cure, below. No gap is visible, lower right.

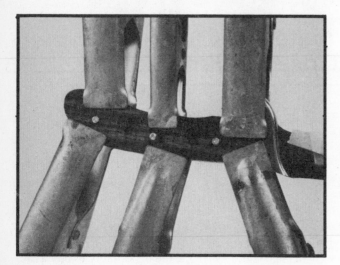

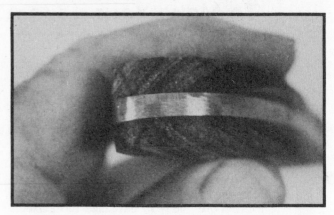

and it saves a lot of time in marking out the area I want to cut. Incidentally, the wood sections that fit on either side of the full tang are called slabs or scales.

After picking the best section of figured wood for the right side, I cut it and mark it on the inside area as "right." Then I select another figured section I feel is a match and mark it as "left." I seldom work the inside areas on the slabs, so that mark remains as a reference and keeps me from getting mixed up.

The finger guard still was in place on the Akonua and it has a slight radius on the handle side that makes this project a bit complicated.

Three holes had been drilled through the tang at the factory and these would be used to hold the slabs in position. One can use knife rivets but I don't. I keep several sizes of brazing rod on a shelf; most of the holes in knife handles will fit one of these sized rods. The rods are of brass and only the end shows when the job is finished. They work

quite well, are inexpensive and add an attractive touch.

I traced the outline on the wood, using the paper pattern. I always cut the wood a bit longer than needed, in case I have problems sanding or fitting properly around such things as curved finger guards.

After the lengths have been cut, I cut off some of the excess at top and bottom with a band saw, to make the coco bolo easier to work with on the sanding belt. The blade of the knife is covered with masking tape for this operation, the unit then placed between thicknesses of heavy leather with heavy copper rivets holding the pieces together at the bottom. This guard is to protect my hands and, when I work with any sharp blade, that guard always is on the blade as protection against cuts.

I use a moderate grit on the belt sander to shape the radius to fit the finger guard. I use the sand-and-fit method until I have a good wood-to-metal fit, then I do it again with the slab for the other side of the handle. When you epoxy

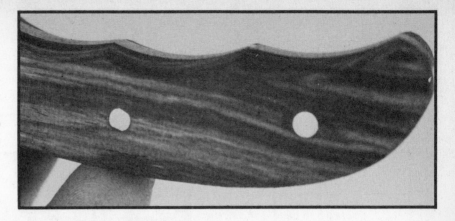

During the initial filing and sanding, excess dried epoxy, wood and clamp marks are removed; pins sanded flush.

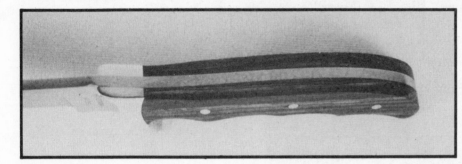

Top of the tang, brass guard and wood handle slabs are ground or sanded down as the work progresses.

Surfaces are still course, but wood to metal fit leaves almost no gap. Grind marks will be sanded away.

and pin the slabs to the tang, you can't go back and make a little change. It has to be right before you epoxy the slabs to the tang.

Sometimes I can make one or two passes on the sander and have a perfect fit. Other times, I might take off a quarter of an inch to get a fit with which I'm satisfied. That is the reason for the half-inch or so of extra length. If I get fussy, I don't end up with a slab that is too short.

Full-tang slabs are the easiest to make for a knife. You don't have to worry about drilling a clean, straight vertical hole as you do with a slip-over tang and, if you want an extremely strong knife, there is nothing more rugged than a full-tang knife.

Both slabs now are radiused and are ready to be drilled and the pins inserted. A drill press is the best method of drilling straight, matching holes. I use the simple method of finding a bit that will fit through the hole drilled in the heat-treated steel tang. Don't try to enlarge the holes in tough

steel, unless you want to see a drill bit turn ruby red from friction. After that, you can throw it away.

Clamp the slab with the radius as tightly to the guard as you can get it and drill the first hole. It makes no difference which of the three it is. Insert a length of the brass brazing rod into the drilled hole. This keeps the slab in position and prevents it from moving while drilling the remaining holes, which can be done in seconds.

Leaving the slab in place, turn the handle over and position the undrilled slab in position tight against the radiused guard. Use the drilled slab as a guide, shoving the drill bit through the slab's holes, through the predrilled tang holes and drill the holes on the bottom slab. Insert the pins after drilling to prevent any slippage that could cause a poor fit. The slabs now are mated roughly to the tang and need to be epoxied.

Remove the slabs from the tang and prepare a batch of good two-solution epoxy. I used Bondo, which worked as

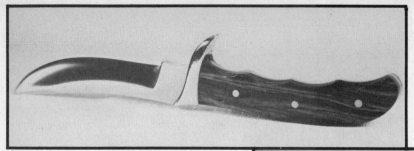

The almost-new knife looks and works well. There is an extra pride in knowing you did the work yourself!

Coca bola wood handle shows the orange and black colors, with some attractive wood grain throughout.

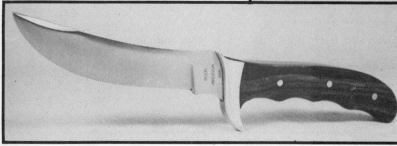

Wood and brass guard have been polished on a floppy buffing wheel to reach an attractive high luster.

advertised and dried clear. I spread it on one side of the slab, placed the pins in the holes, slipped the tang down over the pins and pressed them tight. I epoxied the other slab, placed it on the other side, pushing it tight. You have time to work with this slower-setting epoxy which I feel offers a stronger bond than the quick-setting types.

I had done all you could for the twenty-four hours recommended for drying, except for placing strong spring clamps on the slabs as close as I could get them. Some epoxy will ooze from the pressure, but it provides a tight, clean bond.

When the epoxy has cured, remove the clamps and move to your sanding belt. If you don't have a belt, you can use a sanding drum with a hand drill or rasp and sandpaper.

First, I shape the upper section, as it is the easiest. I never know what the finished handle will look like, but shape it as I go along. You possibly will have to sand into the brass and remove some of the steel from the tang as you shape the wood and metal to match. The radius on the butt of the knife is easy. Just follow the curve of the steel.

The hardest part for me is deciding on the size and shape of the grooves under the tang. I usually follow the grooves in the steel, but sometimes I remove the grooves entirely to give the knife a different look and feel in the hand. That is part of the fun. You can make it any way you like. It's your knife and your ideas.

When I shaped the finger grooves on this Akonua, I moved the handle in a sweep as I ground around the metal. This provides a groove for the fingers.

You probably will have to remove some of the wood on both sides to get rid of the cured epoxy that protrudes and possibly sand out the clamp marks. The brass set pins are

sanded down with the wood and present no problem. If there is a hard part to work, it is the section just behind the finger guard radius, since the sander won't get in there. I ended up by cleaning it with a Dremel tool, then some rat-tail files. Both work.

Sand and shape until you have the look and feel you want on the knife handle. Move it around in your hand and, when you like the way it feels, leave it alone. You are finished. Almost.

I left the top of the coca bola slabs flat, as this felt good and solid when I gripped the handle. It also gave me a good solid ridged grip when I turned the blade up as for gutting.

All that is left to do is the final polishing. Buffing wheels will clean and brighten the brass and that coca bola will polish up beautifully with the floppy buffer pad. You can use a similar buffing pad on a hand drill.

For the finale, you will be sanding hardwood, steel and brass. The wood is softer than either of the others and if you get too heavy on the buffing, the metal set pins may start moving out from the handle as the softer wood is cut away around them. The idea is to polish and finish only. You have removed enough wood and have the shape you want. Easy does it.

With the knife finished, there is none other like it, since Buck Knives uses another type of handle material. You might find a customized knife that will be similar but you do have an original.

Before you put the knife away, use your sharpening stones for a good, clean cutting edge. If you use a buffing wheel for finishing, you will have a paper- or hair-cutting edge, but it won't last. You need to use good stones to attain a long-lasting cutting edge.

A New Handle And Basic, Simple File Work Can Give A Production Knife A Whole New Identity

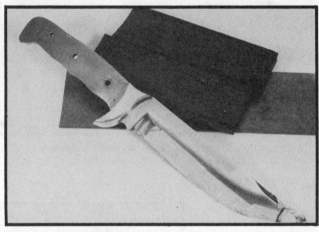

For this handle project, rosewood slabs are selected to be put on the Buck Frontiersman. A sheet of 1/16th-inch brass will be cut to shape and used as attractive liners.

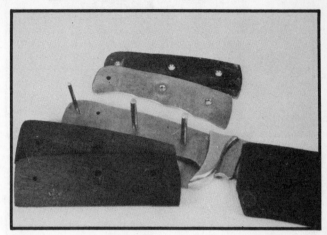

Slabs and liners are cut and roughed out on a belt sander. Three tang pins will prevent brass slippage.

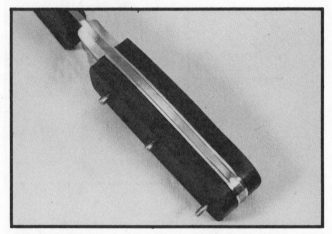

Held by brass pins only, initial sanding and shaping work on tang, liners and handle slabs begns to shape up.

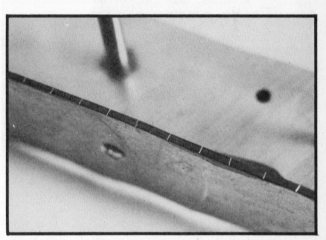

Edges of the brass liners are blackened and scribed at quarter-inch intervals to guide further file work.

AFTER YOU have made a knife handle or two — or three or more — you start thinking of doing them in more complicated styles. One method that isn't too complicated but creates a one-of-a-kind knife involves file art on the tang or an insert of a different material.

Among the good blades with bad handles found in roaming swap meets is a Buck *Frontiersman.* This is about the biggest fixed-blade factory knife Buck makes. The Frontiersman is a good camp/survival knife with a long blade and a full-tang handle. It is tough, rugged and holds a great edge; all the requirements for a working knife.

I dug the knife out of my store of blades and found I had already cleaned it. All I had was just the sharp blade with a full tang, but no finger guard or anything else. Perfect for the project in mind.

The factory model comes with a large, flat finger guard,

but I didn't want one of those. I didn't have the tools to make a curved brass guard similar to the one used on the Kalings, Buck's big top-line knife, but I did know someone who could. We swap back and forth, so I made a call to a friend and offered to swap a chunk of rosewood he wanted for pistol grips. All he needed to do was lathe me a finger guard similar to that of the Kalinga. I'd even supply the brass!

About a week later I picked up a polished brass finger guard that almost fit the blade. My craftsman friend had taken the measurements from a Kalinga, but the blade of the Frontiersman was a bit bigger. But that small amount of steel could be ground down with no problem. I had what I needed to make the file-art Frontiersman knife.

The guard was silver-soldered to the steel tang, but after it was in place, I noted I still had a radius on the guard to fit. I should have thought of this and had the back of the guard

Soft brass is easily filed for a first project. Light buffing or careful sanding removes slivers and burrs.

The brightly worked brass is attractively presented against the darker rosewood. Filework leads down tang.

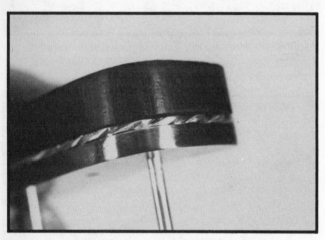

Filing continues around the butt, adding continuity to the liners. Design is limited only by imagination.

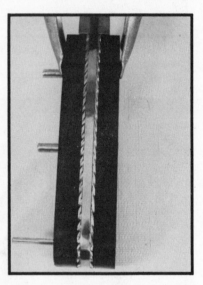

Before cementing tang, liners and slabs are pinned for a trial fit.

made flat for easier fitting.

Digging through my meager supply of hardwoods for the rosewood, I had found a chunk of half-inch slabs. There was a knothole in the center of one section and the wood grain radiated from this knot in a sweeping curve. That would look great for a knife handle, I decided. After a template was made, it would fit the Frontiersman beautifully with some wood to spare. The figure was good, although the wood was a bit dark.

The first step was to cover that sharp blade with masking tape and put it into the open sheath I use when working blades on the sander and buffers. This prevents cut hands.

The slabs were marked on the inside for right and left with a scribe so I wouldn't inadvertently put one of the curved knot sections on the inside. I try to avoid making the same mistake twice.

The first step was to mark the slabs for the best cut to retain the most figure. I cut the wood a bit larger than needed, then went to the sanding belt to cut that half-circle radius to match the guard. The radius was formed and wood-to-metal fit was perfect, for a change. Now I needed something to make this knife different.

After searching several scrap yards and metal shops, I found a small sheet of one-sixteenth-inch brass to use for a liner between the steel tang and the rosewood slabs. This brass would be cut with a file at an angle to give what is termed file art. This was a first attempt and I figure that, if I can do it, anyone can!

The brass was cut for width and a bit longer than required for length. Since I had to radius this brass for that finger guard, I was leaving room for error. The holes through the tang were mated with a matching drill bit and the wood slabs and brass filler all were drilled and pinned with two sizes of pins. The standard Frontiersman has a metal butt cap and the smaller holes in the back used to pin the cap were matched with brass brazing rod of proper size. The pins were cut a bit long and would be ground down later when finishing the handle.

In rough shaping, the brass was sanded to fit the bottom finger grooves along with the rosewood, but the upper edges and butt end were just a trifle higher than the steel and wood. After the rough fit had been made, I colored the top edge and butt end of both brass pieces with a black marking pen. A scribe and ruler were used to mark off quarter-inch lines to give me even marks for filing.

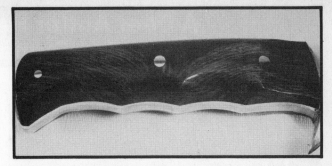

After the epoxy cement has cured, everything buffed, some cement remains in filed cuts. This should be removed while still in uncured, semi-soft state.

Handle wood has been buffed to a high gloss finish. Knot in the rosewood leads the eye to wood center.

The completed project presents an attractive semi-custom knife. Final handle shape may be changed to suit the maker.

While waiting for the marking ink to dry, I inspected a variety of files: flat-edge, one Swiss file and a triangular file. I cut lines on pieces of scrap brass with each to find which angle would look best.

These practice cuts showed me file work isn't as easy as the pros make it look. After checking the different file cuts, I settled on the small triangular file. I held the angle almost on the same line as the brass; just a bit offset. This gave me a good rope effect when finished.

The brass inserts were placed in a solid vise and the file brought down and marks made on the vise to try to keep the same angle on each cut. This worked well enough, but the hard part was keeping the depth of the cuts consistent. I tended to get a few deeper than others and thought of going back and deepening some, but that could go on forever.

I had marked the brass inserts for left and right and made my file marks one way for the right and in the opposite direction for the left, so they would angle down the middle of the tang and complement each other.

I have a folding lock-blade knife in my drawer made by Bill Duff with file art on the back of the blade and down the back edge of the knife. He made the blade/spring joint so tight that, with the file art, you can't see where the joint exists. This knife is a work of beauty, as well as functional.

My first attempt at file art wasn't that bad. I had learned a lot and plan to do much more. With practice, I hope to improve. The file art was carried down the top of the tang and around the butt.

The brass inserts were roughened with some coarse sandpaper and the tang, the brass and the rosewood were coated with two-solution epoxy and assembled. The unit was clamped and allowed to cure for a full day. The brass brazing pins were in place, the extra length to be cut down in the finish process.

The final finish was achieved with the belt sander, some hand sanding and more file work to clean and polish around that curved finger guard. The excess epoxy, the overly long brass pins and the rough edges on the rosewood first were rough-sanded to a shape. The steel tang had to be ground down to meet the top of the brass guard, too.

I learned that I should have protected the file cuts or, at least, cleaned out the epoxy after it had cured since epoxy now is imbedded in the file art. I could clean this out with a Dremel tool or, better yet, a set of dental picks I swapped for some time ago.

I'll leave the epoxy in the grooves until it irritates me, then I'll remove it, one way or another. Next time I see Bill Duff, I'll ask him how to prevent this. If one has questions on knifemaking, handles and this type of work, I always have found the professional knifemakers to be helpful. They don't guard any secrets, since they all do the same thing. Some just do it better than others — and command higher prices.

Final work on the handle, finger guard and insert was done on the buffing wheels. The rosewood polished as I knew it would and the figure looked even better than I had expected. The file art stands out and the dark rosewood with the contrast of brass, then steel makes this a totally different knife. Others probably could do a much better job on the file work, but this is mine and I like it.

This will make a great camp/survival knife and, if I had to, I could cut firewood, cut poles, even field dress and skin a deer or larger animal with it. I normally prefer a much shorter blade — about four inches is enough most of the time — but we should all have a big knife in our collection at one time and this will be mine.

The handle is a bit more slim than the Buck production model and it certainly doesn't look like a factory model and that was my objective.

A Deer Antler Handle Dresses Up
This Damascus Blade

The slot cut into the horn is cut askew to match the Damascus knife tang. Gaps will be filled with epoxy. There is a slight crack in horn, but cement will seal it.

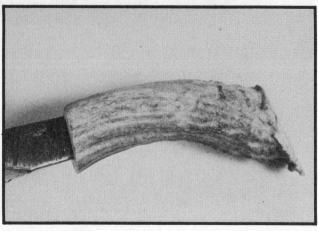

Several trial fits produce a good start. Sanding and buffing have removed roughest surfaces of the horn.

The tang fits into the horn handle to leave about an inch of steel before sharpened edge of blade begins.

A bit of tapering was done on the sanding belt to enhance appearance where the horn meets the blade.

YOU NEVER know where and when you will find a good blade. While touring the trading posts of Wyoming a few years back, I ran across a Damascus steel blade that was crude enough to be interesting. After some haggling, we finally settled on a price I would pay. It was more than I really thought the blade was worth, but far cheaper than I have seen Damascus blades listed for in catalogs.

Now that I had the rough-finished Damascus, I would need a handle material that would accent the blade and still be serviceable for hunting. The appropriate material was found the first day of a winter hunt in the high desert country of Arizona. It was a big three-point whitetail horn. Desert rodents usually find these winter-dropped horns long before I do, but this one wasn't chewed up. The horn was only about a year old and solid white. I would have

preferred a mottled brown similar to a stag handle, but this was from a whitetail, not a stag.

A few months later, I had the antler hanging from the rafters in the shop and, as usual, it dropped on my head at the wrong time. That horn was large and heavy and it hurt. It was time to put it to use as handle material.

This type of handle would be a slip-over stag style. The tang or extra steel behind the blade is narrowed and slipped into a hardwood or any other type handle material one prefers. The horn, already round, makes a natural handle, if it is thick enough in diameter.

Some quick checking with a caliper to see how long the handle length must be to accommodate the tang of the knife left me with no doubts about the use for the horn. It was a natural knife handle for the Damascus.

I cut a length of the horn at the base, six inches more or

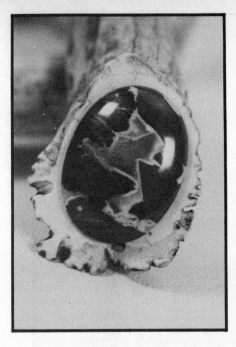

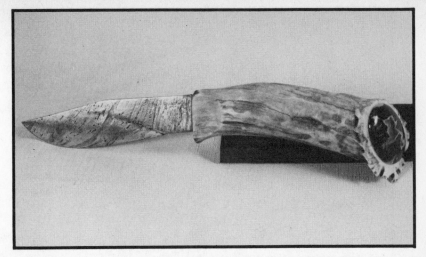

An interesting piece of red and gray jasper, left, is cemented to the butt end of the horn handle, greatly enhancing the appearance of the completed knife. Any gemstone or other decoration may be used on the horn to customize.

less. The tang length really determines the length of the handle along with the size of your hand. I made the cut at an angle to allow the natural curl of the horn to be incorporated into the handle grip. When checking for hand fit, one should check the handle in the normal blade-down position, since that is one way it is used, but I always check with the blade turned up as you would use it in field dressing big game. It should be comfortable both ways.

The antler isn't like a chunk of wood you can throw away and merely cut another from the same board. There is only one horn butt on a horn and I had no others big enough to fit this Damascus blade. I allowed for the widening of the tang as it neared the blade edge and planned to drill the holes to allow the handle to be the entire unit; no finger guards of brass, all horn.

The cut was made and the length checked with the tang. It looked good. Still a bit long, that allowed for grinding after drilling. On a grinding belt, I smoothed the base of the horn butt to give it a solid finish for a later final touch.

To my amazement, the horn was solid, with no pithy core. Many of the cast-off winter horns are quite soft and make better wall hangers than anything else. This one was solid and offwhite in color throughout.

Alignment of the drill hole to fit the tang is the next step. I eyeballed the handle section to determine its widest part and the best way to drill without going through a side of the antler. If you drill too far or are off to one side, you end up with a hole in the end or side to ruin a handle, if it is too big. I have found the only difference between a journeyman carpenter and my wood-butchering is that he knows how to cover his mistakes. I don't.

A drill press and a good adjustable vise make the drilling more precise and you stand less chance of making a mess of this one-chance handle material.

I drilled the hole for the tang as deep as I could with the drill bit one step smaller than the width of the tang. I drilled the top hole, moved the handle material a bit and drilled another hole below that one. Now all I had to do was remove the horn material between the two holes to have a slotted tang hole. I would epoxy the tang in for a solid handle on the Damascus steel blade.

Fortunately, everything went according to plan and no holes were drilled through the outside walls of the horn. The elongation was done partly with a stickleback rasp, then a small rattail file to get the inner tang slot to fit the tang. I did make one decision and ground off half an inch of the tang to make it fit properly, since I couldn't drill the hole slot any deeper. When you grind off part of the tang, you shorten it. Go too far you won't have a solid handle on the blade. A little won't hurt and that is all I took.

You will have to fit and fuss to get the tang snugly into the horn handle, but it just takes time. Don't rush it.

When you have the tang fitting snugly enough that you have to tug to get it out, that is just right. Keep that blade covered, since one tug at the wrong time can cut deeply.

I checked the handle for feel and tried it in every possible cutting position before mixing a two-part, slow-curing epoxy, flooding the handle tang hole with the mixture. Holding the blade, run the tang in and out of the handle slot to work the epoxy into all the nooks and crannies, hopefully not leaving any air pockets that will create a weak handle. I work the epoxy thoroughly in this manner and add more if needed. You might be surprised at how much that slotted tang slot will require.

When you have the cavity around the tang filled and the epoxy is ready to cure, set the knife with the blade up and try to get the right angle on the handle to keep the excess epoxy from running off the edge of the horn by the blade. In this case, I managed to keep a small ridge of soft epoxy built up by the blade and it remains there. It helps hold the blade and keeps the end of the horn from splitting.

Horn is tough but also brittle. If you get too heavy-handed and bang and strike it with a hammer to get that blade into the handle, you can split the material. Even with gentle working, I saw a natural split running from the edge of the horn to the center. This was natural, caused by dry-

No two pieces of antler are exactly alike, even these from the same animal. In this case, the handle goes extremely well with the Damascus blade material.

ing, but it wouldn't take much to split it out. The epoxy filled the crack, though.

When the epoxy has cured, I wait at least one full day. The next step is to shape the handle with a belt sander or, if you don't have one, a rasp and sandpaper will do. It just takes a bit longer is all.

I ground a groove on the forward bottom edge to fit my finger. This acts as a finger guard. The sides of the handle were slanted to give them a bit of shape, then grooved to align with the blade. Some of the little craggy bumps had to be removed, since they were a bit too high and actually hurt the hand when I gripped the handle. Work slowly and make each cut or groove so it feels right.

The final product looked great; the section of whitetail antler accented the rough laminated Damascus blade and I felt the combo was plenty tough and rugged enough for any use. I used my buffing wheels to polish the horn to a high luster and almost called it quits. It didn't need a plastic finish, lacquer or anything else. Polished horn only gets better with age and handling. Horn does shrink, but on this handle, it would never be a problem.

That flat white base bothered me; it needed something a bit better than just flat white. I can't scrimshaw and had nothing that would fit in brass or coins. Sometimes you can use an old coin to accent such work, but I had nothing big enough.

I visited a lapidary shop, hoping to find a nice chunk of turquoise to cap the horn butt. I found it, but backed off when given the price. It would cost more than I had paid for the blade!

I found a cabuchon of jasper that was a bit undersized, but looked good with its deep red color along with some gray ziggy lines and a gray center section.

The finished knife looks great. There is nothing brassy or shiny about it, except the polished horn handle and the red jasper on the butt. It feels good in the hand and is about as simple a knife handle as you can make.

You may not wander the high desert country, but you can buy horn sections and butts at gun shows and through some of the catalog companies. You usually have to take what you get, but if money is no object, you could buy a nice chunk of stag horn. This is beautiful stuff and great to work with.

The only thing that I wish is that I could have found the horn when it was on that monster buck. He is big and I'll look for him next year. I might get lucky and skin him with my horn-handled Damascus knife.

Stranger things have happened.

Old .50 Caliber Machine Gun Cartridge Cases Fit The Hand Well For A Knife Handle!

The .50 caliber shell, a potential knife handle, is dull and tarnished now. Shells are to be found at swap meets and gun shows, reasonably priced. Files and a sanding drum are the tools to use for project.

The original handle material has been ground off the tang. The taped object to the right is a homemade blade and hand protector slipped over the blade.

RUMMAGING AROUND in a bin of spent cartridge brass in a scrap yard, I found a batch of .50 caliber cases. Back in the late Forties, I had the dubious position of tailgunner on a B24-type aircraft that afforded me the privilege of firing a pair of twin air-cooled fifties at various targets while airborne. Fortunately, we never went into combat, as most tailgunners had a life expectancy of about five minutes.

When I found the .50 brass, I knew it would be a quality product, but how could I use it? I was searching for brass to use for spacers in a knife handle I was making. The brass cartridge cases were tapered and wouldn't serve for that, but I picked out a dozen or so that seemed in good shape. Some of the throats had been mashed and all had dings caused by the firearm's ejection system.

Earlier that week, I had been reconnoitering a local dis-count store and had run across a number of thin-bladed knives in the kitchen section that were labeled as vegetable knives. They didn't intrigue me as kitchen tools, but each did have a serrated blade that was long and skinny. A perfect fish filleting knife for about a dollar was something I couldn't pass up.

When I returned to my shop, I placed the brass from my scrounging expedition on the workbench. The knives were there and the idea surfaced of mating the skinny blade to the .50 brass and making a letter opener or, better yet, a set of unusual steak knives. The blades were more than strong enough for steak slicing and they would make great conversation pieces.

The idea became reality in a short time. It didn't take many tools or much time and you can do the same, if you can find the .50 brass. I understand the purists now are shooting .50 rifles in single-shot benchrest competition.

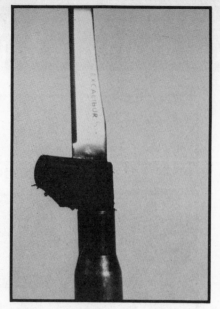

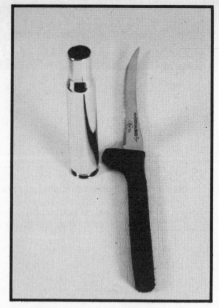

The original handle material was a kind of rubberized substance. Enough is left on the tang to slip into the mouth of the .50 caliber brass case.

Additional shaping and sanding will be necessary in the hand guard area.

If a reloader's case tumbler is not available, the brass cartridge may be polished with buffing wheels.

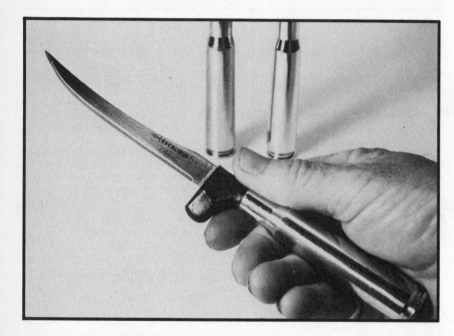

The original rubberized handle material provides a snug fit in the empty brass. No adhesive was used for this project, but a good two-part epoxy may be added.

That doesn't interest me, but knives do.

I took one knife with its rubber-like moulded handle to my belt sander. This is an old 4x36-inch shop sander that I picked up years ago and have used frequently. A 40-grit belt made fast work of the handle material, as I cut it down to a diameter of half an inch to fit the neck of the .50 brass. The neck had been smoothed and made uniform by running a pair of needle-nose pliers around the inside of each neck to form a nicely rounded throat. This miked out on my inside/outside calipers to .50-inch and I used the same calipers to check my sanding on the rubber handle.

When the calipers were getting close to fitting on all sides of the handle, I knew the neck of the brass should be a tight fit. I inserted the handle into the rounded throat and, as it fit, I shoved until the handle was inside the neck and body of the brass casing as far as it could go. I had to remove some of the length of the original handle to make a tight fit. The handles of my new steak knife set retained their rubber finger guards to prevent a finger slipping off and possibly being cut.

Sand and fit until the handle can be forced evenly into the brass neck. About a half-inch of the original handle was removed to allow the finger guard to fit snugly against the brass neck.

The only problem left was to smooth the guard and make a groove that would fit the finger and feel right when cutting. I used a rattail file, then sanded out the file marks.

The brass had laid around for many years and was green

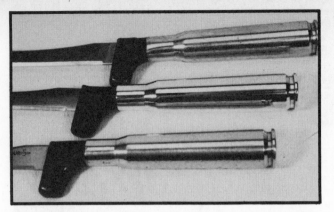

The bright brass polish can be retained with a coating of Varathane over the brass and finger guard.

Stamping at the end of the shell indicates it was loaded sometime in 1955. Dates can be mixed or matched, according to the whim of the builder.

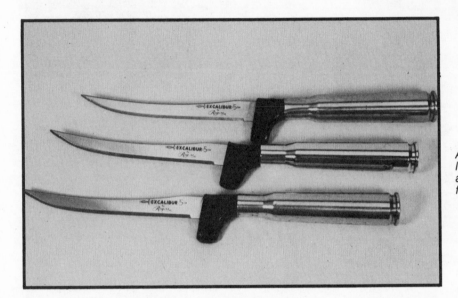

A set of three unusual steak knives led to a second, equal number to accommodate guests. The knives never fail to elicit comments from all.

with corrosion in some areas. I turned to that buffing wheel set I had made years before and use constantly. One wheel is a 3M deburring sander, which are sold in fine, medium and coarse grits. I used only the fine grit and this removed the tarnish to leave the brass with a matted finish.

The other wheel on the buffer unit is a floppy cotton finish pad. I use this in conjunction with white buffing compound that made brass mirror-smooth in no time after cleaning off the corrosion with the 3M wheel.

In a few minutes of buffing, I had a highly polished brass .50 shell in hand. The entire project took less than thirty minutes. It will take longer if you use hand tools, but the only difference between power and hand tools is time.

The finished handle of the vegetable knife — now a steak knife in the making — was inserted once again into the polished brass. There remained one problem: how to keep the brass shiny. I made four knives total for the steak knife set, waxing one finished knife heavily with Trewax. This is a carnauba wax and good for almost any waxing need. This didn't last long and the acid from hands and a few washings soon turned the brass to a dull oxidized finish. Not what I wanted at all.

The knives were buffed again and the brass and rubber finger guards sprayed with a matte-finish Varathane spray. This did the job and will last for quite a while. The brass isn't shiny, but is muted a bit and looks even better. If you prefer the higher polish effect, you can use the gloss finish also available in spray cans.

I laid the set on my buffet and there hasn't been one person who could walk by and not pick one up, asking what they were used for. They know it is a big caliber shell and it does get some wild stories started.

I lucked into finding my .50 brass cases, but you can find them too. Some of the mail-order houses such as Dixie Gunworks in Union City, Tennessee, might have them or something similar in their catalog. I have seen a few brass cases at gun shows, but they usually want more than the dollar a pound I paid for mine. The entire set of four steak knives cost me about six dollars total, not counting my time.

You might not find a serrated blade knife such as I used, but any small-tang fixed-blade could be used. I didn't have to cement the handles into the brass, as they are sanded to a tight fit. However, you could use any small blade, cementing it into a brass shell with epoxy or casting resin. It would last forever.

Knife blade shapes seemingly are limited only by the imagination of the maker. In this case, form must follow function, as the size and shape of a blade is directly related to its intended use. This group is Western Cutlery's.

Chapter 8

THE SHAPE OF THINGS TO COME

Selecting A Knife Blade Shape Is A Matter Of Deciding Its Use

THE BEGINNING knifemaker probably will look at a piece of steel and ask himself, "What type of blade do I want to make?"

The obvious answer is built around another question: "What do you want to do with the knife once it's finished? How will it be used?"

If you're a fisherman and want a knife for filleting trout, that calls for one shape. If you're going into the jungles of the Amazon — those that are left and haven't been turned into grazing lands — you'll want something a lot more sturdy.

If you are a hunter and are interested in cleaning game in the field, you'll probably want a blade that's no more than four inches in length and probably follows the drop-point design that Bob Loveless, the King of the Custom Knifemakers, and his copiers have made popular.

If you're going into a combat situation, a Bowie probably will be your choice, but one also has to recognize the limitations of whatever design he decides is for him. While Jim Bowie may have worked over a batch of enemies and done himself proud at the Alamo with a foot-long Bowie designed by his brother and made by blacksmith James Black, it's somewhat doubtful that he used the same knife to clean many rabbits for the frying pan.

Twenty years or so back, virtually all so-called hunting knives boasted thick, heavy, lengthy blades. In retrospect, it would seem that the manufacturers of the day felt that everyone who bought such a knife, with the idea of hunting, would have to use it sooner or later to save himself from a Cape buffalo or an elephant by stabbing it to death! If you'll look back to the old catalogs, virtually all of the commercial knife manufacturers seemed to follow this logic: Buck, Schrade, Western Cutlery, Case and a host of others.

A good deal of this philosophy probably went back to the days of the pioneers, when a frontiersman probably had only one knife and it had to be one with which he could do just about anything that his way of life would demand. He probably could skin and clean a jackrabbit with some degree of trouble; he surely could field dress a deer and he probably could defend himself against an aggressive Indian brave, if he'd run out of ammunition. The truth is, such

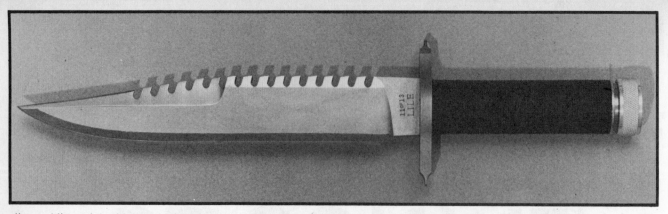

Jimmy Lile makes this survival knife to include sawblade teeth cut into the back of the large blade. This design is from the movie "Rambo — First Blood" and Lile went on to make several high-priced replicas.

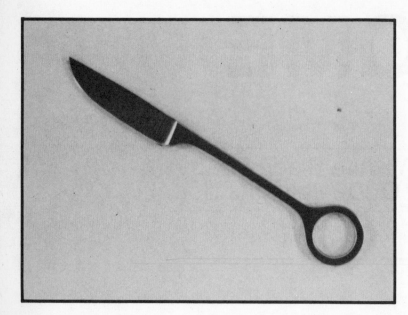

Knives are made in all sizes and shapes, from the large Lile survival model, above, to the little lightweight trout knife, left. The trout knife is all stainless steel, fits in tackle box.

individuals could fillet that trout with a large Bowie-type knife, too, but when done, the fish probably looked like a pound of chopped liver. However, if it cooked in the frontiersman's frying pan and made a meal, he probably didn't care much about how it looked.

If you want to go back to the Middle Ages and take a look at the Crusaders, they favored heavy daggers with long blades. Their swords — the legendary Excaliber, included — were heavy, unwieldy creations that were designed to carry a lot of force to slash through another knight's body armor or perhaps even put down his horse. The Turks, on the other hand, favored sharpness and cutting qualities over strength and settled for thin, curved blades that had some of the attributes of modern-day razor blades.

Ka-Bar, for example, is reputed to have gained its company name from a scrawled message from a frontier type saying he "K a Bar." That, according to legend, translates to the fact that he had killed a bear with one of the heavy-duty knives.

The Ka-Bar Marine Corps combat knife introduced in World War II was a thing of beauty, with its ten-inch blade and leather washer handle and each of them became a prized possession to the Marine to whom it was issued. Both the authors of this tome have carried such a knife in the jungles and rice paddies of Asia. Lewis has the same knife which he carried through three wars, but he is the first to admit that its greatest use was in knife-throwing contests whereby he was able to win cigarettes from others to maintain his habit. If anyone ever used a Ka-Bar in hand-to-hand combat, we have not been able to find any record of it. That, though, doesn't mean it didn't happen!

As mentioned earlier, it took Bob Loveless and some of the other top custom knifemakers to set the trend of shorter sturdy blades. The experienced outdoorsman found that a blade of 3½ or four inches could do anything with game that a ten-inch blade could do — and more handily. All too often, they learned, those extra inches of steel simply got in the way and were more a hinderance than a help. As one

Right: The replica Celtic sword by Sean McWilliams of Solid Wrought Iron is definitely a special design. It is twenty-two inches long of forged W-1 steel with brass fitting and buffalo horn handle. The blade is from a Celtic sword design dating from about 300 B.C.

Two knifemakers come up with different designs for the same purpose. Tom Morlan made the curved, semi-Bowie at left and Jeff Morgan, the hiltless model.

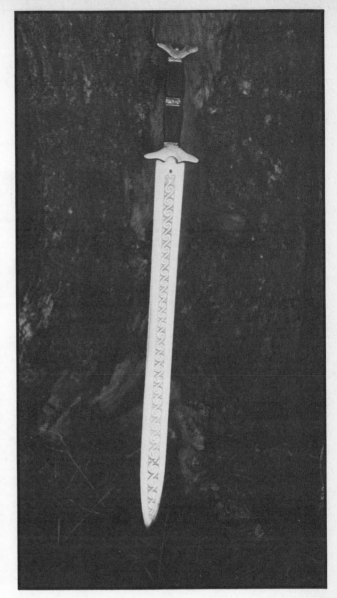

professional guide put it, "With ten inches of blade, there's just that much more you can cut yourself with, if you're trying to field dress an elk!"

The commercial knifemakers have kept a constant eye on the doings of the custom knife crafters in recent years and have adopted many of their basic designs. One factor that the average individual might not consider lies in the fact that economics are involved. If one is producing thousands upon thousands of knives, a lot more steel goes into the making of a run of knives with ten-inch blades than those with four inchers. The difference adds up to a batch of money on the balance sheet at the end of the year. True, you may be able to get more money for a longer knife, thus recovering the cost of the steel — if you can find enough customers to buy it. But the man on a budget will tend to buy the shorter, handier knife and the manufacturers can sell it at a more reasonable price.

In this regard, a number of custom knifemakers concen-

trate on ornate Bowie-type knives that they know are never going to be put to practical field use. Instead, they will be displayed in glass cases as part of a collection. Most of these custom makers offer a specific length and width of blade at a price. If one should want a wider, broader blade, the custom knifemaker usually charges extra for this at so much an inch. Not only does the steel cost additional, but he is required to do more work on a longer blade. He expects to be paid for it.

In more recent years, custom knifemakers have found another bonanza in the blood-and-guts motion pictures about mercenaries, hoods, outlaws and general troublemakers. In these epics, the hero invariably has a special knife that he has designed and had made to meet his own particular ideas on survival against all the elements and any kind of enemy. The "Rambo" series is a good example, with Sly Stallone carrying a different and more impressive knife in each film. Arnold Swartzennegger, in his

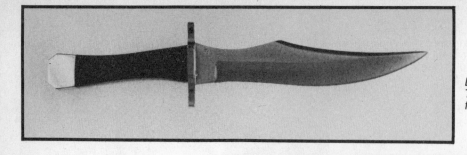

Dan Fitzgerald photographed this Tom Morlan Bowie design which also features a coffin-shaped handle.

Right: This is Cold Steel's version of the Bowie knife, called the Trail Master. The blade is long and heavy enough to chop down small trees.

An original Morseth boot knife is the one on top, with a Japanese factory reproduction beneath. The quality of the Morseth is obvious.

series on soldiers of fortune, has followed a similar trend, each successive film featuring a larger and more exotic knife. They're great for seemingly hacking up members of the Screen Extras Guild in hand-to-hand combat scenes, but again, we don't recall any sequence in which either of these characters has had to fillet an iguana for purposes of sustenence.

Nonetheless, such custom crafters as Jimmy Lile, Jack Crain, Herman Schneider, Gil Hibben and others have been paid large hunks of money for creating such exotic chopping tools — and in some cases, have made even more by reproducing exact copies and selling them at premium prices.

When it comes to folding knives, the field isn't that broad, since there is only so much one can do in designing a blade that will fold into a handle. Still, the manufacturers keep trying. The Wyoming Knife Corporation, for example, has one they call the Powder River II folder that works on a series of pivots with the blade ultimately being encased in a compartment of aircraft aluminum. When it is unfolded properly and all of the swiveling completed, the knife case becomes the handle.

The folks who produce this one boast that the aircraft aluminum alloy handle material has been heat-treated and stress-relieved, but we're still trying to figure out just what advantage that has, since one is not likely to be trying to get a cutting edge on the handle!

The oft-mentioned Bob Engnath of the House of Muzzleloading has a catalog that features well over a hundred different blade shapes. These are available at nominal cost and probably would be the best way for the beginning knifemaker to go.

If you want a combat knife, he has a blade that measures 7½ inches that was designed by himself and a former

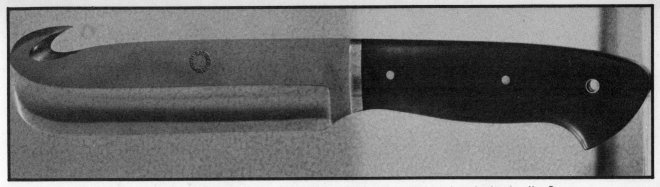

The strange-looking knife above has a specialized purpose; it is an elk field dressing design by Jim Sasser.

Factory knives also come in all shapes. These Al Mar knives are derived from the Tanken, a Japanese term meaning short sword. The blades are of AM-6 steel and the handles are of DuPont's black Zytel material.

Green Beret buddy who "proved the prototype in the jungles of West Los Angeles." This one is a totally nasty blade with a full-length double grind that is cut for a double guard and has a tapered tang. This one sells for about $40 and is made from ATS-34 stainless steel.

At the other extreme, Engnath markets a blade he calls the Chubby, saying that "this ugly little thing is one of our best sellers." It originally was designed to use up those little ends of bar steel that were too short for a regular knife. The blade on this one is only three inches long, but it's wide and thick for heavy-duty cutting. It also is made from ATS-34 and sells for about $22.

If you just have to have something big, ugly and impractical, Engnath will sell you the blank for an item he calls The One. It's his version of Resin Bowie's double-ground Louisiana fighting blade, the design predating the Bowie allegedly made in Arkansas by James Black. "This one probably is closer to the true Jim Bowie knife than any other design," Engnath claims. It is made from three-sixteenths-inch stock and features a tapered top grind. The blade measures about 9½ inches overall. Add four-plus inches for the handle and you're dealing with a real widow-maker. Engnath makes this one from ATS-34 or 440C stainless and sells it for $37.95, at this writing.

At the other end of the scale is one he calls his Mouse Skinner. This is a tiny hunter style with a three-finger type handle and a tapered tang. The blade measures only 2½ inches in length, but it would make an excellent caping knife, if you are called upon to do that kind of intricate work in preparing a game head for mounting.

Engnath proclaims that his blades "are totally hand ground. Profiling and rough grinding are done with a coarse grit belt that takes the stock off in a hurry."

Then each blade is trued up on a 120-grit belt, finally

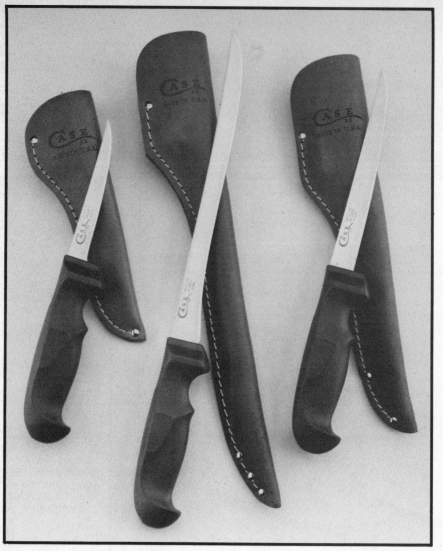

Fish knives are almost always long, slender and flexible for slicing out those tasty fillets. The three Case knives are factory made, but can be produced by the custom maker.

being semi-polished on a 220-grit belt. From there, each blade goes to drilling, hand filing or decorating, if the pattern calls for it. Heat-treating is handled by a professional firm that assures quality.

"After heat-treating, we check for straightness. We don't feel it's necessary to clean up any color, though the first-timer may be shocked to find his 154CM a deep purple or 440C looking like a rainbow," Engnath admits. This can be caused by the various hardening and tempering processes.

"That's as far as we go," the California knife supplier states. "Any serious polishing or buffing could easily double the selling price and you wouldn't appreciate the professional's work nearly as much if you didn't get a chance to do the rubbing."

In spite of his seeming flippant attitude toward marketing, Engnath is highly respected and supplies materials — including blades — to any number of professional custom blademakers.

In the last year or so, — thanks to Al Mar and such custom craftsmen as Bob Lum — there has been a good deal of interest in the so-called Tanto blade design based upon the knives carried by the ancient Japanese samurais.

Engnath stocks a number of these designs, most of them designed by Lum, who incidentally, is of Chinese ancestory as is Al Mar.

More recently, Engnath has discovered what is called the *yakiba* blade. The Japanese term means "flamed" or hardened edge. Engnath spent a couple of years in perfecting this type of blade and now offers several designs, most of them Oriental in nature, with a cutting edge with a Rockwell hardness of about 58C, while the rest of the blade is relatively soft, in the mid 40C range.

"This gives a high shock resistance and allows the blade to bend quite a bit before suffering damage," the supplier explains. It also can be polished in such fashion that the hardened edge is plainly visible to the eye; an extra decora-

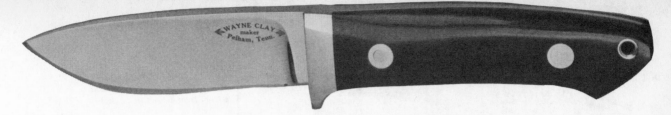

Wayne Clay, of Tennessee, turns out this clean Loveless-style drop-point knife, popular with outdoors people.

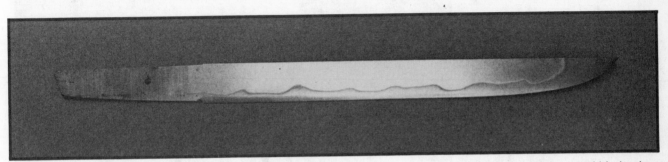

The Japanese-style sword blade above is difficult to make for the beginner, so Bob Engnath offers them as shown. Note the unusual heat treatment line just above the blade edge.

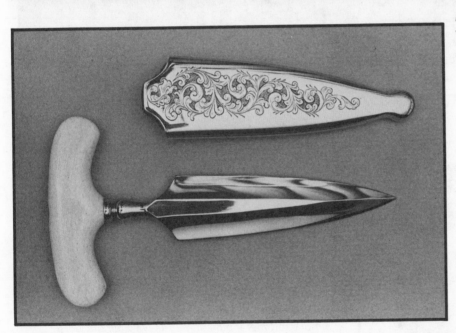

Custom knifemaker Sid Birt makes the push dagger and metal sheath of 440C steel, ivory and silver. The blade measures five inches.

tive touch, if that's the sort of thing you're after.

"While the yakiba blades are entirely unique, we don't make any outrageous claims for their capabilities," Engnath warns. "They are simply steel and all steel has certain limitations that cannot be exceeded."

If you want to build your knife of Damascus steel and don't have the ambition or the equipment to sweat over a hot forge, shaped blades of this material also are available. House of Muzzleloading has quite a variety and Damascus USA has still more. Keep in mind, though, that Damascus is labor intensive and not cheap, even when the basic blank has been forged in some underdeveloped country!

Going back to the beginning, the shape of a knife blade is pretty much up to the individual. If you're looking for blades that can be used for serious using knives, there are several sources mentioned or you can make your own. At the other extreme, if you're looking for an exotic blade for a Malay kris, a Filipino bolo, an Australian boot knife or some other off-the-wall shape, Bill Adams of Atlanta Cutlery seems to have an endless supply of these unusual shapes, as well as the other materials such as hand guards, handles, et al., to help you turn out that one-of-a-kind wall hanger that will be a conversation piece forever. The address for Atlanta Cutlery is 2143 Gees Mill Road, Conyers, GA 30207.

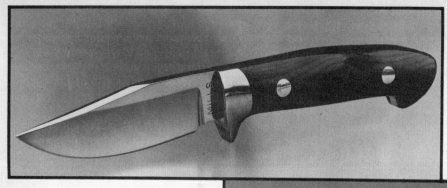

Custom knifemaker Andy Mills makes this full, untapered tang knife using stainless steel bolts and nuts, left.

Ted Dowell has a loyal following for his custom knives. He gets the bullseye effect on his knife and ax combo, right.

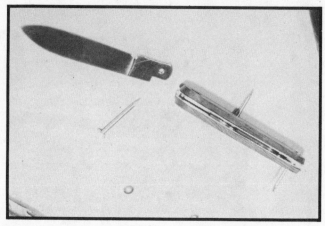

Simple soft metal pins and birdseye washers were used to build the Atlanta Cutlery folding knife, above. The pins are clipped, peened and filed down smooth.

Cutler's rivets are the simplest devices to use on these slab-sided handles. The rivets are made of copper and are hammered together after assembly. The two hidden-tang models, left, use threaded nuts through butt caps.

Chapter 9

HOLDING IT ALL TOGETHER

Strength And Appearance Make The Difference When Attaching Handles To Knives — There Are A Number Of Choices

UNLESS YOUR KNIFE is without a handle, utilizing only the shaped tang, or it uses a cord wrap as a handle, you will need some sort of bolt, pin, rivet, cement or combination of materials to hold the handle slabs to the tang area. This applies to folders or sheath knives, as we saw in our first simple knife construction project. The choice of handle materials is wide and the choice of something to hold it all together also is extensive.

Selection of the proper method of attachment depends upon the handle slab material and on the type of knife. A folder usually will use pins or rods, without any cement added. A look at most commercially made knives will show that there are exceptions to that rule; many do have the handle material pinned and cemented. Our own folding knife project did not use anything except the pins, slightly peened.

There are several good brands of two-part epoxy on the market. We used the Devcon five-minute epoxy on one of our projects and ran into some trouble, because it set up too fast. Bob Engnath recommends using a slower-curing variety, unless there is some overriding reason for a fast set.

We also learned a lesson that we would like to share. During construction of a full-tang, slab-handle knife, we were using five-minute epoxy cement and a pair of large solid-head bolts. This is the type of bolt that requires countersunk holes on one side — actually a dual countersink to accommodate the configuration of the bolts. Furthermore, the nut end has internal threads into which the bolt screws. The female threads have no outlet.

In our efforts to get plenty of the cement on all surfaces, we got the mixture into the female end of the bolts. That was the first mistake. The epoxy would not compress and could not force its way out of the nut hole.

As we struggled, the five-minute epoxy was hardening fast. By the time we decided this arrangement was not going to work, the cement had hardened to the point that we could not get the bolts out nor the slabs loose from the tang.

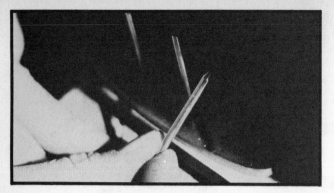

These handle pins are made of simple brass welding rod. Inexpensive, they will hold any knife together.

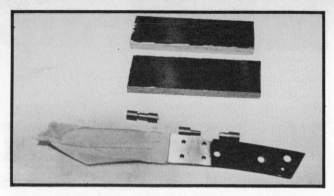

These threaded bolts and nuts will require larger tang holes and the handle slabs will have to be countersunk.

We still had about a sixteenth of an inch space between the handle slabs and the tang, and the bolts were still sticking out too far.

Eventually, we had to saw the slabs and bolts off, ruining all of it, then we had to grind off the excess epoxy still adhering to the tang. It took a lot of time and was a mess. When we went back to it, we went with simple pins and epoxy. With the pins, the five-minute cement was satisfactory. We should have listened to Engnath's advice about using the longer-curing type for knife projects.

Epoxy cement will bind almost any material to any other material, but there are certain precautions to keep in mind when using it. Some cements are dark gray in color and some are clear. Most knifemakers use the clear type, because the dark coloring can stain or at least leave marks on some natural handle materials. You wouldn't want to stain a choice piece of real ivory or sambar stag, both becoming difficult and expensive to come by. With some medium-color wood, the darker line of epoxy might be desirable, looking a bit like a liner between the tang and the handle slabs.

The best advice we can give when using any type of cement is to follow the package directions exactly. If you purchase a brand you haven't used before, take a minute to read the directions. Changes are made in chemical composition from time to time and the same brand of epoxy may now be different from what it was two or three years ago.

Excellent knives have been made, using only epoxy cement to hold on the handle material. A typical hidden or spike-like tang knife may have only cement to hold on the handle, there will be no pins or rivets through it. Many kitchen knives are so constructed, but remember to use epoxy with a high melting temperature or such knives cannot survive an automatic dishwasher.

Using only epoxy cement to hold the handle slabs to a full-tang knife may not always work well. With a good coating of cement on them, the slabs often tend to slip out of alignment as they are clamped. You can make them well oversize and grind down the slabs later, but using pins or bolts will provide a tougher hold, as well as add to the attractive appearance of the knife when complete.

The simplest material to use, of course, is a soft brass. These are offered by several suppliers, already cut to approximate length. Regular welding rod also can be used,

cut to whatever length is needed. If you were going to make several knives, this would be a less expensive material.

Pins may be stainless steel, too, since most makers will want to match the pin material with their bolster, thong hole liner or have them complement the handle material. Some handle colors look better with brass, while others go well with stainless steel.

Not every maker agrees that tang pins should be slightly peened after the epoxy has cured. Bob Engnath warns that, especially on some natural handle materials, peening soon will crack and split the material. This is especially true, he says on real ivory, mother of pearl and even some of the Micartas. Use the pins to fix the position of the slabs, but don't try to peen them.

All sorts of rivets, bolts and screws have been used by various knifemakers. Recall the pins and birdseyes which we used for the simple folding knives from Atlanta Cutlery. The handle slabs already were precision drilled and counter-sunk for that method. For your own knives, if you decide to make a folder or to use a similar system on a sheath knife, you will have to drill and cut countersunk holes in your handle materials.

Bolt head counterbores are available from suppliers. One that Bob Engnath sells fits three-piece bolts and counter-sinks .280-inch; another is available for 5/15-inch bolt heads. It will accommodate handle bolt nuts to most reasonable depths in wood, stag, or manmade phenolic material. The hole is flat-bottomed to prevent splitting any of the more delicate handle materials and requires a pilot of #19 drill size. Careful users may use it in a hand drill, but best and most accurate results are obtained by using it in a drill press with a depth stop.

You may make your choice of bolt or pins from among the many types available. The three-piece bullseye is a standard type that consists of a length of threaded rod with a pair of round, .280-inch diameter nuts. The nuts can be tightened from either side and countersunk over a quarter-inch deep, if that is required. The 8-32 rod will slide through a #19 hole just right. These are available in brass or stainless steel, heads or rods. To use these, the handle should be drilled for a #8 hole.

Another choice might be the double blind nut. This is a separate solid head nut on each end of an 8-32 threaded rod. These also are available in brass or stainless steel, in three head sizes. The heads are slotted and the bolts are

Here, we have a choice of brass or stainless steel pins, cutler's rivets and/or two-part epoxy cement. The epoxy hardens in five minutes, too rapidly for our purposes.

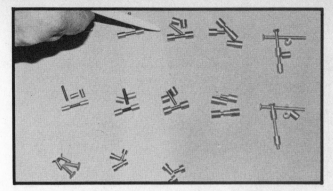

This is a porton of the types of handle fasteners from which the maker may choose. Most are available in brass or steel, in a choice of several diameters.

adjusted easily for different handle thicknesses. These fit into a handle hole drilled for a #8 bolt. The head sizes are 5/16-, 1/4-, and 4/36-inch.

Another bolt-and-nut style of stainless steel or brass has one side with a solid head machined onto a length of 8-32 shank. The other end is a slotted through-nut with a screwdriver slot. When finished and sanded down, the threaded nut end will show a bullseye configuration. The shaft fits through a hole drilled for a bolt.

Next is the standard solid-head nut and bolt. Be sure to get the professional quality, manufactured to the highest standards. The Luke brand is recognized as one of the best. In brass or stainless steel, these solid-head styles require a 15/64-inch or .220-inch tang hole and a 5/16-inch countersink. All threading on this type is internal, so they are not recommended for thinner slabs. Some suppliers also have a solid-head bolt in a larger size that is of stainless steel only. These require a 15/64-inch tang hole and a 3/8-inch countersink. This type may be hard to find.

Yet another choice is the short head and bolt. This special arrangement has an internally threaded screw slot bolt on one end and a male-threaded bolt and slotted nut on the other. These are used by makers who do not epoxy their handle slabs to the tang and who leave the screwdriver slots exposed so the knife may be disassembled at any time. Their use requires a .220-inch handle hole drilled through the tang.

Double-acorn nuts and threaded rod bolts also are popular options with many knifemakers. These are available in brass and stainless steel. With these, once they have been tightened and the epoxy cement cured, the nuts are ground and sanded flush with the handles and they cannot be removed. At the ends they present a plain, round face in either material. They are available in three diameters for the nuts. The threaded rods are all the same size: 8-32.

Another choice might be the set similar to the double acorns, but this one has one nut smooth on the end and the other slotted. When they are sanded down, however, they present the typical bullseye effect on both sides. The slot makes it easier to tighten down the bolts during construction.

When using stainless steel pins on knives with bolsters, especially folding knives, most makers will use what is called 416 stainless wire cut to proper length. When ground and polished, this material matches the appearance of the stainless steel bolsters. When done well, the 416 pins are nearly invisible when finished.

Speaking of bolsters, friend Engnath has a slick trick for pinning them on knives. He suggests that before peening the pin or pins holding the bolsters, one should countersink the hole from both sides to about half the thickness of the material; use a drill just a few thousandths wider than the existing hole. A vise and a drill press are needed for this operation, as the work will tend to climb up the drill bit.

When the pins are peened, everything will be locked in place as the pin expands to fill the slightly larger hole. Be sure to file or grind the pin ends square before beginning to hammer on them or the pin may bend instead of spreading evenly. Leave about one diameter length of the pin sticking out of the bolster before peening. The bolster also may be soldered in place around the pins to prevent water or blood from seeping in around the pin to cause corrosion later.

While peening bolster pins, use a medium hammer and tap lightly and repeatedly. Pounding too hard may cause you to miss or push the pins off-center. Use your anvil on the bottom against which to peen.

When you have finished hammering, the pins may be ground and shaped along with the rest of the bolster. Hand-rubbed, the pins should be nearly invisible. Use this technique only on bolsters; handle slabs surely will split with this kind of treatment. Bolsters will not remain in place, if held only with epoxy; they must be pinned or soldered.

An inexpensive slab handle knife similar to the Green River style will benefit from the use of standard cutler's rivets. These may be hard to find, as they are not so commonly used these days. Cutler's rivets are two-piece, with a male and a female end. They lock firmly together when hammered. To use them, a loose hole should be drilled so the handle scales will not split when the rivets expand. They are generally available in small and large, of either brass or nickel silver. They are quite inexpensive, when you can find them.

Keep in mind that, for most knives, the tang holes can be drilled slightly larger than required, as they will be filled with epoxy for assembly. If the handle slabs are drilled with too large a hole, the epoxy may show around the bolts or pins and be visible proof of sloppy work. Clear epoxy will be all but invisible, if used in small amounts. Holes drilled with a drill press, at precise angles, should not present that problem.

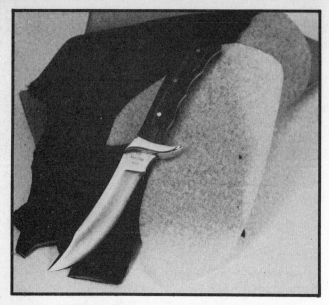

The Buck Akonua is a rather large fixed-blade knife with curved shape. A custom sheath for this design offers challenges. Pattern is cut from polyurethane.

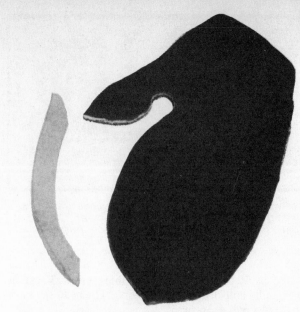

Pattern of sheath front section reveals a channel cut into it to accommodate sweep of safety strap. Curved leather plug will flop over to right of section.

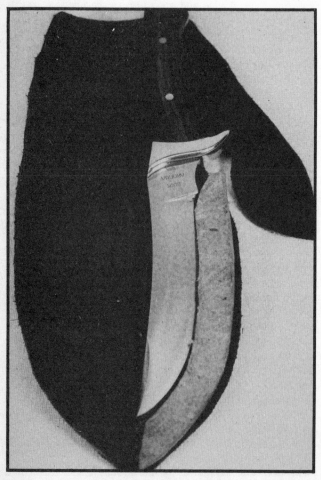

A heavy, rough leather plug which follows blade curve is laid out along edge, on inner side of sheath material.

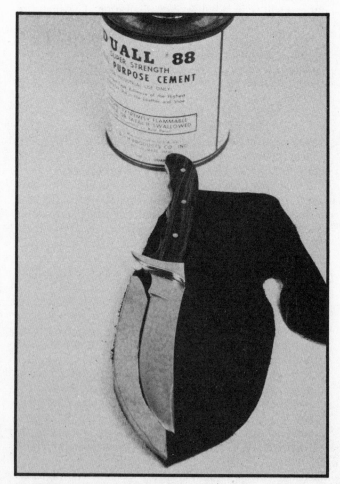

All-purpose cement is applied to both surfaces of plug and sheath section. Any slight adjustments or moves must be made now as parts will adhere after drying.

Chapter 10

SHEATHS AND POUCHES

When Your Knife Is Built, You Can Buy A Ready-Made Sheath, Or Make Your Own

THERE PROBABLY are as many sheath variations as there are knives, since each knife deserves a bit different treatment when making the sheath to fit it. That sheath should be made of heavy leather to make the blade safe to carry.

Home craftsman Bob Learn has made any number of sheaths over the years. In the pages that follow, he discusses his efforts:

The Akonua blade on which I had been working was finished and I wanted a sheath that would cover the shining handle and brass so as not to reflect in the field. If you get close to game, the last thing you want is a ray of reflected light spooking the animal into the next county. The simple way to prevent this is to cover all or most of the knife with leather.

Before you cut any leather, first make a pattern. This can be changed many times and the cost is nothing compared to a side of leather.

I found a new pattern material, a light piece of polyurethane form such as the type used for protecting glass and breakables when shipping. I received some in a package and I took it to the shop, where I found it flexible enough to fold over a blade, yet sufficiently stiff that I could trace around it. I now prefer it to my old method of using single-sided cardboard.

Craft paper, show card or any such material will work

for the pattern, but one should work that pattern up, move it around on the leather, before making the final cuts. You can replace patterns, but not leather.

One sheath that I liked from the day Buck Knives introduced it is the style they use to encase their two top-line knives, the Kalinga and Akonua. This is a one-piece sheath that has a finger-snap guard to enclose the curved finger guard of the knife and prevent the knife from falling out, even if the snap comes loose.

I modified that sheath to make the snap closure work from the back of the sheath rather than the front! The snap could be opened accidentally in moving through brush; by placing it on the inside against the leg, it is almost impossible for it to open, except when you need it.

After I had the pattern designed to my satisfaction, I added some rivet holes so I wouldn't forget them, then proceeded to work the pattern on the ten-ounce brown, oil-tanned latigo leather I planned to use. This is heavy stuff that will never fold on you, yet one often can use sections for a sheath that wouldn't be used for a belt or handgun holster.

The final item needed for the basics is a heavy plug. This fits along the edge of the blade and is sewn or riveted into the sheath while it's being made. This protects the knife edge from cutting the seam on the sheath — and possibly cutting you. For this, I use sections of heavy sole leather

Outer and inner portions of sheath are glued together and stitched with leather plug inside. Stitching may be crude, but is effective. Insert knife at each stage.

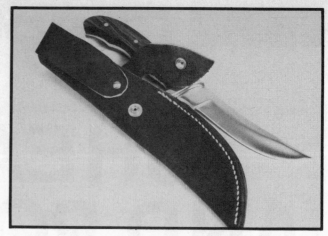

Belt loop may now be glued and riveted onto inner surface of sheath. Stitching does not interfere here.

The safety strap curves around, over the hand guard and snaps in place. Any excess leather may be trimmed.

The addition of the heavy leather plug at the blade edge results in a thick sheath when finished. All exposed edges will be treated with darker leather dye.

Completed custom sheath holds the big Buck knife firmly and safely, protecting knife and wearer.

that I buy in a cobbler's shop. I can use pieces he can't, so he is usually happy to sell them to me by the pound, which goes a long way.

There are only two pieces to this sheath: the body and the plug liner. After you have everything cut out, make your final check to determine whether you allowed for the fold over of the leather and will not have it come up short. That is one reason for making a pattern.

I use a leather cement my cobbler friend gets for me. It is called *Duall 88* and is used in the shoe business for just about anything that needs gluing. It is an excellent contact cement.

Cement the plug along one side of the inner section of the sheath. I usually run the cement on both sides of the plug and on each inner edge of the sheath, then let them cure. This contact cement can be worked wet, but when you make contact, it is there almost forever, believe me, so be certain of proper positioning before you place your leather

in contact. You also can use Barge cement, which I favored for years, or any other brand of good contact cement.

After the two sides have been folded and the contact made, I try to clamp the edges with a couple of boards and clamps for a time to let them set solidly. Don't use a spring clamp directly on leather, as the clamp marks will stay there forever and you don't want that on this sheath.

You still have a few small items to tend to in finishing the sheath. For example, you need to place a leather belt loop on the back of the sheath. This can be done with lighter weight leather of the same color, since it isn't necessary that it be terribly tough. I make the strap, fasten the upper in a loop style to make it go over the belt easier. I cement, then rivet it in that position. Bend the loop, give it some slack and cement and rivet the bottom. It will fit a two-inch belt, if you wear them that wide.

The snap holder is part of the pattern and, as a part of the sheath, you need to be able to attach the snap. I use the

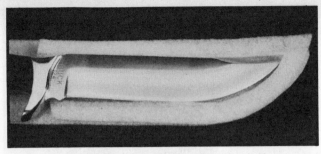

A thin foam material is ideal for pattern formation with the blade laid out on it. Leave plenty of extra space around blade for placement of leather plug.

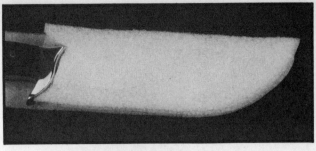

The custom sheath maker is able to cut the pattern to precisely fit the knife, something not feasible by production means. Pattern fits guard exactly.

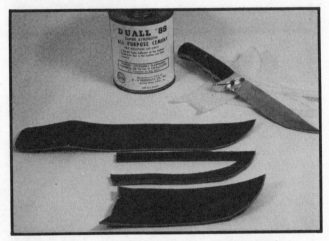

Four joining surfaces, the central plug, outer and inner components are coated with Duall 88 cement.

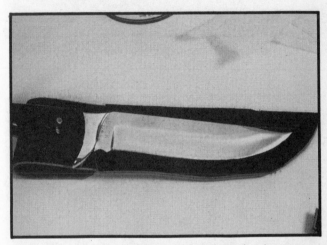

Blade fit is tested a final time before last glued side of sheath is fastened. Adjust as necessary.

Baby Dot-style snaps available from MacPherson Leather in Los Angeles, but one also needs a snap-setting tool. This tool is inexpensive and will last just short of forever. It's also available from MacPherson, 420 S. San Pedro Street, Los Angeles, California 90003.

Mark your center on the strap tongue, punch and set the top round head section of the snap. Take the strap around behind the sheath with the knife in it and press firmly to get the location for the male section of the snap. This method never fails to give me the right setting for the snap.

After the snaps have been tapped into position, you still have a decision to make. You can mark off spaces an inch or less along the seam of the sheath and set rivets or take it to a saddlemaker or shoe shop to have them use a heavy-duty leather sewing machine and stitch the seam for you.

I used to rivet sheaths, since it isn't hard, but the sheath must be wider to allow the rivet width. Now I prefer a narrower sheath, so I let the cobbler run a stitch and pay him a dollar or so to do it. You also can hand-stitch the sheath, but with that heavy leather plug in the seam, you must drill the holes first. It's easier to have a professional stitch down the edge, then run a backstitch to prevent it from unraveling.

A final touch for the sake of appearance is to use leather dye or even shoe polish to stain the leather's cut edges, especially along the seam. This makes the sheath look more professionally made. I use a cotton dauber to run black dye along the big seam edge, being careful not to get it on the body of the sheath. This is an alcohol-based dye and it will stain anything it touches — including you.

When you wear this sheath afield, there is nothing to snag or catch on limbs or brush. It isn't a fast-draw style, since you have to reach behind the sheath to release the snap and, if you prefer, you can move the strap to the front by merely reversing the pattern on the leather. As a reminder, you also must be careful to lay the pattern properly on the leather when cutting. I have one great left-handed sheath among my collection. I goofed when I cut the leather.

THE LAYERED SHEATH

The bigger the knife, the stronger the sheath needed. The Buck Frontiersman is a big knife, with a blade seven inches long, and thick. This is the type of blade that properly requires a multiple-layer sheath.

The multi-layered sheath is just that, comprised of three layers of leather. The back section usually incorporates the belt loop. The inner layer is a full, heavy leather plug that totally encloses the blade, while the outer layer is the finish side that is seen.

In making a pattern, determine then whether you will be riveting or stitching the seams. To rivet, you will need three-quarters to one inch of leather around the edges of the blade to allow for the width of the rivets. I planned to stitch this model, so I made the edges a minimum of half an inch.

Among the odds and ends of leather I've saved, I found a

For the two-piece sheath model, entire length is stitched after gluing, before forming loop.

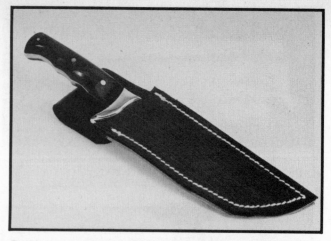

Belt loop portion is folded under, ready for cement and rivets. Riveting tool reaches into sheath pouch.

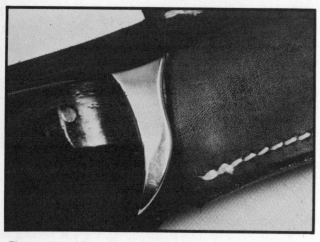

Finger guard fits snugly against planned curve in top portion of leather sheath, patterned ahead of time.

Plug and sheath leather edges may be smoothed down with grinding wheel or belt sander and dye finished.

heavy ten-ounce piece that had been antiqued to make it look different from the normal leather finish. Dyed black as the inside, it was a good choice for the sheath I had in mind.

To make the inner or plug pattern, I find it easier to lay the knife on the pattern material and trace around the entire blade. Using a compass, I make a line of at least one-half inch around that line to establish the inner and outer marks for cutting the leather.

The back section of the sheath is made to encompass the total width of the blade and so is the front section. I made a minor deviation in that I allowed for the downsweep of the finger guard and cut the front section to fit this. I didn't want the finger guard going inside the sheath, but meeting the front section. This way, the entire knife handle is exposed.

Allow a longer top on the back section for installation of a belt loop about halfway up the length of the handle. You can cut this rear section to be the full length of the handle, then incorporate the loop, if you prefer. One factor will be the size of the leather with which you are working.

Take a good look at the handle and blade and plan the sheath to fit that particular style. The next step is merely to cut out the sections on the leather. One of the advantages of the multiple layer is that you can use smaller pieces of leather than with a full wrap-around style, thus utilizing your leather to better advantage.

After the leather has been cut for the front and back, the plug is next. It can be a real problem due to thickness. I have used a jigsaw to cut it on occasions. This done, lay out the pieces and check them for positioning. The plug will be a bit on the skinny side and will need special care during the cementing or it can slip out of position.

Place the plug section — both sides coated with contact cement — on the cement-coated area of the back section. I start at the tip of the sheath to be certain the two sections mate properly, then move up the right side with the tip facing me, working what will be the back edge of the knife. As the leather meets the cemented section, it will grip and hold, so take it easy; you can't move it at this point.

The blade edge of the plug next is moved into position and the two cemented surfaces pressed into position along the edges. It helps to run a line with a marking pen along the interior lines that match the fit of the blade, using this as a guide when cementing. With the entire plug solidly in place, we're ready for the face of the sheath.

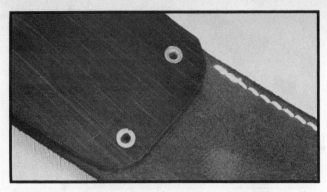

Belt loop portion is radiused at corners for better appearance and strength before attaching two rivets.

Safety strap is riveted to outside of belt loop and male and female snaps are located before securing.

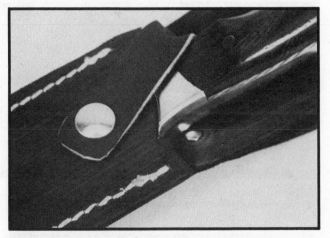

The safety strap should be made of thinner, lighter leather as it is the only moving part of the sheath.

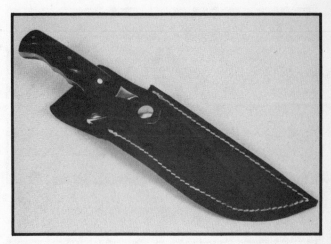

Knife is held safely while handle is fully exposed. This is the design to show off an attractive handle.

The outer edges of the underside of the sheath cover have been cemented at the same time as the other sections, so it is simple to place this on the plug, which already is cemented in position. Don't get in too great a rush, since this cement will grab fast and hold. If you get it out of line, you might have to cut a new section.

After all three pieces are in position, I lay heavy weights on the sheath or clamp the edges to ensure a solid joining. Don't use clamps on the outside of the leather, however, unless you first cover the leather with wood or metal to prevent clamp marks on the sheath's surface.

At this point, you can insert the blade into the sheath to check for proper fit. There really isn't much you can do, though, except make a slight fitting cut since the sheath is formed.

The remaining step is to fold over the extended length of the back section to form the belt loop. I usually make these about two inches so it will fit over a web belt. It also fits the nylon straps on my fanny pack, but you can make adjustments to meet your own preferences. This belt loop is cemented, then riveted, since one can't get to the required area for stitching it at this point. The rivets work well and are out of sight.

You probably will want some type of loop or strap to hold the handle of the knife to the sheath. This isn't a tight-fitting sheath, so the knife could come out. I used a similarly colored but lighter weight bit of leather to make a loop to fit over the curved finger guard. The loop is riveted to the back of the sheath — be careful you don't rivet through the belt loop — and brought over the guard. A snap is fitted to that end of the loop.

The male end of the snap fixture will be placed on the front of the sheath and you may have to take a piece of metal, insert it into the sheath to give it a solid backing to set the snap base. You could punch and set the rivet base before you place the front section on the plug, but as long as you can get to it, you don't have to worry about setting rivets or snaps.

This particular sheath was completed as far as design and basics were concerned. A quick trip to the cobbler shop, a dollar fee to run a stitch around the edge and the sheath was ready for the field. This makes a strong and safe means of carrying any large-bladed knife. That heavy leather plug along the outer edges will prevent the knife edge from getting to you or cutting the stitches.

If you prefer to bind the edges with a rivet system, this is easy and fast, especially if you don't have a friendly cobbler close. The riveted sheath is made a bit larger to allow for the rivets, but they work equally well.

Another advantage of the multiple-layered sheath is

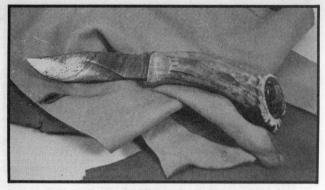

An unusual blade and an unusual handle demands a fancier sheath: buckskin and oak-tanned leather.

Tools required include an adjustable caliper, rivets, leather hole punch and a sharp razor-blade knife.

After the leather has been cut to shape, the blade shape is outlined on the surface with pen or pencil.

Outer outline of sheath body is coated with cement and cured for five minutes before pressing together.

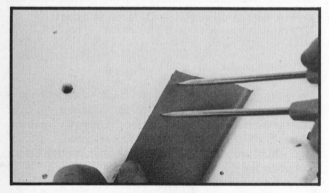

Caliper marks rivet locations. With no leather plug inside, rivets help prevent blade cutting through.

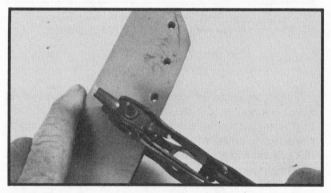

With hole punch adjusted for proper rivet size, locate the caliper marks and punch through leather layers.

some of the poorer sections of a hide such as the legs or neck can be used for the full plug. All that is required is that it be thick, hard leather. The leg and neck leather often is just that and you would have little use for them otherwise.

THE MOULDED SHEATH

Should you make a one-of-a-kind knife, such as my own Damascus horn-handled knife, you need to think about the sheath in which you will carry it. You'll find design ideas, as you look through books and catalogs. I do that, too, but seldom find what I want, so I merely jot down designs until one looks right.

The knife I mentioned is a simple blend of horn and steel, so I wanted a sheath that would be simple to make but dif-

ferent from those in the commercial marketplace. The sheaths made by most companies are designed for mass production and you won't find many variations. You can let your imagination run wild to come up with a wild-looking, yet safe, sheath.

After cogitating for a bit, I decided on a fringed leather sheath, using some buckskin from deer kills over the years. The horn handle knife sheath would be from the same animal.

This type of sheath is simple to make, but would violate my own safety rules, as in this case, I wouldn't use a plug on the blade edge of the sheath.

I dug into my pile of old leather and found a small section of tough, heavy hide. It would be heavy enough to protect

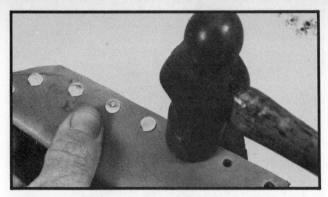

Rivets are set with ball peen hammer. Rounded head is used to pound rivets flush with leather surface.

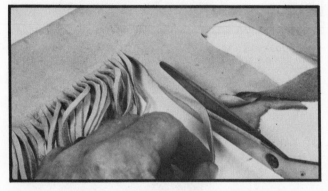

Enough excess deerskin is left beyond knife shape so that fringe may be cut with careful scissors.

A deerskin belt loop is easy to construct and may be set on sheath to position knife higher or lower.

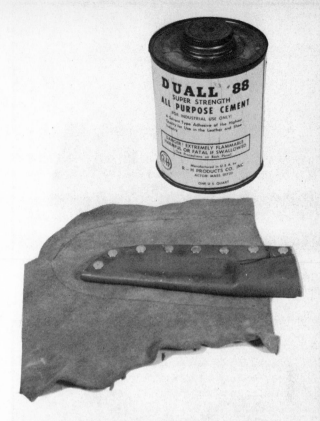

Inner sheath and outer deerskin will combine for a customized, moulded sheath. Glue coats surfaces.

No stitching or riveting is visible on the finished product, but a strong, rigid sheath is on the inside.

my body from the blade, but I planned to add to its safety. The leather, incidentally, was of the natural type such as the oak-tanned variety, since this would be a moulded sheath.

Place the leather on the workbench, put the blade on the leather and cut it at least three-quarters of an inch from the blade edge for the outer edge of the leather. Mark the back edge of the knife on the leather, then remove the knife. Allow enough leather on the upper section to come up over the handle section at least an inch. Fold the leather over and cut along the line you marked on the outer edge. Work on the flesh or rough side of the leather; the smooth or hair side will be the visible side when finished. Make certain you place the blade correctly or you may end up with a left-

handed sheath.

Mark the outer edge on the smooth or hair side. Using a compass, mark the leather at one-inch intervals down the edge where you will punch and set rivets. When you set the rivets, pound them flat, since they won't show. If you leave the rounded top, it will bulge the cover later. These rivets — and the next step — will serve as protection against that sharp blade.

After the rivets are set, you have the sheath body. That is all it is at this point; merely a leather holder and nothing more. Immerse it totally in water and allow it to soak for an hour or so. While the leather is soaking, coat the knife, handle and all, liberally with a good paste wax. You will have to position the knife in the wet body to make a moulded-

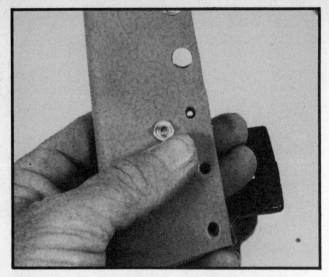

The bottom, male portion of rivet protrudes into hole which must also accommodate top cap of rivet.

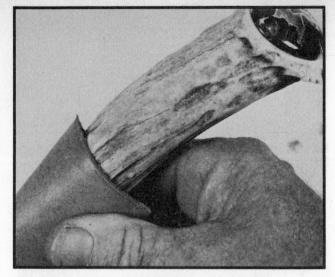

The moulded sheath is more a pouch style, because knife will be held in only by friction, not straps.

A strip of deerskin may be inserted through the belt loop and used to retain knife inside sheath.

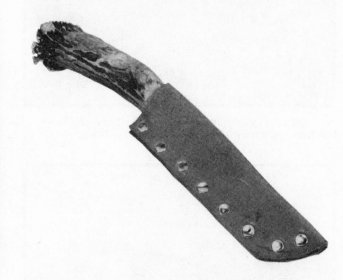

Heavily coat the blade with a good paste wax before inserting it in sheath. Soak sheath and knife in pan of water for twenty minutes, remove and let dry.

style sheath that is different from the others. The wax protects against rust.

When the leather has become soft, take it out of the water and immediately place the waxed knife into the leather body, pushing it to the bottom as hard as you can. The upper section of leather should extend over the top, covering part of the handle. Place heavy-duty spring clamps along the edge by the base of the handle at the blade section and another on the back edge where the leather is meeting the handle. This will leave clamp marks, but don't worry about that at this point.

Allow the leather to dry totally before removing the knife. when the leather has dried hard, remove the knife, noting how it snaps out of that leather holder. When you remove the knife, the leather should remain in a rigid state and feel hard to the touch.

There is some flexibility, but not much. This moulded sheath will constitute the base for the exterior leather we

now are ready to apply.

If you have some gold-colored or natural tanned deer skin — often called buckskin — you can use pieces of it to make the outer covering of the sheath. I had part of an old hide I had used in making a shirt. I settled on a leg area, since the shape fit what I wanted. If you don't have buckskin, you can buy sections of it in most leather shops or use split cowhide. It works, too.

Cut the buckskin larger than needed for the sheath, trimming it to fit over the back side of the moulded sheath. The front will lap over the edges quite a bit, since we will fringe this after the hide is cemented to the hard sheath base.

Cover the entire hard leather surface with contact cement. I held my sheath with a clothespin to dry, since there is no way of laying it down without picking up hair or dust. Coat the inner side of the buckskin only where it will cover the sheath leather. Don't coat the area to be fringed, since you don't want it to adhere to anything.

The golden-tanned Colorado deerskin makes a nice complement for the horn-handled Damascus knife.

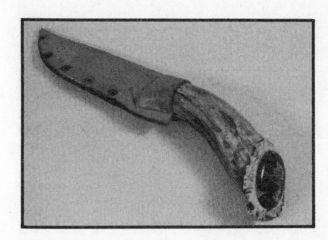

The inner, hard leather sheath is moulded to shape. Unsightly clamp marks will be hidden by deerskin.

Three knife styles and three sheath styles demonstrate what the custom sheath maker can do. On the left is the three-layer design which exposes all the handle, then the wrap-around which conceals the handle and the buckskin with fringes. Last style seems to match the horn handle.

After the proper setting time — I usually wait five minutes — take the hard leather body and lay the deerskin on the back bottom edge. Pull it tight and slowly move it over the entire back surface, then over to the front side. The tighter you pull, the smoother the hide will lie on the hard base. You can't pull the leather apart, so pull it hard!

When you reach the front mating edge, be certain there is some cement on that edge, since the cement is all you have for holding this cover on. There is no stitching, no rivets.

When the leather has been set on the hard base, you still will have a long flap — mine was about six inches — hanging over the edge. The upper section of the sheath will be covered with the buckskin, too. This one had a bit of extra buckskin overlapping above the base unit, but I left it that way. I can always cut it off.

With a pair of sharp scissors, start cutting strips on the flap of buckskin to create a fringe on the outer edge of the sheath. I usually make the fringe about one-quarter inch or so in width. Try to make them even in size and be careful that the buckskin doesn't slip and you cut off the fringe you are working on. Do this around the entire outer edge of the cover.

When the fringe has been cut, you still need to add a belt loop to carry the knife. Using a section of the same leather used for the base, fold it to make a simple loop, being certain it is long enough to fit your belt. Punch a hole in the strap and the back of the sheath at the upper back edge to attach the strap to the body of the sheath. Before you rivet this in position, cover the loop with a section of buckskin to make the entire sheath look the same. Position the covered belt loop and tap the rivet home.

You now have a one-of-a-kind knife in a one-of-a-kind sheath.

A buffing wheel, above, may be used to put a fine, mirror-like finish on a knife blade, faster than hand-finishing. Great care must be exercised, however, because of the possibility of danger and serious injury while in use. Always use eye protection when buffing or polishing and observe all safety procedures for power tools.

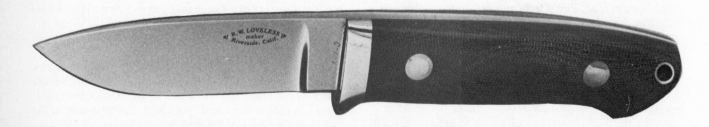

Bob Loveless is one of the best-known custom knifemakers who enjoys a strong demand for his products. The bolsters and blades are hand-finished, with no flaws to mar the artistic and utilitarian appeal of Loveless knives.

Chapter 11

POLISH AND BUFF

Recent Technological Developments Make These Tasks Easier Than Ever!

FEW OPERATIONS in knifemaking provide such a dramatic difference between run-of-the-mill appearance and true professional-quality custom results than correct polishing and buffing.

Polishing is a term which describes metal removal. It involves the removal of pits and scratches, uneven surfaces and imperfections with the aid of abrasives. Accomplished with stones, paper or cloth, applied by hand or used with a power source, coupled with sheets, wheels, discs or belts, polishing is the preparatory stage for buffing.

Buffing is more the displacement of metal than it is removal. Extremely fine grit compounds are used to bring out the natural color and luster or sheen of the piece. It is performed most commonly with a buffing wheel of loose or stitched muslin, running anywhere from 1750 to 3450 revolutions per minute. The compound is applied to the wheel while it is turning. Many commercial buffing operations buff steel with wheels moving at 7500 sfpm (surface feet per minute), but this equipment is costly and not likely to be used by the amateur knifemaker.

Although power equipment allows the worker to polish and buff metal more rapidly than by hand, most will not have access to such machinery, so we will concentrate on hand polishing. Power equipment should not be used by one not completely familiar with its hazards. It can be dangerous. A knife blank, even in its unsharpened stage, can catch in a wheel and become a screaming missile capable of killing or maiming.

However, talented amateurs who wish to use power equipment for polishing and/or buffing of knife materials, should be aware that excessive heat caused by placing the work against a fast-moving wheel can destroy the work just as easily as improper heat-treating.

Many knifemaking authorities suggest the use of heavy gloves while polishing metal on electric-powered wheels. Gloves prevent the worker from realizing when the work is becoming too hot, however. Instead, keep a pail of water close by the machine and work with bare hands until the metal becomes too hot to hold. If the blade becomes too hot to hold, it is nearing a temperature which could render the blade useless. At this stage, you have already put too much work and time into your project to have it ruined. Water will cool the metal quickly and your work can continue.

A substance called glanz woch, left, is imported from Germany. Used with an unstitched buffing wheel and turning at 700 rpm, it will clear up surface irregularities, giving a high sheen without danger of metal burn.

Among the many buffing wheels used, the hard felt and stitched muslin, right, are two of the most popular.

If you are looking for some fast, easy way to polish any rough metal surface to that mirror sheen achieved by a professional custom knifesmith, you won't find it here. Hand polishing with any abrasive stone or paper is time-consuming and tedious. Custom results can only be expected with a certain amount of expertise and a large measure of patience. It is the latter that presents the greatest challenge to the beginner because he generally has no frame of reference from which to draw. However, it is the single most important ingredient necessary to produce any custom knife.

Patience, a self-taught trait, is achieved only when one is determined to complete the job using his or her highest skill level, then follow a method and schedule to accomplish it. Typically, many of us, when working on any project that requires a great deal of time, may complete ninety percent of it, then become anxious to finish. We hurry the final ten percent. This almost universal trait separates the amateur from the professional. The pro has learned through sad experience that the final ten percent of a project is the most critical. He forces himself to slow down and finish with as much care as he used at the beginning.

One method that works in teaching patience to amateur knifemakers is to lay the project components out on a table

Custom knifemakers have embraced the Burr King brand of belt sander because of its reliability, versatility. While such a machine represents a sizable investment, it has multiple uses for knifemakers, gunsmiths, others.

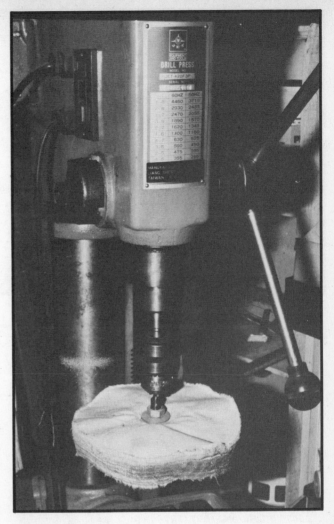

The glanz is most effective when used on a slow moving unstitched wheel turning at 700 rpm. A variable speed drill press is an ideal set-up for this arrangement.

or bench, then estimate the time required to complete the project. Now quadruple that estimate. If only the simplest hand tools are available, such as stones and wet-and-dry abrasive paper, and the maker desires a mirror-finish blade and custom-quality handle, he should figure on forty to sixty hours of work for satisfactory results!

Once the project has begun and the amateur has committed himself to devote four times as many hours as originally anticipated, there is less tendency to become frustrated as the hours drag by.

Another way to achieve professional results it to pace oneself. If you begin to feel frustrated or become bored,

you should get away from the work for a while. Take a walk around the block, or leave the project alone for a week, if necessary. This technique will help keep the project from becoming an unhappy chore and enable you to produce a custom knife worthy of your best effort.

POLISHING WITH ABRASIVE PAPER

Polishing metal for long periods of time with abrasive paper is a boring task, but there is no better way to obtain professional results. It requires total concentration. When wet-and-dry paper is used, it will last longer and cut faster

The Micro-mesh cloth abrasives are available in a number of grades, some extremely fine. The material may be used on any surfaces, natural or man-made, wood or metal, blade or handle. The finest grades will not damage soft plastic finishes.

Tool and die supply houses are some sources for a wide variety of useful polishing stones. They range in grits from 50 to 1200 in various shapes.

if used wet. Kerosene is a good cutting agent as it will not rust the metal.

Obviously, the rougher the surface of the metal, the coarser grit one should use to begin polishing. If there are pits and obvious uneven surfaces in the metal, one may begin with 50-grit, working through to the finer grits until the final finish is obtained.

For those new to knifemaking, the term, "grit," refers to the particles found on one square inch of paper. The lower the grit number, the larger the particles, thus the faster it will cut the metal.

Regardless of the grit used, it always should be employed with a flat, semi-hard backing, such as rubber. Polishing without backing can cause high and low spots that will be impossible to remove without some backing later.

The paper always should be moved back and forth from the tip or point of the knife to the back or hilt. If the paper is moved across the metal at an angle, when the next finer grit of paper is employed, the scratches will be more obvious and difficult to remove.

Knowing when to shift from one grit to the next finer one must be learned from experience. A beginner should plan to spend five to six times longer, using each grit, than he feels necessary. Scratches may not show in the metal when one switches from 180-grit to 240 or even 320, but when polishing is begun with 400-grit, those old 180-grit scratches will jump out like a flashing beacon.

One of the biggest problems in polishing with wet-and-dry paper is the uneven size of each grit particle. Because they are uneven, the most prominent ones wear down first. The lower and still sharp-edged particles create new scratches as the work progresses. This problem can be quite frustrating.

There is another product now available to knifemakers,

Polishing stones are most effective when held in both hands, applying equal pressure. The stone is pressed lightly and drawn toward the worker.

Wood, hard rubber or metal backing is used with cloth abrasive or the traditional wet and dry sandpaper.

similar in appearance to wet-and-dry paper, but it is vastly superior. It has been used for years by airlines, tool and die makers and surgical instrument manufacturers. Even the violin guild members in Europe use a type of it to final-finish expensive wood instruments. It is called Micro-Mesh MX — the type used for metal — and will achieve much better results than wet-and-dry paper in considerably less time.

Micro-Mesh MX is scientifically engineered to bond its cutting crystals firmly, yet flexibly, in a latex cushion. The system allows the crystals to move, depressing enough to seek a common level and rotating their planing levels into alignment for more uniform cutting. This product is manufactured by Micro-Surface Finishing Products and produces a grit cloth, sheets, rolls, discs and belts ranging from 100-grit to 1200-grit rating. No other hand abrasive produces a finer finish.

Micro-Mesh is nearly three times more expensive than a sheet of regular wet-and-dry paper. However, since a sheet of MX lasts four to five times longer than the wet-and-dry paper and polishes faster without causing new scratches, it is more efficient. It also is more economical in the long run.

Another peculiar property of MX which serves in attempting to gain a mirror finish is that even the rougher grits put a higher shine on the metal as it cuts. By the time one has need for the fine grits, there are no deep scratches and most of the final polishing has been completed. Both Micro-Mesh MX and regular Micro-Mesh — the latter for polishing wood, fiberglass, painted surfaces, oil and polyurethane finishes — are excellent.

POLISHING WITH STONES

Initial polishing work on metal blades to remove high or

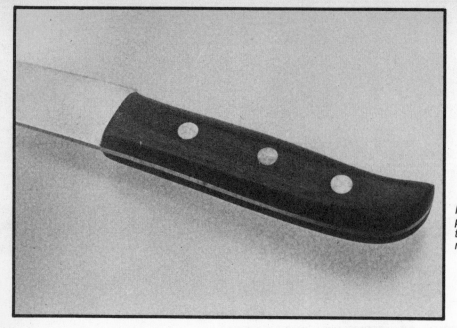

Pakkawood knife handles are easily polished to a desired sheen using the glanz woch. Handles of this material are also dishwasher safe.

E. MORGAN
Thousand Oaks, CA.

Emil Morgan likes to use stainless steel for his blades and impregnated, laminated wood for handles. He polishes both surfaces to smooth, even finishes. A highly polished knife not only looks well, it is less affected by elements.

low spots, pits and imperfections can be accomplished faster with artificial stones than with abrasive paper. The Norton Company produces stone in several sizes and shapes, ranging from coarse to fine, that lend themselves to this task. Another type of artificial stone used in the tool and die industry is more porous than the Norton stones. These work well because they quickly wear to contour to the surface shape being polished. To find these stones, check with your local tool and die supply outlet.

Oilstones should be worked from one end of the metal to the other and held much like a file when draw-filing. Holding the oilstone at its ends, using equal pressure with both hands, will help create a more uniform surface. Any scratches created by the stone will run longitudinally along the blade and can be removed during additional fine polishing.

A problem for beginners working with oilstones involves their proper care. Improper care translates to less than satisfactory results and even additional scratches in the work. An oilstone, like any tool, must be properly maintained and correctly used for optimum results.

New stones should be soaked in oil for several days before first use, unless they are specifically listed as an oil-filled type. The cutting action of artificial stones such as those made by Norton will be more efficient if kept wet with a solution of oil and kerosene. However, many natural stones should be kept wet with water. Be sure to understand which type you have on hand.

Maintaining oilstones is not difficult. Use a cloth to wipe off dirty oil after completing the metal work. If they gum up or become glazed, soak the stones in gasoline, naphtha or other solvent to restore cutting capability. Beware of these

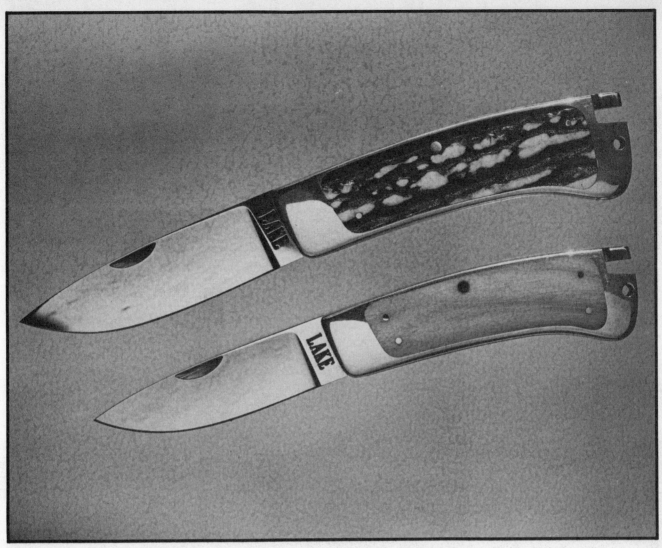

Custom knifemaker Ron Lake is best known for his beautifully finished folding knives, eagerly sought by collectors. The flawless fit and finish is all the more difficult to achieve with this use of inset, softer handle materials.

petroleum products; they are volatile and dangerous.

If residue adheres to the stone's surface, it can be removed with wet-and-dry paper against a hard flat backing such as a piece of wood. Soak the stone again and it should be like new.

Maintaining silicon-carbide stones requires different tactics. If they become clogged, they are cleaned by placing the stone in an oven with an old pan underneath to catch the oil and dirt. When it looks like most of the surface crud has dripped off, pull the stone out of the oven, wipe it thoroughly with a cloth and store it away in a sealed jar, half-filled with light oil. With proper care, stones will work more efficiently and last years longer.

Most of the tools and methods used to build custom knives have been borrowed from gunsmiths. Unfortunately, some of these tools and methods lag woefully behind those of other industries that have found ways to complete similar tasks faster, with better results.

If you are a golfer, you may have noticed that even low and medium priced golf woods have a finish and sheen the equal of any expensive custom rifle or shotgun stock. The golf equipment manufacturer gets this custom finish with a soft muslin buffing wheel and a buffing compound imported from Germany called *glanz woch*. It should be an invaluable aid to custom knifesmiths and gunsmiths offering a multitude of applications.

The *glanz woch* compound allows the knifesmith to attain a fine mirror sheen on a variety of surfaces, including oil- or plastic-finished wood, synthetics such as pakkawood and natural materials like ivory and mother of pearl, faster and safer than with any other method.

This German compound's superior finish capability is

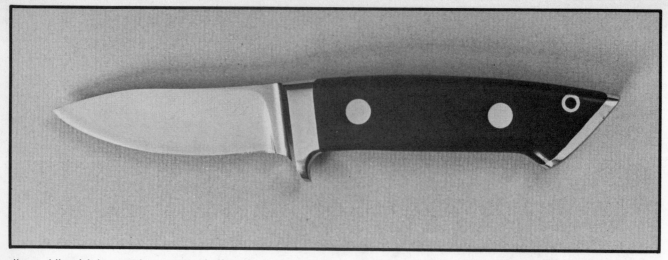

Jimmy Lile of Arkansas is a custom knifemaker of long experience who knows the value using the proper equipment.

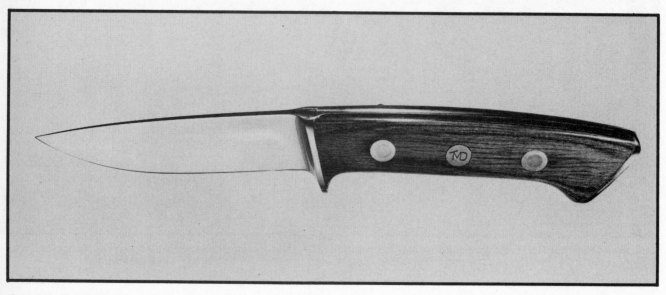

Oregon's Ted Dowell is another custom knifemaker with many years of background using hand and power tools to turn out excellent knives. Dowell often uses natural wood or wood Micarta for the handles of his mostly working knives.

maximized with the buffing wheel turning at a slow speed. Heat created by placing the work against wheels turning at 1750 rpms and faster makes it difficult to reach satisfactory results without burning through oil- or plastic-finished wood surfaces and scorching synthetic and natural materials. Because the compound works with a wheel turning at less than 1000 rpms, there is less chance of damage. The wheel is up in a drill press turning at a moderate speed. Custom results are possible on any surface in less time and without damage.

When it comes to power equipment for polishing or buffing knife material, the Burr King abrasive belt grinder has become the standard by which all others are judged. The Model 960, with its special knifemaker attachment, is used by more custom knifesmiths than any other power tool.

This machine may be operated in either a vertical or horizontal position, using a two-inch-wide, seventy-two-inch length belt. There is an adjustable belt-tensioning positioner allowing for loose-belt work. The knifemaker attachment consists of two-inch and five-inch contact wheel; six-inch backup platten is tangent to both wheels.

This attachment may be used for flat grinding, profiling and tapering tangs. It is also removable for contour and loose-belt grinding, polishing and deburring. This machine also can be used for precise hollow blade grinding currently in vogue among custom knifemakers.

With the availability of belts for the Burr King running from 24- to 800-grit, no other piece of power equipment performs as fast or efficiently.

A polishing-buffing wheel powered by an electric motor can be of loose or stitched muslin, soft or hard felt, cork or layered leather. Each wheel, coated with a particular grit and so marked on its side, should be trued up before buffing.

Texas custom knifemaker, Jack Crain, above, is well known for his designs used in several action movies. His blades are hand finished, using no power tools. He includes his distinctive Crain logo on his knives.

SAFETY FIRST!

Whenever power equipment is used, whether by the professional or amateur, special safety rules must be followed to prevent serious accidents and injury. Here are some:

1. Know and understand the tool you are using. Learn the tool's intended application and limitations and don't attempt to exceed them.

2. Make certain all power tools are grounded before turning on the electric current.

3. Do not remove any safety guard. Electric grinders have see-through plexiglass viewing shields. They are placed there to protect you and your eyesight and should not be removed.

4. Always check any piece of machinery to make sure wrenches or keys have been removed before pressing the *on* switch.

5. Keep your work area clean and uncluttered. It's too easy to trip or stumble over something that doesn't belong near power equipment. If metal is dipped in water during polishing, the floor can become slippery and extremely dangerous. Keep the floor dry and use a non-conductive mat.

6. Concentrate on what you're doing or get away from the machine. More accidents result from wandering minds than equipment malfunction.

7. Use power equipment in well lighted areas. Working in the dark with electric tools is begging to be called "Stubby" or "Lefty" in the future.

8. Never allow children close to any power equipment while it is in use.

9. Remove all loose clothing or jewelry when using power equipment.

10. Allow the tool to do the work. Attempting to apply too much pressure or forcing the tool to do more than it is designed for will almost guarantee an accident.

11. When changing belts, bits, cutters or blades, always disconnect the power source first.

12. Always be aware of which direction a tool is turning before applying the work or you may end up polishing your chest and forehead.

A knife must be kept cutting sharp unless it is to be simply a piece of art to hang on the wall and look at. A sharp knife is a simple, efficient tool that will accomplish many things for its owner. Ceramic rods are one of the best methods.

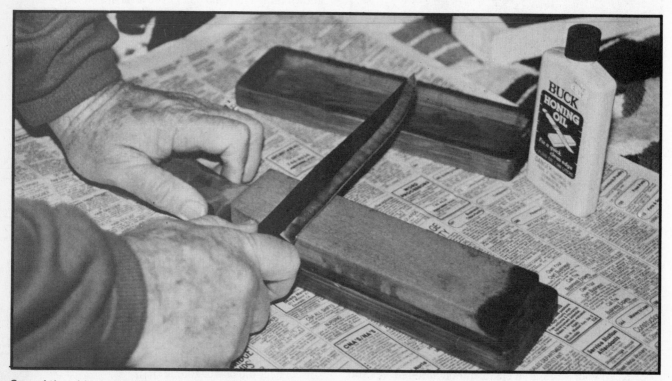

One of the oldest and still the best sharpening methods is to use a natural Arkansas soft stone and plenty of honing oil.

Chapter 12

SHARPEN THAT EDGE!

A Knife Is Nothing Unless It Is Sharp — But A Good Edge Takes Practice And Maybe Some Help

AFTER YOU HAVE made a few knives or have gained the reputation as a knifemaker among friends and relatives, you will find you have become the "duty expert" on sharpening blades. Whether you are or not, you will want to be able to do a credible sharpening job on your own knives; and your spouse will expect you to keep up the kitchen cutlery.

Sharpening a knife comes easily for some, difficult for others and never comes to a few. For some, the task seems easy; for others, the edge never is right. There are as many opinions on the best method for sharpening as there are knifemakers.

Put in its absolute simplest terms, sharpening a knife is the removal of enough blade metal along the edge so that it becomes sharp enough to cut whatever is required of it. Saying that is much simpler, usually, than doing it. Removing the metal is not so difficult, but removing just the right amount, in the correct, optimum angle and maintaining that same cutting angle throughout the entire length of the blade is what makes the job frustrating and — eventually — gratifying.

Complicating the task is the formation of what is known as the "feather" or "wire" along the sharpened edge. If we should examine the knife edge through a strong magnifying glass, observing a cross-section of the blade, we probably would detect the feather. It is a minute sliver of metal that tends to hold on to the edge, moving to the opposite side of the sharpening stone as the blade is stroked along it. It may not be visible, but it will interfere with good cutting or slicing action. The feather must be removed as a final step to sharpening. We'll discuss several easy ways to do this after we have mastered the basics of sharpening and honing.

Some will tell you the only way to get a really sharp edge is to use a buffing wheel or power sanding belt. Many professionals use such power machines and get excellent results. But for those of us with minimal experience and training with power tools, it is best to avoid them when sharpening blades. Buffing wheels, especially, can be highly dangerous to the careless or untrained rookie, often resulting in serious injury. Even the professionals get caught now and then, sometimes crippling themselves for life. The quick power tool hone job is not worth the risk and we advise against attempting it.

The simple carborundum, natural stones or other non-mechanical sharpening devices will do an excellent job. The job may take a while longer, but you will get a good cutting edge. Furthermore, the chances of ruining your newly constructed knife are nil. Too much heat from a fast-

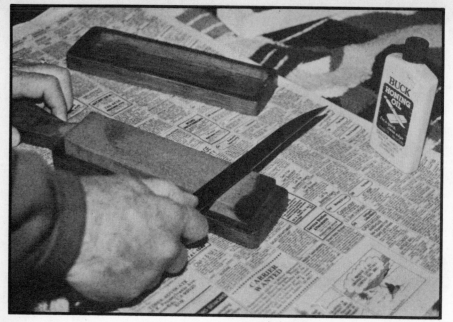

The knife blade to be sharpened is drawn across the surface of the stone with considerable pressure, as if trying to cut a slice off the top of the stone.

Natural Arkansas stones require plenty of honing oil on the surface which floats away tiny steel and stone particles which build up as the blade is sharpened. Honing oil is thinner than regular lubricating oil.

turning buffing wheel can ruin the temper of a fine blade in a second and the knife never will be any good again. Think of all those hours of labor!

Getting a sharp cutting edge on any knife is, as we said, a matter of removing metal from the blade a few grains at a time, until the sharpest edge is reached. This is an over-simplified explanation and the actual task is more complicated. The angle of the cutting edge depends on such things as the size of the blade, its intended use and the type of steel. Final success depends upon maintaining a constant angle between blade and stone throughout the entire sharpening stroke.

With some knife blades, there seems to be some unknown or unidentified properties in the steel which make re-sharpening almost too difficult. One might test the blade against another and find that both are hardened to within a point of each other. They may be made of the same steel formula. But one sharpens easier than the other. It may be the angle of the edge, the length of the blade, the curve of the blade, even the handle material, but one still is more difficult to sharpen.

Some blades seem easier to hone on a ceramic rod or natural stone, than others. No doubt there is some logical, scientific explanation, but we will not pursue it here. In-

The difficult part of sharpening a knife edge is keeping the angle between blade and stone consistent and accurate for the job to be done. This knife is being held at a rather steep thirty degrees, which seems right for a kitchen knife.

A tiny natural stone carried in a plastic case may be just right for touch-up of a small pocketknife.

While the small touch-up stone in question may work on a large knife in an emergency, it is not the thing to use under most circumstances.

stead, let's consider a number of methods and sharpeners which have been tried and have proved successful on our knives.

Keeping that identical angle on each stroke, throughout each stroke, is the difficult part, though some people can do it each and every time while some cannot. Nonetheless, it is the key to a really good cutting edge. There is partial agreement among knifemakers as to what is the correct angle. Estimates vary from seventeen degrees to thirty degrees. Part of the decision must hinge upon what the knife will be called upon to do. A small pocketknife might require a more shallow, seventeen-degree edge angle, while a heavier hunting knife or kitchen carving knife will work better with a sharper angle; twenty to twenty-five degrees, perhaps.

Were one to examine a knife edge using a strong magnifier, one would see that the edge is anything but perfectly smooth. A so-called razor edge is not what works best on a carving or field knife. A close look will reveal a sort of saw edge — tiny teeth or ridges — along the metal. These teeth give the edge a slight bite to easily cut through tough meat, cardboard, rope, or whatever may be encountered. A butcher cuts meat all day and does not attempt to hone his knife edges razor-sharp.

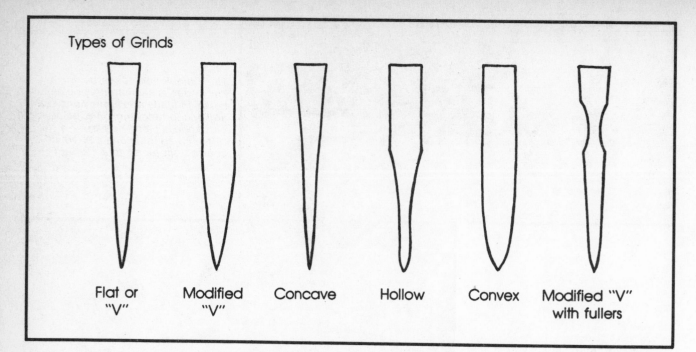

Types of Grinds

Flat or "V" Modified "V" Concave Hollow Convex Modified "V" with fullers

Various angles and types of edges are described in text. Each has a specific use, appropriate for the blade shape and size, above. There is no universal knife edge for all.

The giant knife factory, Buck Knives, is one which supplies knife honing kits, which include various hardness stones and excellent honing oil.

We all have seen the knife sharpener at gun shows and fairs who brings an edge right down to where he can shave the hair on his arms. But such an edge may not be best for the tasks at hand. And such an edge is likely to be delicate in nature, requiring too many touch-ups in the middle of a long field-dressing job.

A blade hardened to a Rockwell reading of more than 58 or 60 on a C scale most likely will be difficult to sharpen. Stainless steel blades generally are tougher to re-sharpen than tool steels, which are usually heat-treated to a lower, softer reading. Some of the folding knives we used to carry would take an edge with only a few strokes across the stone, while one of the new, large survival knives will take considerably more work.

As an over-simplified rule of thumb, stainless steel blades are more difficult to sharpen than tool steel blades, such as 01. Tool steels used to be more common for knives, but not so today. We know several custom knifemakers, though, who still swear by the virtues of tool steel for blades.

Stainless steel generally is hardened to a higher Rockwell C scale reading than tool steels. Many stainless steel blades will have a reading of 58 to 62; maybe a point or two higher. Most tool steel blades — and some stainless — are held to 52 to 56 C. These will be easier to sharpen, but usually will not hold an edge as long during cutting work.

Before we begin to sharpen a knife we have just made or one of our many household knives, take a close look at the blade grind to determine what kind it is. If it is our own cus-

Knives with special blade shapes, such as Outdoor Edge's Game Skinner, right, present special problems when sharpening. The sharply curved blade and guthook need special care.

Close, magnified examination of a knife edge will reveal that the cutting edge is actually a minute saw blade.

tom knife, we'll know what it is. But most of us have dozens of other knives around the house which always need to be sharpened.

Looking at a blade in cross-section, there are at least a half-dozen different blade grinds with which we may have to contend. The first and most common is the flat or V grind. This blade is tapered from the spine to the edge in a single, unchanging line. Only the last cutting edge may have a slightly sharper angle to it. The flat grind, as we know, is one of the easier blades to make, so there are a lot of them around. Typical kitchen cutlery blades nearly all have flat grinds. They are rather easy to sharpen. They seem to need honing more often, but that may be because they are used more often.

Next on the list is the modified V grind. This, as it sounds, is similar to the flat or V grind, but the taper from the spine to the edge is not so long. The taper begins away from the spine, about half-way through the blade. Once started, the V taper moves straight to the edge without any curve or interruption. Because of the additional steel left on the blade, this grind results in a stronger blade; it also is slightly heavier. The blade is stiffer and is a good all-round shape to use. Modified V blades are a bit more difficult to sharpen, but they tend to hold an edge longer. This grind is popular for general utility blades and hunters. Extra care should be exercised during sharpening or the design properties may be lost by honing at the wrong angle.

Another cross-sectional shape which was popular dur-

As the tip of the blade is approached, the handle must be raised to maintain the correct honing angle.

If a holder or mount is not included with the sharpening stone, rough paper towels will suffice.

It takes practice and concentration to maintain the correct angle of the blade edge. Use enough oil.

ing and just after World War II, but not so often these days, is what is called a modified V with fullers. Most of us refer to these fullers as blood grooves. We have heard that term so long, many of us have come to think that is what they are supposed to be. Their only real function is to lighten the knife by a small amount.

The grooved-blade design still is seen on the Ka-Bar design we have come to associate with the old USMC fighting knife and we see some Buck knife designs which have adopted the look. Ease of sharpening and strength are about the same as for the modified V design. The design is rather difficult to produce for the beginner, however, and ought to be left to more advanced students.

The hollow-ground blade is rather common, especially on some large fixed-blade knives. Many factory-made hunting knives use the hollow grind. It is another design that is not for the beginner, but many professionals have mastered the technique and we have seen some really beautiful hollow-ground custom knives which bring top prices.

As the name implies, the hollow grind results when a portion of the blade profile below the spine is ground out in a concave manner. The hollowed-out portion usually is less than half the blade depth, leaving a good bit of spine for strength.

Hollow-ground blades hold an edge well and usually are easy to keep sharpened. They are pretty, too. The problem

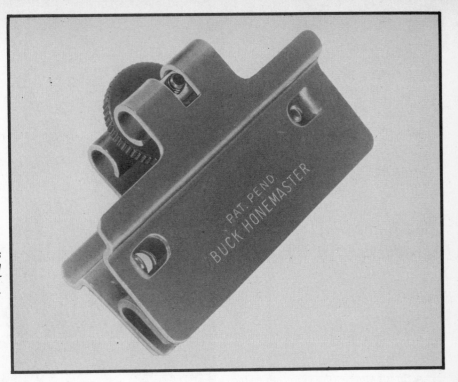

Buck Knives, Honemaster, right, is one answer to the problem of holding the blade at the precise angle for sharpening throughout each stroke.

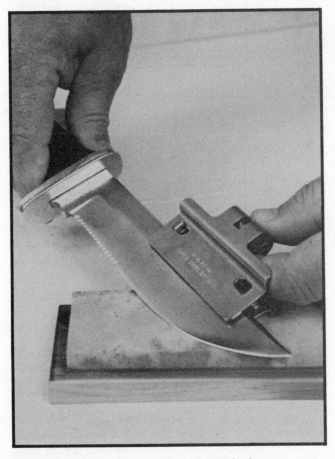

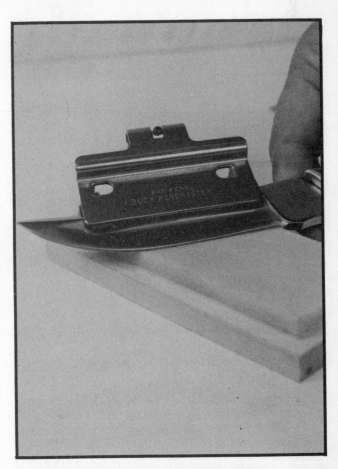

A blade such as this one with a serrated edge near the hilt may be sharpened with the Buck Honemaster attached, using care on the stroke.

The Honemaster, above, is attached to a blade slightly longer than the attachment. Smaller blades cannot be used with the Honemaster.

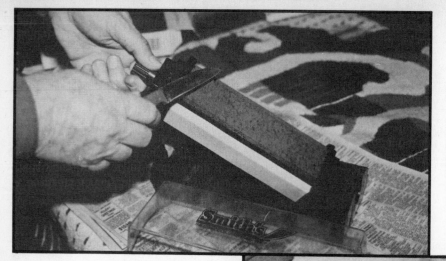

The Smith Multi-Hone features four stones, each with a different grit, ranging from coarse, through the finest, hard stone. All are carried in a plastic case with dust cover.

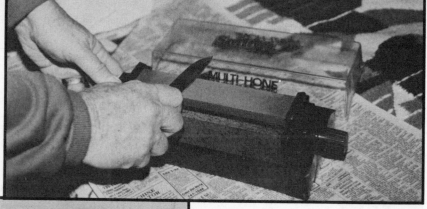

As each of the four stones on the Smith Multi-Hone is turned to the bottom of the carrying case, it is bathed in a reservoir of honing oil.

Four stone faces of the Smith left, or three of the Buck model; each has a special use. With either unit, the knifemaker has all he needs to sharpen knives.

is that, with the hollowed-out blade shape, that much metal is gone and the blade may be just that much weaker under stress. Careless buffing on a power wheel is the quickest way to ruin a fine hollow-ground knife blade.

Similar to, but slightly different, is the concave grind. The concave blade is hollowed-out, but the curve starts farther up on the spine, leaving less metal in the profile. Sharpening and care are similar to that for the hollow grind, but the blade is a bit weaker than the others. However, concave blades are excellent slicers. They often are incor-porated in the best kitchen cutlery and in fine restaurants wielded by experienced chefs.

The convex shape is not found on knives — unless by accident. The convex is for axes, hatchets, machetes and the like. The blade, usually heavy and massive, is used primarily for hacking, chopping or splitting. Sharpening a convex blade is time-consuming, because usually there is a lot of sharpening to be done. Consider your axe by the woodshed and how dull and chipped the blade probably is.

A large ceramic sharpening stone, left, will handle most any large knife. Ceramics are easy to clean up, needing no honing oil; ideal for the field.

Here is an idea that will not work! Spyderco knife features a serrated edge blade, excellent for slicing through tough belts and ropes. But edge presents sharpening problems.

Convex blades usually are sharpened with a file or a round sharpening stone. The work can be done on a coarse, slow-moving grinder, but care must be exercised not to let the metal get too hot. The size and weight, too, of most convex ground tools complicates the sharpening task. The loggers of old could put an edge on a double-blade axe in only a few seconds. Reportedly, they could even shave with the blade. It isn't likely many loggers shaved and cut down trees with the same type of edge, however.

Perhaps we remember the old carborundum stone our grandfather used to have affixed to the workbench. With it, he could put a cutting edge on any knife, be it the little Boy Scout knife you carried or grandma's best carver. These artificial stones were good; they still are, but there have been improvements along the way and there are other methods and materials available to us. Also, grandfather had a great deal of practice and experience at sharpening that most of us may not have.

Let's start with a standard bench sharpening stone made of carborundum. These stones, still popular with some

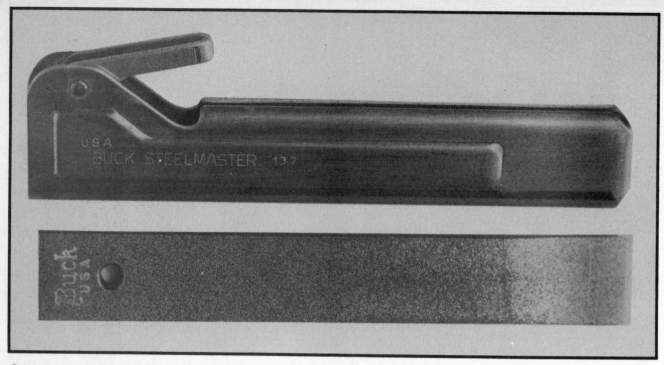

Buck Knives' Steelmaster is easily carried to the field, folded into its metal holder. To use the steel, it is unfolded and locked into place as it pivots out to left of holder. Unit is strong, may be used as a chisel.

Ka-Bar knife company offers honing oil and a medium-size honing stone which Ka-Bar calls a Chromostone.

knifemakers and workers, are available in several sizes, ranging from a short, thin model intended to be carried into the field for touch-ups, to six- eight- or twelve-inch bench models. A pretty good rule of thumb on stone size is that the longer the blade, the longer the stone should be. It is possible to sharpen a large kitchen knife on a four-inch stone, but it will take longer and require more skill to get it right. After a bit of experience, we have learned that sharpening any knife, large or small, is much easier when using a bench stone eight or more inches long. Smaller stones and rods have their uses.

After the purchase of a good stone, we soon realize that, for best use, it has to be held down firmly so it will not move in use. Some stones are sold with a wood, metal or plastic holder or base. The base may be C-clamped or otherwise fixed to the workbench or kitchen table for sharpening. It is not necessary to use a really heavy clamp to hold down your stone, because you will not be using that much pressure. Too heavy a clamp has too much arc in the bow which can protrude above the level of the stone face, interfering with the sharpening action.

Stone holders may be purchased or, as many do, made in the workshop. The simplest is merely a big flat board a couple of inches longer and wider than the stone. Then a framework of quarter-round moulding or other narrow wood is nailed and glued to the top of the board. The frame should provide a tight and complete grip on the stone. You don't want the stone sliding around inside the frame as you are stroking the knife across it.

Another holder can be made from a much thicker piece of wood which is hollowed out for the stone. This requires a rather soft piece of wood, with a tight, even grain that won't

A flat sharpening steel is easiy carried in the field for re-sharpening use. The flat shape may be used in opening up a game animal, as well as when sharpening. No water or oil is required.

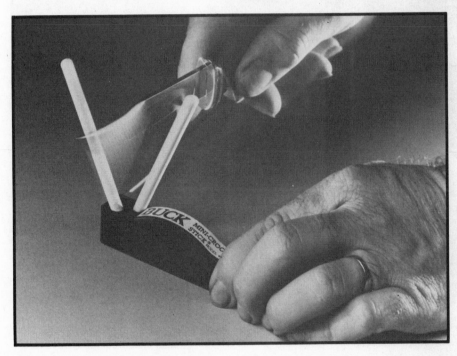

Buck's Mini-Crock stick is a compact unit, easily carried to any location, ready for use. The ceramic rods do a quick edge job.

crack after awhile. For this holder, you need some skills with hammer and chisel, but the job shouldn't take more than an hour to finish. If you have one, a router will make quicker work of the job.

The wood holder, either type, can be painted or stained and sealed when finished. You will be using a lot of honing oil, and eventually, the wood will become soaked with it. Sometime in the future you will have to build another.

The wood pattern can include a handle on the bottom, which may be clamped down on the bench or simply held in one hand, while the knife is in the other. Also, a wooden lid

over the stone will keep dust and dirt off its face when it is not in use.

Most of the metal or plastic holders are equipped with rubber feet for a non-slip grip on the bench or table. Also, most of these stands are built up high enough that you may hold them down with one hand while safely moving the knife across the stone with the other.

Most of the commercially available stone holders or stands also have some provision for keeping the stone well oiled even when not in use. A thin fiber or sponge rubber pad between the stone and the holder may be kept saturated

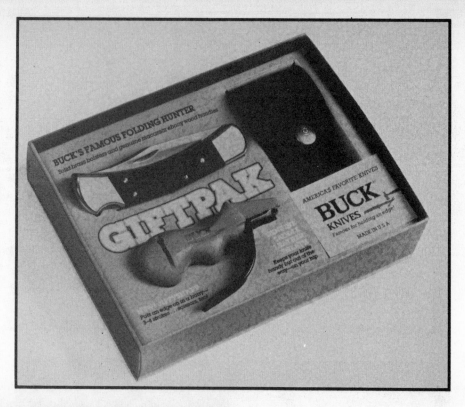

The Buck Folding Hunter, right, comes complete with a belt pouch and a sharpening device called a Jiffy sharpener. Buck is aware of the importance of a sharp blade for each of its knives.

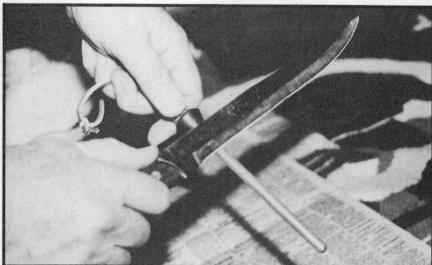

The honing steel has a dual use: it will do the sharpening as well as remove the feather or wire edge from a knife previously stoned.

with oil and will, in turn, ensure the stone is kept moist with honing oil. Such an arrangement may be added to your homemade holder, too.

Honing oil is essential for most stones, man-made or natural, to provide the lubrication for the knife blade and to continually float away the minute particles of metal as the knife is sharpened. The oil holds the metal particles in suspension and floats them off. Without it, the particles can embed themselves in the stone and cause irregular gouges in the knife edge.

Ceramic, diamond faced and some other man-made sharpening surfaces do not need oil. They are lubricated and cleaned with water.

Once we have examined and determined the type of blade profile with which we are working and have spread a liberal amount of honing oil on our stone, there is yet another step before beginning the actual process of blade sharpening. We need to decide upon the angle of the sharpened edge; the angle between the blade and the stone. There are several opinions as to which of several angles is the best.

Part of the answer to that question is to ask another: How thick is the blade and to what use is the knife to be put? The smaller the angle — say, ten degrees or less — the finer the edge, but the weaker it is. Such an angle might be appropriate for razor blades, broadhead arrow heads or, at

Some makers prefer a smooth brass rod to remove the feather from an edge, right. A good edge is a final step in making your own knife.

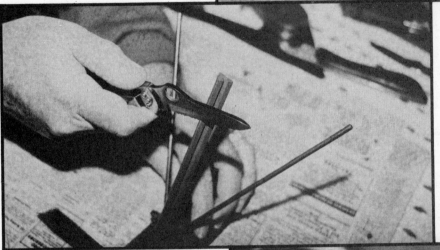

Sharpening serrated edge blades is a special challenge. Spyderco offers its own solution to the problem with its sharpening kit, including triangular cross-section rods to reach into the negative serrations.

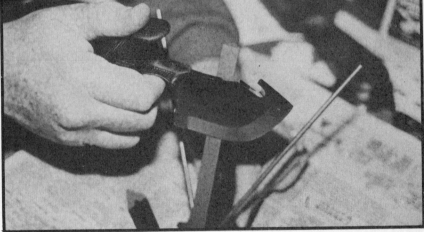

Bringing back the edge on a skinning knife with a sharply curving edge is facilitated by the Spyderco sharpening system. Several grits and composition rods are included.

eight degrees, scalpels and other precision tools. For some uses, such an edge is desirable, but it will not last long and needs constant re-sharpening.

From there, we might go on up to thirty degrees of angle. This is almost a wedge, useful for splitting or chopping. It would be too sharp an angle for skinning, but might work well if your job was to cut into cardboard boxes from time to time. An edge like this would tend to remain sharp through a lot of hard work.

Some say an angle between seventeen to twenty degrees is best for the general-use knife we might carry around all day. Folding-blade pocketknives generally have finer blade angles than large hunting or survival knives.

If you are uncertain as to what angle to choose, examine the existing blade edge closely. While sharpening, try to duplicate the angle already there, unless the knife never before has been sharpened, as will be the case with your non-kit knife construction project. Twenty to twenty-two degrees is a good compromise, we think.

Maintaining the same angle throughout the sharpening stroke on both sides of the knife is difficult. If the blade is allowed to rock even slightly, the edge will be rounded rather than a sharp, clean cutting angle. It won't have the micro-saw surface which does the cutting.

Professionals at this business can sharpen any knife at a proper angle in a few minutes, because they have had years

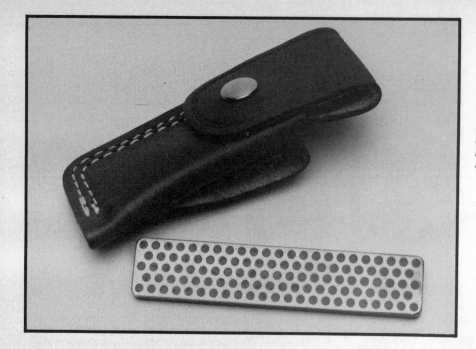

Here is one of the DMT field stones, carried in a handy belt pouch for instant use. Diamond-impregnated sharpening surface needs no oil.

DMT stones in various sizes and shapes are useful for sharpening all kinds of edges, including knives, scissors, arrow heads and other precision tools.

The technique of sharpening a blade on a DMT diamond surface is the same as for any other abrasive stone.

of practice. You can get a feel for the angle with practice, too.

Hold the knife handle in your strong hand, then place the fingers of the other hand a bit more than halfway down the blade, closer to the tip. Move the blade across and into the stone as if you were trying to slice a thin layer off the surface. Maintain the same angle and pressure throughout the stroke. Make a half-dozen strokes, pushing the blade away from you, then reverse the blade to make the same number of strokes toward you.

Use the off hand to maintain pressure along the length of the blade. As you near the tip, you will have to raise the blade handle to maintain the correct angle. This is the tricky part and is one of the areas where many go wrong.

Be sure to maintain the angle and the pressure throughout the stroke all the way to the tip. Make the same number of strokes on each side while keeping the stone well oiled.

You will notice that after several passes, the oil either begins to soak in, run down the sides or seems to thicken up as it turns color. This indicates the build-up of metal residue

The deluxe edition of the Spyderco sharpening system is all neatly enclosed in a soft leather carrying case.

The Spyderco kit includes a base or holder, right, carrying case, three sharpening grades or grits and brass hand protectors. Kit can be carried anywhere.

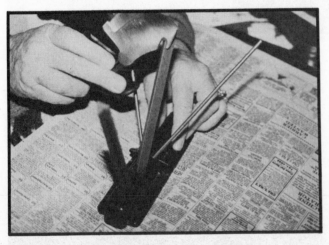

An intricate guthook blade is easily sharpened on the Sypderco system. Triangular-shaped sharpening rod will fit into hook area. Brass rods protect user's hands.

Serrated-edge blades may also be sharpened using small ceramic rods to reach into hollow-ground surfaces, above.

The E-Z Sharp system is another with a positive sharpening angle maintained by mechanical means; all carried in a pouch.

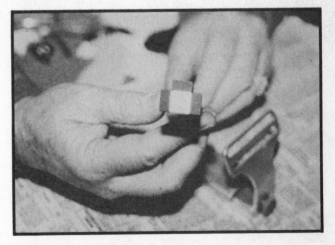

Three grits on three sides of a mounting block are used on the same jig of E-Z Sharp.

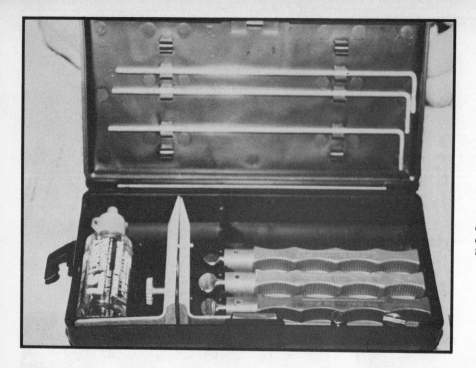

The Lansky sharpening kit is complete in a carrying case, containing everything needed for honing, including the oil.

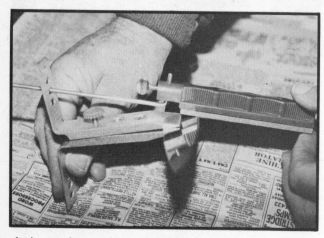

A sharpening angle, one of four choices, is selected and the rod is slipped through the hole. The sharpening stone is afixed to handle.

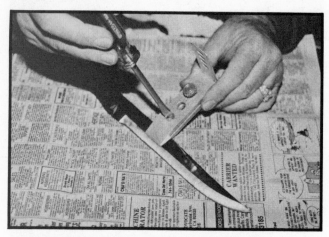

Various blade thicknesses are accommodated by the Lansky sharpener, but the holder must be thoroughly tightened to prevent any slippage.

The E-Z Sharp system, above, operates similarly to the Lansky with a clamp and an angle guide.

and stone grit. Don't let too much of it build up on the surface before cleaning it off and applying fresh honing oil.

Work slowly and carefully at first. Get a feel for what is happening. Some pros advocate using considerable pressure while sharpening the knife. The amount of pressure depends, in part, on hardness of the blade steel. Harder steel, of course, requires more pressure. Some older kitchen knives and folders have relatively soft blades and will sharpen with minimal pressure. You will have to experiment a bit, at first.

Keep at it until the blade begins to feel like it wants to "bite" into the stone, then wipe off the excess oil from the knife and test the edge. With care, the craftsman can test the edge with his fingers or you may draw the blade lightly across the thumbnail, feeling for snags as it passes along. Others will want to try the traditional slicing of a sheet of paper or shaving hair off an arm. All these tests are rather dangerous and should be tried with care.

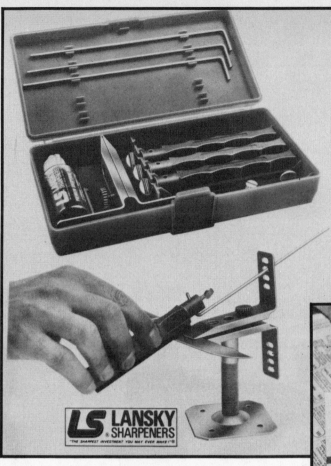

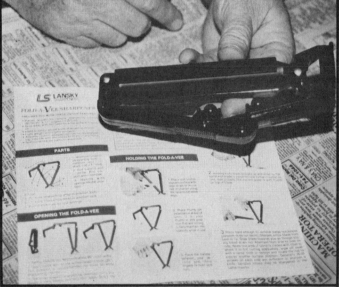

Lansky offers several optional pieces of equipment for its system. One of the most useful for knifemakers would be the bench mount, left, for the most positive operation.

Lansky calls this field sharpener a Fold-A-Vee, which comes with detailed instructions for use. It is shown in its folded, carrying mode, which protects the sharpening surfaces from damage.

If the edge is not to your satisfaction, wipe the stone clean, re-apply oil and take a few more strokes with the knife. With a good light source — something like a gooseneck lamp at the workbench — we can use the reflection to determine the evenness of the edge. Look carefully for any rounding of the edge and missed spots, especially near the tip. Feel for the feathering along the edge; it looks almost like a tiny wire on the edge. It will have to be removed if it develops.

When the edge has been sharpened on the stone to your satisfaction, you may wish to finish the work or put an even finer edge on the blade by going to a steel or ceramic rod. Using a steel has the added benefit of quickly knocking off the feathered edge, if there is one. A ceramic rod is usually finer than a steel, but also is useful in removing the feather.

Ceramic sharpeners — whether blocks or rods — have a number of advantages over oil stone. They require no oil for use and therefore are excellent to carry in the field.

They clean up easily with water and kitchen cleanser. A small rod makes a quick touch-up to an already-sharp blade. The bad news is that they can break if dropped or abused and they are not cheap.

While many knife people swear by the old carborundum stone, others insist that there is nothing better than the natural Arkansas sharpening stone. The Arkansas stones are mined, sawed, shaped and finished to standard size and used all over the world for sharpening knives and other cutting instruments.

Arkansas stones are available in different hardness ratings: soft, medium, hard and extra-hard. Anything other than soft is used for special blades and instruments, such as medical scalpels and razor blades. They do not leave enough of a bite to the edge for most knife blades. The soft Arkansas stone is the one most often recommended by those who do a lot of knife sharpening.

The natural stones are used in much the same manner as

The Fold-A-Vee is opened and the stone surfaces are on the inside of the V. The blade is stroked vertically to hone each side.

The hand which holds the unit is completely outside the danger area. The Fold-A-Vee may be opened out and locked into one of two sharpening angles, depending on type of blade.

the man-made carborundums just discussed. Each needs to be placed in some sort of wood or metal holder so as to be held solidly while drawing the blade across. The surface should be kept well oiled to float away the tiny metal particles. Clean the surface often, as the dark, gritty grindings build up. A stone six to twelve inches long is easiest to use and will handle even the largest survival knife or long kitchen carver. This type of stone will benefit from being soaked in oil before it is used the first time.

Because it is a natural material, the Arkansas stone is not immune to breakage or damage. It may break, if dropped on a hard floor and probably will chip if slammed around on the bench. It should be covered when not in use to keep off dust and dirt.

A. G. Russel and Smith Whetstone, both of Arkansas, are two of the largest suppliers of specialized knife-sharpening stones, but there are many others.

Smith offers man-made sharpening stones, also. This company's solution to the problem of keeping plenty of oil on the honing surface is a clever design involving four different grits on one block. Each stone is fastened to each side of the block, with all held in a plastic holder with an oil well at the bottom. Each stone face, as it is turned to the bottom, is bathed in oil. The desired surface is then rotated by a knob on the end of the block to the top when it is needed. The unit has a plastic dust cover to help keep it clean and solid mounting feet which hold it firmly while working. The device provides a single unit with four dif-

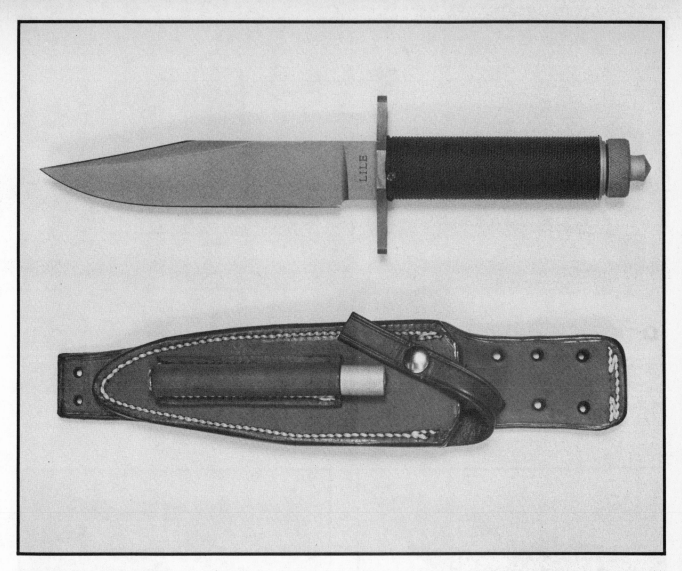

Jimmy Lile is one of the best known custom knifemakers, who often features large survival knives in his designs. This 6½-inch blade Bowie-style knife has a combat matte finish and includes a small sharpening steel carried in a pocket on the sheath.

ferent stone grits, each eight inches long and ready for use. Even longer units are available, mostly from commercial sources.

Small Arkansas stones often are found in survival packs or in pouches as part of the knife sheath. They are used primarily for touch-ups, but could be used for complete sharpening in emergencies. Most of us will not be carrying honing oil into the field, so the stones should be started and used with only water for lubrication.

Ceramic or steel honing rods are easy to attach to a knife sheath for the field. The steel is more difficult to break than the ceramic and is ideal as a touch-up device. When performing long cutting tasks such as field-dressing a deer, these devices come in handy. Commercially made sheaths, with these provisions can be found at gun shows and swap meets, if making your own seems too difficult.

Honing steels and rods may be carried separately in belt pouches or in the backpack. Most knife companies offer a variety of such devices. Some are round; others are flat, rectangular, large or small. They are available in several grits in those shapes. Most are man-made abrasives that with care, should last a lifetime.

Other field sharpeners and larger whetstones for the shop are produced with a diamond-impregnated surface which will file, hone or lap almost any hard surface material, using a slight amount of water. They will sharpen steel, tungsten carbide, ceramics and glass. With proper care, they will last many years.

One of the best known producers of this type is Diamond Machining Technology (DMT). Their whetting devices consist of a thin layer of perforated steel moulded onto a plastic base and covered with diamond particles that are embedded in nickel. The perforations are there to speed sharpening and to aid in removing the fine grindings. They are available in several sizes for the shop or the field. They do a good job, but must be kept clean for best results.

The early model of the Nighthawk, imported from Germany by Bianchi International has a small pocket stone on the side of the leather sheath. It is too small and difficult to hold to be of much use for major sharpening, but can do touch-ups.

The new U.S. Armed Services military bayonet is built by Buck, with a nylon sheath made by Bianchi. A touch-up stone is attached permanently.

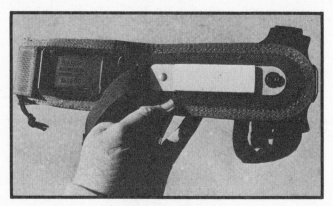

Bianchi's newer Nighthawk II features a more eleborate nylon sheath with a larger more practical sharpening stone attached.

The problem of maintaining the correct, consistent angle between the blade and the sharpening surface has several solutions among several cutlery companies. For those who do not have the experience or skill to hold the correct angle throughout the honing stroke, there are some mechanical gadgets to do it for us.

Buck Knives has a simple holder which clamps to the back of the blade and uses its thickness to construct the correct angle with the stone. As the edge is moved across the stone, both the knife edge and the holder are on the stone surface. This keeps the blade at the same angle throughout the stroke, preventing a round edged surface. The device works well with larger knives, but small pocket-

knife blades do not leave enough area exposed to the stone for effective sharpening.

Another knife company, Spyderco, sells knives with serrated as well as regular blades; the serrated edges present special problems for the sharpener. Their solution is a base holder which accommodates interchangeable triangular rods of different grits. The rods all are housed within the base unit and may be carried into the field or stored at home.

The Spyderco sharpeners are made in fine, medium and coarse grit, a ceramic, extra-fine rod is included. The tri-angluar cross-section shape permits serrated edge blades, including such things as bread knives and pinking shears to

Schrade Cutlery's honing kit includes a two-sided, two-grit stone, honing oil and polishing, wiping cloth sections.

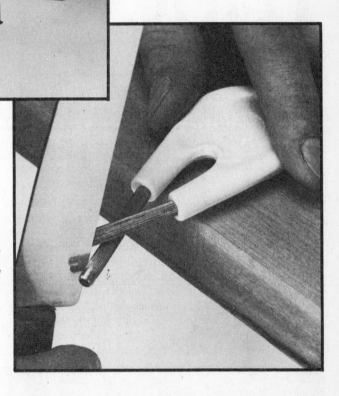

This little device called Quik-N-Sharp is an attempt to assist the worker to fast, accurate blade sharpening. The handle is pressed down on a desk, bench or table and the knife edge is drawn down across the steel rods.

be sharpened. The base unit is drilled to hold the rods at the specific sharpening angle. A metal guard protects the hand as the blade is drawn down across the rods. The correct honing angle is achieved by keeping the knife blade absolutely vertical during the entire stroke.

The Spyderco set-up also includes a diamond-surfaced panel which slides over the triangular rod for final honing of edges which must be extra fine. The unit is versatile and compact to carry. For knives with serrated edges, the Spyderco sharpener is a must.

Another system designed to keep knives and stones always at the same angle is offered by Lansky. Included in this system is a special stone for knives with serrated edges.

The Lansky system is a honing stone guide and clamp which maintains the exact angle with each stroke. The angle can be adjusted through thirty, twenty-five, twenty or seventeen degrees by inserting the guide rod into the appropriate rod pilot hole. Once set, the angle cannot change, unless another pilot hole is used. The stroke across the knife edge is the same throughout.

The system has a knife clamp with four angled guide holes, three color-coded, slip resistant finger-grooved hone holders and oil stones designated coarse, medium and fine grit. Three guide rods are included, with Lansky's honing oil and instructions. Several other grit stones and bench holders are optional items. Everything is packed in a fitted plastic case.

Lansky also has a lightweight portable field or shop sharpener using a locked-in V system for rods. The Lansky Fold-A-Vee sharpener folds down into a compact carrying unit. When opened to either seventeen or twenty-five degree sharpening angles, the blade is stroked down across the enclosed rods. The knife must be held vertically as the blade is drawn along the rods. The hand holding the Fold-A-Vee is completely outside the unit, protected from the knife blade.

We have tried and used each of the sharpening devices discussed in this chapter and found each does a job. Sharpening is more an art than a science. Doing it right requires considerable practice; some of us need more than others.

Chapter 13

THE DECORATIVE TOUCH

Scrimshaw, Plating And Engraving All Can Add To The Beauty Of A Knife.

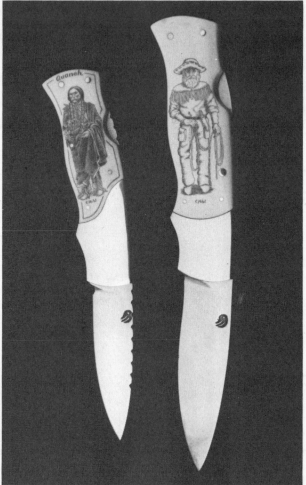

A HOST OF decorative measures can be taken with a knife you've made yourself. Some are relatively simple and others might be best left to a professional. However, one doesn't really know the extent of his artistic abilities, unless he tries.

This brings to mind recollections of the late Slim Pickens, the actor, who died several years ago. Pickens was an avid outdoorsman and also was an enthusiastic knife collector. In addition to all that, he had outstanding abilities as a con man. That's the reason we learned to lock up all of our knives — well out sight — when we heard Slim was coming

Custom lockback folding knives were made by Sean McWilliams. Scrimshaw is by Carole McWilliams, who works closely with him on such projects. Material used was elephant ivory. (Left) Stan Hawkins is well known among custom knifemakers, who appreciate the scrimshaw work he accomplishes in his small studio.

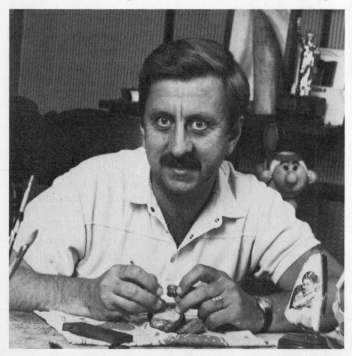

to visit. If a knife, no matter what the quality, was in sight, Pickens could give forty-seven reasons why he needed that particular knife. Each one was exactly what he needed at that specific moment. It wasn't a case of believing any of those reasons, but we usually gave Pickens the knife just to shut him up!

Slim had made his early living as a ranch hand in the Central Valley of California. That's the area where all of the Oklahoma refugees settled during the Dust Bowl days of the Thirties. They drifted into the valley more than fifty years ago, but the Oklahoma accent still prevails. If you sit in a coffee shop, close your eyes and listen to the conversations around you, it'll seem as though you're in Oklahoma City!

Eventually, Pickens drifted into rodeo work and became one of the bull-fighting clowns who run around the arena, trying to distract the angry bulls and oftimes are instrumental in saving a downed bull rider from being trampled or hooked by a horn.

After that, Pickens signed up with Republic Pictures to play comic sidekick to Rex Allen, the last of the B-Western era's singing cowboys. When that era ended, he began to play small roles in bigger films.

But when your rock-bottom price is $5000 for a week of emoting before the cameras, you may not work as often as you did as a rodeo clown or even in B-Westerns, filming half a dozen of them a year back to back. That led Slim Pickens into life as an artist, although he would growl at anyone who called him that.

He began to sculpt, choosing as subjects the things that he knew. He turned out sculptures of cowboys, horses, rodeo scenes and a host of similar subjects. They were good enough that limited-run bronze castings of his work began to sell for several thousand dollars each.

Once, when we asked him about his work and what made him feel he could be a sculptor, his answer was simple: "I didn't know I could until I tried."

This usually is the case with such work as scrimshaw, etching, engraving, fancy file work and the other artistic touches that tend to set a knife apart: You don't know, until you try. And what may seem crude and unprofessional to you, may strike others in a different way. Picasso, some feel, proved that point.

Raj Singh of Art Jewel Enterprises looks over a shipment of elephant ivory that has just arrived at the Illinois headquarters. The tusks in foreground have been polished.

Cutting ivory is a careful business and has a degree of danger. Note that this cutter wears a protective face mask against the toxic ivory dust caused by saw.

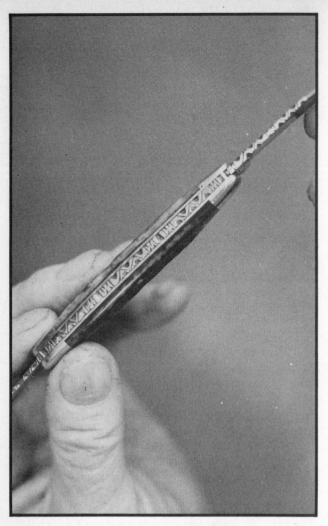

Intricate file work such as this on the back of a knife can be beautiful, but if done poorly, can ruin values. Most knifemakers do such custom work in their own shops.

Over the decades a small cadre of artists has continued to practice as scrimshanders, but it has been only in the past two decades — since the popularity of the custom-made knife — that this technique of enhancement again has gained popularity.

Today, types of scrimshaw have been developed even further. While the original may have been some rather untalented scratches on a bit of elephant ivory, the line cuts filled with India ink or some type of dark dye, modern dyes are being used to reproduced full-color figures. In fact, some of the work is so detailed that, unless inspected closely, it appears to be photo etched.

The difference in what appeared originally — nearly two centuries ago — and what is available today is the difference between a group of bored sailors working on a piece of ivory and today's trained artist, who has selected scrimshaw as his medium of expression.

Bill Pugh is an old-timer in the custom knife business and recognizes the preparations that must be made if his knives are to be works of art and beauty when completed.

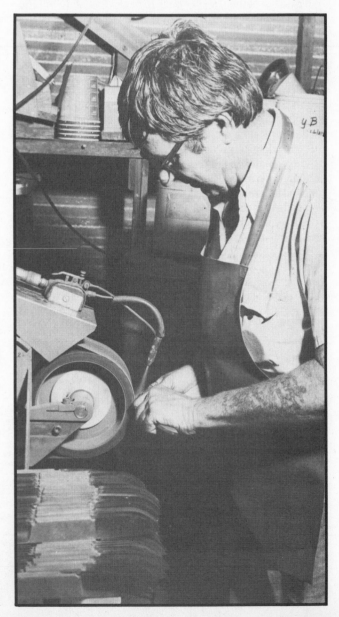

But if you are going to try any of the decorative techniques listed above, we'd suggest you use scrap materials to learn. There is not much point in using elephant ivory at $35 to $50 a pound as a practice medium, when a piece of Micarta will serve just as well. Before you attempt to engrave or even etch the blade of the knife you've just finished, it's logical to try your newly acquired tools on some bits of scrap metal. The same is true of file work. Don't screw up a good knife until you know you can handle the job. If you find you just don't have the talent, but still want the knife gussied up, find a pro. Every community has its artists and a local art dealer should be able to give you proper leads.

Probably the best way of describing scrimshaw is to call it a time-honored art. The technique probably goes back to the era of the caveman, when they scratched crude scenes and figures on bits of bone or perhaps a piece of broken tusk from a mastodon.

But scrimshaw probably did not come to be considered art until long after the Yankee whaling fleets began to ply the seas. It was these sailors, more than 150 years ago, who began to carve patterns on what was primarily ivory as a means of relieving boredom at sea.

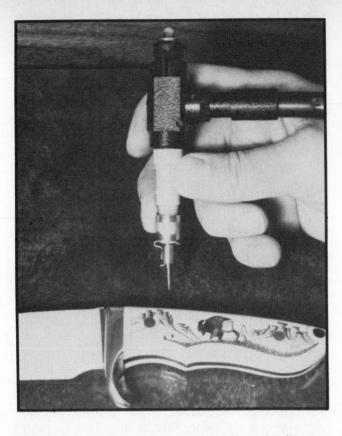

Scrimshander Dale Fisk uses a flexshaft-driven hammer powered by a small motor to accomplish some of the rough work on his figures. The material is woolly mammoth tusk found in Alaska; it is millions of years old. (Below) An array of equipment used by Fisk includes a pin vise that holds ordinary sewing needle, carbide tip tool scribe, #11 X-acto blade with rounded tip for slicing, Higgins' drawing ink and another X-acto blade in short pin vise.

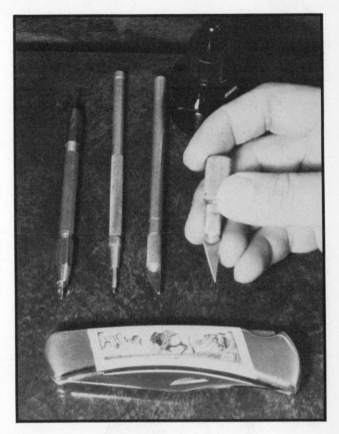

Woolly mammoth tusk was used to produce this figure on a custom skinner from the Buck Knives' custom shop. This was Fisk's prototype for a limited edition series.

As mentioned, there are alternatives to the use of elephant ivory. For example, the Eskimos of Alaska and northern Canada have been doing scrimshaw work for centuries on walrus tusks. These tusks were used as primitive tools in their society and it would appear that many an Eskimo hunter carved figures on his tusk implements so they could be identified as personal property.

Horn of various types has been used by any number of scrimshanders. This includes the horns of water buffalo, cattle and even the antlers of stag, elk and deer. Some, of course, are better than others. In each instance, polishing and buffing are required to present a smooth, shiney surface on which to work, and it is imperative that the craftsman wear some sort of protective mask over his nose and mouth, as the dust from these horns can be highly toxic — as also is the case with elephant tusk ivory.

At first glance, buffalo horn appears to be a solid substance. However, horn is nothing more than compressed hair. Even the horn of the rhino is compressed hair. This rare animal is being slaughtered to near extinction in Africa by poachers solely for that horn. Taken to the Orient, it is ground up and sold as a sexual stimulant. Ten years ago,

Jim Pugh has developed a series of intricate wildlife heads that add a decorative touch to his knives. Each one is cast by means of the familiar lost wax process. Spacer in the ivory handle reduces the tendency to crack.

Custom knifemaker Tom George favors a sweeping, almost Oriental design, using intricate file work on back of the blade as an added custom touch.

Chinese traders would pay $5000 for rhino horn. Today, the Arab oil sheiks of Kuwait have come to prize this same material for use in making knife handles. They are paying as much as $30,000 for a single horn! Moral: Don't practice scrimshawing on rhino horn!

The tiny hairs in the horn of the water buffalo have been pressed and compacted into a solid, but there are hard and soft layers in this material much as with wood, giving it a definite grain. Those who have worked with water buffalo suggest that the horn should be cut at a slight diagonal. This leaves the material with a smooth-looking appearance, without the grain being obvious.

The polished horn takes on a semi-translucent appearance, but in attempting to attain this finish, there is the likelihood of overbuffing it. This can cause the surface fibers to separate. The result is that, when India ink or any other type of dyeing agent is used to fill the carved cuts in the horn, it may spread in and in predictable manner, following the path of the loosened fibers.

Scientific techniques have been developed for flattening the horn into sheets that then are cut into billets measuring about four-by-six inches. These can be used to make knife handles, pistol grips and numerous other decorative items. The flattening process, however, sometimes produces cracks, so if you are going to invest in flattened water buffalo horn, check it carefully for these cracks before you plunk down too much loot.

The horns taken from cattle are found in a variety of shades, ranging from white to full black; others appear to be translucent. The problem with scrimshawing this particular material lies in the fact that the grain is tough and can deflect the point of your scribe, causing an unwanted cut.

Sambar stag is a favorite material for fashioning knife handles. It comes from India and is likely to become in short supply, since the Indian government has placed a ban on export of these antlers.

The material is tough and durable, with a rough outer layer. When this has been ground away, the substance beneath ranges from off-white — what we might call Navajo white if comparing it to a house paint — to a flat gray tone. The problem here, of course, lies in the fact that the substance is rather porous and scrimshaw inks tend to spread into these pores, destroying any effective approach to art.

We discussed various materials with Harbans Singh, who operates Art Jewel Enterprises, Incorporated, at 460 Randy Road, Carol Stream, IL 60188. He imports and markets a number of materials of an exotic nature that have found favor with custom gunsmiths and knifemakers. Included in his array of products are elephant ivory, sambar stag, water buffalo horn, mother of pearl, ebony and others.

Since our native North American deer and elk horn tend to be even more soft and porous than sambar stag, we suggested the possibility of impregnating this type of horn with epoxy to fill the pores and provide a less grain-ridden material. While Harbans Singh didn't reject the idea that it could be done, he felt that the cost would become prohibitive.

The ulimate answer appears to be that, if you are going to use one of these antler materials for a knife handle, leave the surface in its natural state.

Bone is found on a number of factory-made knife handles, but it tends to be difficult to cut. The result is a heavy-handed design even if the craftsman is an experienced scrimshander. Bone also contains a number of interlocking small pores that tend to serve as a blotter. When the lines cut in bone are inked, the fluid invariably will seep into the adjoining pores, spreading and discoloring other areas of the handle. Let's settle for the fact that bone is less than satisfactory as scrimshaw material.

We've seen some interesting scrimshaw on mother-of-pearl, but these examples have been done, for the most part, on the grips for handguns. To start with, this natural material is quite brittle and any great amount of pressure from a cutting tool tends to break or chip it. Also, because mother-of-pearl is quite hard, the scrimshander usually finds it necessary to use cutting tools with either carbide or diamond points. These tools, incidentally, are quite expensive.

As with many other materials, the dust from such shells is quite toxic. If you really want to try your hand with mother-of-pearl, be certain to wear an adequate face mask to protect your nose and lungs.

All of this tends to bring us back to the point where we started: to Micarta and the similiar plastic materials. Ivory

Custom knifemaker Ron Lake designed and made this knife, but engraving is by Steve Lindsay, a Nebraskan. A majority of custom makers send their knives out for decorative touches.

The design of this knife, while unusual, still remains simple. Thus engraver Byron Burgess, Eureka, California chose a simple, but forceful, pattern for its decoration.

Custom craftsman Herman Schneider built this knife in a standard drop-point design, then commissioned William Metcalf to scrimshaw the intricate Bicentennial design.

Micarta long has been considered a more than adequate substitute for elephant ivory. In fact, it has a number of advantages. It will not dry out and crack, for example. Real ivory does. And we can testify that there are few things quite as disheartening as to pay a batch of money for a handmade custom knife with an ivory handle only to discover a year or so later, after the ivory has dried out, that a long, unsightly crack in the handle has damaged the artistry of the piece — and assuredly has lowered its value.

Micarta is a material developed by Westinghouse for use as an electrical insulator, but it was not long before craftsmen discovered its properties and began to use it for making handgun grips, then knife handles. The material is available in various thicknesses, ranging from one-eighth up to a full inch.

What is called paper Micarta is made by combining layers of white paper with a phenolic resin which are subjected to pressure and heat. Then there is what is called linen Micarta. It is produced by the same methods, except that layers of cloth are substituted for the paper. The latter material may be stronger, but it is full of pores and is not a good medium for scrimshaw work.

Micarta is available in a number colors, including black, brown, tan, green, blue and maroon. If of paper Micarta, all these colors can be scrimmed easily. Of course, with the darker shades, the cuts must be filled with inks of contrasting colors if the work is to stand out. We recently saw a knife with a black micarta handle which had its cuts filled with silver ink. It was beautiful, indeed, but there may be some question of how long the silver ink would last, if the knife were to be used with any frequency.

The advantage of scrimshaw, of course, is that the filler ink or dye can be replaced simply again filling the scribed lines with the contrasting liquid and wiping off any excess.

While other colors are used with frequency, most customers seem to prefer white micarta, as it has the look of ivory and, with the passing of time, tends to yellow, eventually taking on the look of elephant ivory or that of an ancient whale's tooth.

Other manufacturers have come up with similar materials, but some are not necessarily as good for the scrimshander's work. There is a phenolic-based substance, for example, that is gray in color. Its problem lies in the fact that it is layered with asbestos — and we all know what asbestos

Greatly enlarged, the work of William Metcalf shows the detail that goes into carefully scrimshawed scene.

While the work on the upper knife appears rather bold, this is due to the fact that the rams and tufts of grass are in color; rocks in background remain black and white. Dragon figure on a knife made by Jim Craig was scrimmed by Mike Ochonicky. Much intricate work and attention to detail was required in figure.

In scrimming this scene of an Indian buffalo hunt on an elephant tusk, Mike Walker was careful to make his work follow the curvature of the material used for this medium.

can do to the lungs. One is better off leaving this type of material alone completely, but if you *must* use it, be absolutely certain you are wearing the best protective mask that money can buy!

Another type of phenolic sheeting is loaded with fiberglass. Not only does this one leave strands of exposed fiberglass to louse up the scrimshaw inks, but it also can be most uncomfortable when it gets on your skin. This particular material also is tough on saw blades, ruining one after a few passes, according to those who have tried it.

There are other plastics, too, that are used by scrimshanders, including the filled material that is used as artificial marble. It comes in various rock-like colors and textures and is available in various thicknesses. The problem with this particular material is that the filler is silicon, which plays immediate hell with cutting tools.

Polymers also can be used for making knife handles and seem to take scrimshaw cuts and ink quite well. This is a material that also can be cast in various shapes, but like Micarta, it doesn't work quite as well as real ivory. Those plastics with a proper filler material tend to cut better than if one is working a piece made from pure hydrocarbon.

In cutting these plastics, one usually will find that a minute ridge is pushed up beside the cut. This may not be

No matter how intricate the work, if the ivory is not worked properly, protected after completion, cracks can ruin value of a knife.

evident to the naked eye, but it is visible through a magnifying glass. The inner edges of this ridge help to hold the scrimshaw inks, but with use, the inks also tend to wear away quickly. If one tries to re-ink, the cuts seem to spread. Recutting is an obvious answer to the problem.

Working real ivory presents a whole set of problems in itself, but perhaps the greatest is in using power equipment to cut it. Excess heat from a saw blade can ruin the piece.

As mentioned earlier, cracking of ivory as it ages is a big problem, but there are some steps that can be taken to minimize the possibility — or, at least, delay it.

Larry Peck of Hannibal, Missouri, was careful to have the figure of his Indian follow flow of handle.

On this ivory-handled knife, Larry Peck utilized space available to full advantage.

Ivory carving is an ancient art and Eskimos still do it on walrus tusks in the Arctic regions. This technique is unlike scrimshaw and requires a different set of tools.

Fresh-cut ivory should have the cut ends coated in wax, glue or epoxy, and these pieces stored in some sort of container that will allow them to dry, but not too rapidly. When the moisture from this animal material dries too quickly, it tends to split. In the desert states such as Southern California, Arizona and Nevada, chances are that a finished knife eventually will have the ivory split. The heat and lack of moisture in the air can do damage in only hours.

Preparing raw ivory for knife handles is a painstaking operation as is the care and curing. Bob Engnath, who supplies many knifemakers with materials, has written an excellent book that covers this subject. It is titled *The Second Scrimshaw Connection* and is available from The House Of Muzzleloading, P.O. Box 6217, Glendale, CA 91205.

You're probably saying, "Yeah, man, I know more about ivory, Micarta and all that stuff than I ever really wanted to know, but how do I scrimshaw?"

Well, probably the first thing we should discuss has to do with proper tools. The early scrimshanders — those sailors from the whaling fleets — might use one of the needles designed for sewing sailcloth. The eye end of the needle would be forced into a piece of wood that had been shaped for a handle or the seaman may have swiped an awl from the ship's carpenter and sharpened it to as fine a point as possible. This type of tool does work, but the results are pretty crude by modern standards of artistic endeavor.

Bob Engnath, who has become something of an expert in these needs, recommends a standard hand sewing needle that is held in a machinist's pin vise. The point of such a needle will cut in any direction desired and it is sharpened easily. He recommends a #11 needle. If you want heavier lines in your work, use a larger needle.

Others favor the use of a drill rod, but this is of relatively soft metal and must be heated to a temperature of about 1350 degrees Fahrenheit, then quenched quickly in oil. The rod, properly hardened, can be filed to the point wanted. If you're using a heavier length of drill rod, it should be filed to the desired point prior to hardening.

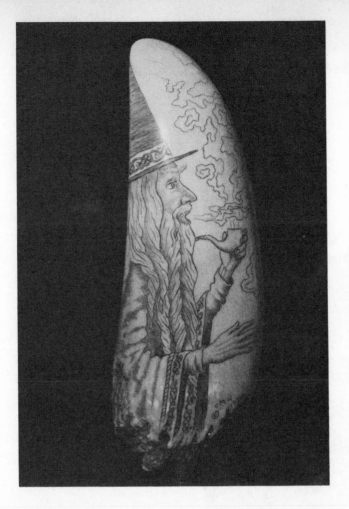

Carole McWilliams used a bit ot broken elephant tusk to create this figure. It surrounds the entire tusk, smoke from wizard's pipe becoming a dragon on reverse side.

For deep carving rather than scratching, any number of modern craftsmen favor old dental tools, but these are too thin to handle intricate work. The sewing needle, with its attached handle, remains the favored tool by most and demands that one develop a light touch, if the needle is not to snap off under pressure.

Proper lighting also is a prime necessity for scrimshaw work and should be arranged so that it shines directly to spotlight the piece of ivory, Micarta or whatever, while the material is being worked. Thus, even the faintest scratch should be visible under the bright light. Bob Engnath suggests a shaded light that does not shine in the scrimshander's eyes, and he recommends small lights of high intensity.

Some sort of magnification is a requirement, too. The lens should be situated over the work in such position that the artist can see the minute detail clearly as he makes his cuts and scratches. There are several compact units with their own built-in lights that range up to ten-power in magnification. However, most of the professionals favor a magnifying glass of about three-power.

Before you've been at this type of work for long, you probably will collect an array of tools that you have discovered are useful for special jobs. Some, for example, will use an ordinary single-edge razor blade for certain cuts.

So now you have your tools laid out and you have an idea of the type of design you want to try on that knife handle, but where do you start?

The old whalers usually just grabbed a bit of whale tooth or walrus tusk and started scratching. Today, usually in museums, there are outstanding examples of this technique; the majority, though, turned out to be extemely crude and the subject didn't always look at all like what it was meant to be.

A technique that is recommended for today's beginner is to make or find a sketch that strikes your fancy. It probably will be too large to display on anything as small as a knife handle, so you have to reduce it. That's where the modern image reducing Xerox machine or similar type of copier is put into play. By making multiple reductions, each smaller than the one before, one usually can get the image down to a size that will fit the handle material.

The reduced image is glued to the material to be scrimmed, then one begins to punch small holes through the paper, following the lines of the illustration. When the entire outline has been punched out in such fashion, the paper is removed and the needle used to connect the dots with the desired width of scratches and cuts.

If you find the image is not what you imagined it would be, it's a simple matter to use sandpaper or emery cloth of fine grit to polish out the marks and start over.

This should be enough to get one started in the scrimshaw art. Your talents — if you have any — will develop, as you become more familiar with the basic requirements and you will develop your own techniques and special tools.

Good scratchin'.

Most modern scrimshanders use what is called a diamond hone to sharpen their scribes. This is a small rectangle of manufactured stone that has industrial diamonds imbedded in its surface. In sharpening the scribe, effort must be taken to see that the point is consistently round. If it is not, the uneven point may tend to grab and scrim lines where you least want them.

Carbide scribes are available, but the majority of craftsmen tend to steer clear of them when working ivory, Micarta or other comparatively soft materials. It is virtually impossible to sharpen a carbide scribe to the point that most want for fine lines or for stippling effects.

Some artisans use X-acto knives, but controlling these wide blades is a chore that takes a great deal of practice and the instrument must be held with firmness. If the knife is held loosely in the hand, your outlines probably will appear shakey when inked in.

Others prefer to use the same tools employed by engravers. These gravers, used normally for cutting steel, are used with a push-type stroke, being held horizontal to the work. However, they must be kept extremely sharp, for a dull graver will easily gouge or tear ivory and even Micarta, resulting either in a ragged line or damage that is beyond salvage.

The State Of Plate...Or How To Give A Richer Look To An Otherwise Adequate Knife

THERE IS nothing that gives an item — including a knife — the look of richness that is provided by touches of gold or silver. Since both of these metals are too soft and too expensive to use in their pure state for butt caps, hand guards and the like, it is the usual practice to use another metal, then to coat it with the more precious metal.

When manufacturers want gold plating added to an item, they usually send it out to a company that specializes in such work. However, there is an inexpensive plating kit available that can be used by the amateur or even the professional. In both uses, the results come out the same.

This basic kit is available for under $50 from Texas Plater Supply, (2453 W. Five-Mile Parkway, Dallas, TX

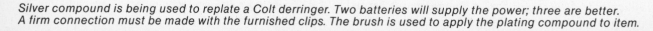

Silver compound is being used to replate a Colt derringer. Two batteries will supply the power; three are better. A firm connection must be made with the furnished clips. The brush is used to apply the plating compound to item.

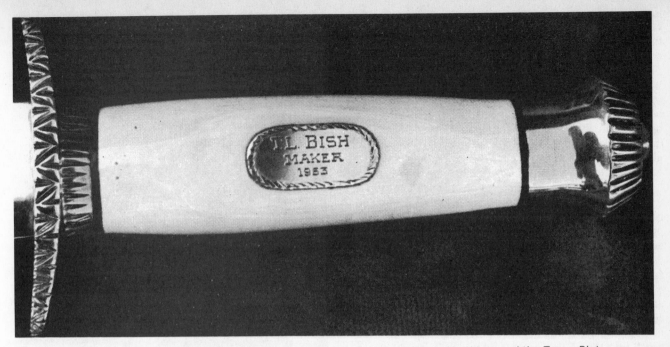

Tommy L. Bish, who specializes in restoration of antique arms, made this knife, then used the Texas Plater pro kit to gold plate the butt, cap the hand guard and the name plate which he set in the handle of elephant ivory.

75233). Professional gunsmiths have used this kit for years to restore the plating on expensive firearms, using specially prepared gold, silver, nickel, copper or brass compounds.

Tommy L. Bish, a gunsmith who has specialized for years in antique restorations, has used this kit with great success, renewing finishes on guns that have had the plating worn away through continuing use or perhaps the application of harsh polishing mediums.

The power supply for this kit is nothing more than a pair of #6 dry cell batteries that are hooked in series to provide a minimum of three volts. If you want the batteries to last somewhat longer and perhaps accomplish the plating sequence a bit more rapidly, three or four of these batteries

make a better power source.

Actually, Texas Platers offers five different kits, which range from the Hobbyist Special, a kit containing minimal supplies through the Gunsmiths Special, which is used by professionals and is priced accordingly. Needless to say, the prices vary with the amount of supplies included. Since the prices tend to fluctuate somewhat with the current prices of precious metals, one would be advised to write to the organization at the Dallas address for a current price list. The compounds used in transferring gold to a metal surface give you a 24-karat finish; the other plates are equally authentic. Refills of any of the metal compounds listed earlier are available, too, from Texas Platers Supply.

But getting back to the dry cell batteries. Once they are

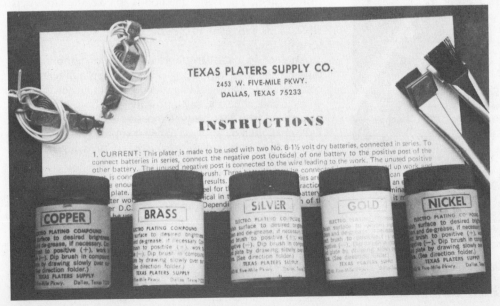

Texas Plater kits are made for the amateur, others for the professional. This one has copper, brass, silver, 23-karat gold and nickel compounds as part of the kit.

connected properly in series, according to a supplied diagram, the brush, which has a metal handle acting as an anode, is connected to the identified positive pole; the object to be plated is connected to the negative pole by means of a wired clamp that is included with the kit.

Before getting further involved, perhaps one point should be made clear. If you want to plate the hilt or another part of your knife that is made of aluminum, don't bother sending for the kit. None of these precious metals will adhere to aluminum, which must be anodized rather than plated, if one wants to change its natural finish.

With the components properly hooked up, a first step is to be certain the metal to be plated is absolutely clean and has been polished. It probably will come as no great surprise to the average home craftsman that, should the metal surfaces bear any coating such as wax, oil, dirt or other foreign substance, the plating will not adhere to the metal's surfaces.

"The procedure for using this kit is simplicity itself," according to Tommy Bish. "With the batteries wired in the correct sequence and the knife part that is to be plated connected properly to the negative pole, one simply dips the brush into the plating compound which is supplied in a small marked bottle. Be certain that the bristles and the underside of the anode are well covered with the material."

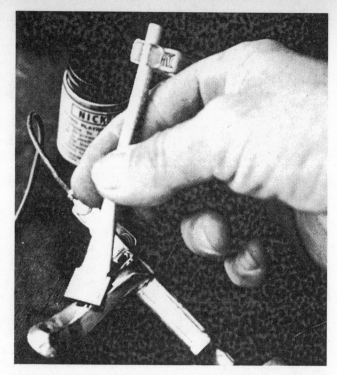

The compound must be applied to the new metal with a series of long strokes so that the application is even.

Tommy Bish found that the nickel-plating compound with the kit could be used to preserve tools against rust.

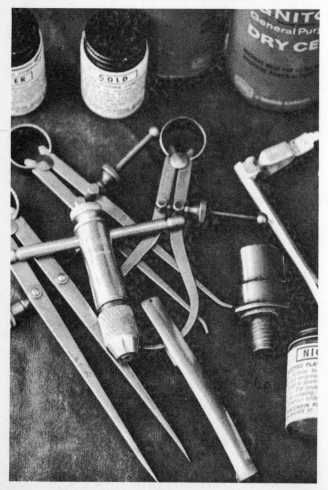

One must use a small circular motion with the brush against the metal that is being plated. The bristles must always be in light contact with the work and one is required to keep the brush in constant motion; don't ever stop or you'll end up with a messy, uneven job.

One must dip the brush into the bottle of plating compound at short intervals to keep the bristles loaded. One should brush each square inch for at least thirty seconds, but if you want a heavier coating, simply brush the area for a longer period of time.

Another point that should be made is the fact that neither gold nor silver plating adhere well when applied directly to iron or steel. The better method is to coat the knife part with the copper material, then cover the copper finish with silver. This will result in the gold or silver standing up better with use.

Another tip that Bish offers for the sake of durability is to tape off the areas not being plated. When application is completed, a coating of clear lacquer from an aerosol can — available at nearly any hardware or hobby shop — can be applied. But this lacquer should be sprayed only as a light mist, then be allowed to dry completely. Don't overspray or you may end up with unsightly runs that spoil the desired effect.

Another method that Bish has used, when an aerosol was not available, has been to apply the lacquer with a brush of soft mink hair, but the lacquer must be applied in a smooth, even coat — and sparingly. Once the lacquer has dried completely, he adds to the protection by applying a coating of pure carnoba wax.

Bish was one of the earliest of the outdoor writers to recognize the importance of good cutlery in the world of hunting and shooting. Early on, he began to use some of the techniques he learned in gunsmithing to improve his custom knives that he has made and collected.

For example, he suggests that, if one wants to give the plated surface a soft matte finish instead of the natural high luster appearance of freshly applied gold or silver, this can be accomplished by rubbing the plating ever so lightly with fine steel wool or crocus cloth.

"This process must be accomplished with an extremely light touch, however," he cautions. "Both gold and silver are exceedingly soft metals and, if one gets overly enthusiastic in his rubbing, he may find the plating disappearing."

When the plating compounds are not in actual use, the small jars should be kept tightly closed. This prevents the compound from drying out. When the job is done, the plating brush and the underside of the anode in which the bristles are mounted should be washed clean, then allowed to dry completely. The wiring clip that connects the brush to the batteries also should be washed to clear it of any of the plating compound, as well.

"I learned the hard way," Bish recalls, "that even the slightest amount of compound left on any of the components will have an adverse effect the next time you want to use the kit."

One never should use a brush that has not been cleaned thoroughly and is totally dry. Bish also has found that one should use a different brush with each of the different solutions for the best effect. Also, his personal experiences have shown him that nickel plating is the most difficult of the various compounds.

"I learned through continuing experimentation that if I add a few drops of water to the nickel compound, then raise the voltage up to twelve volts by adding more batteries, the nickel will adhere better than if applied in the same manner as the other metallic compounds."

At first, he thought this was simply that, because the solution had been diluted and was thinner, it worked better, but he since has come to consider the fact that the added water may provide an improved conductor for the electrical current. He also notes that the added voltage to improve adherence qualities of nickel would tend to lend some credence to this theory.

Another technique that Bish developed for his own purpose is to tape off areas on steel or iron so that just a set of initials remains visible on the bare metal. Any of the various compounds then can be used to fill in the desired set of initials, stripping away the tape after the plating has hardened properly. He uses masking tape for this, since none of the plating compounds will adhere to this material.

"I've been using this kit in its various forms for more than twenty years," this experienced craftsman reports. "In that time, not all of my projects have ranked in the total success column and several have had to be redone. However, each time something went wrong, I later discovered that the problem had been human error on my part rather than any fault with the kit."

For example, he once found that the plating simply would not adhere to the metal on which he was working; closer investigation showed that the current had been reversed, the brush and the knife part being hooked up to the wrong wires. In other instances, he has found that he has had broken wires leading from the current — easily replaced,

When three batteries are used, the plating compounds adhere to the subject metal for rapid job completion. If current is low, the results are less successful.

of course — or bad connections that caused the unit to fail to live up to its advertising.

In other instances, he has discovered that the bristles of the brush were not loaded heavily enough with the plating compound; in other cases, he has found the brush had not been cleaned properly and that the old compound was being mixed with a different one. This doesn't work, either.

The batteries, of course, must be up to strength; insufficient power will negate the effort or, at best, slow it considerably. And a big problem in the beginning was finding that the piece of metal he wanted to plate already was coated with a layer of lacquer; this efficiently masked the metal from the compound. Once the lacquer was removed, the kit worked famously. As he discovered, if one follows each of the rules laid out in the accompanying instruction sheet, there should be no major problem.

In addition to using the plating kits to renew the finishes on firearms — chiefly handguns — and to embellish knives, Bish also has used it to gold plate watch cases, jewelry, even items as small as screw heads.

Going a step beyond, he has used the kit to plate any number of his tools, usually giving them a coating of nickel or copper to protect them against rust.

"Actually, there are any number of uses for this little kit," he proclaims. However, if one is going to get into plating entire rifles, broadswords or larger items, it's likely that a different type of plating unit — some of them costing $1000 or so — will be required."

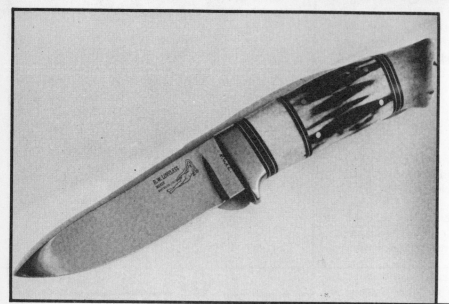

Bob Loveless makes highly sought, simple knives for use in the field or in collections. He makes sure each is decorated with his name.

Some time back, Smith & Wesson offered knives in their line, some of which were highly decorated. This Collector Series, limited to a thousand knives, was acid-etched on the blade, sculpted on the guard and pommel, engraved on escutcheon.

THERE ARE countless custom knives with scenes or designs etched on their blades, this decorative touch adding to the beauty and value. But, in virtually all cases, it is not the custom knifemaker who does this sort of work. He sends it out to a professional etcher, who is set up to do this specialized work and has the expertise to see that a pattern on a blade doesn't go astray and ruin an expensive knife.

There are a number of these individuals around the country — but far fewer of them than there are good engravers. One of the best — who will take on specific jobs, using your own design or creating one for you — is Leonard Leibowitz, a graduate of the New York National Academy of Design.

While some etchers create designs from photos or some other reproductive process, Leonard Leibowitz usually creates his own in an effort to make the artwork follow the flow of the knife design. Thus, even though several customers may choose the same basic design, there are individual touches in his work that make each of the etchings an original piece of work.

Leonard Leibowitz, who can be contacted at 1202 Palto Alto Street, Pittsburg, PA 15212, maintains a reference file of big game animals, Western scenes, action figures and those from mythology from which to draw his ideas. He also can etch a customer's portrait, slogans, names, initials or just about anything else one might desire incorporated in his pattern. In addition to etching on hardened

While hand-scribing any design, one may steady the cutting hand with the fingers of the opposite hand.

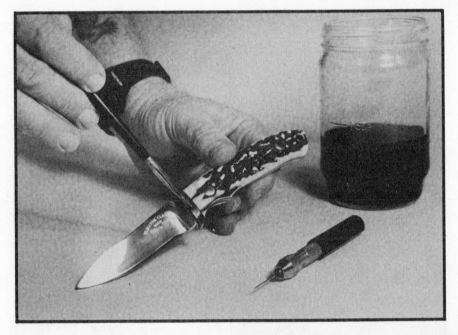

Etching a small area, a clean cotton swab may be used to coat section repeatedly with acid until desired depth is reached. Metal surrounding is coated with shellac.

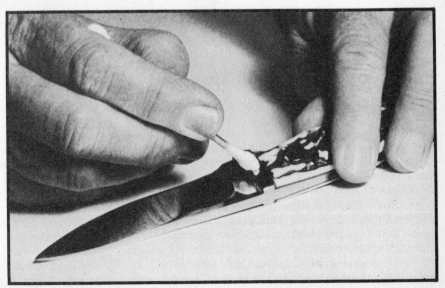

A.G. Russell's little boot knife is etched with oak leaves and acorns along its two-edged blade.

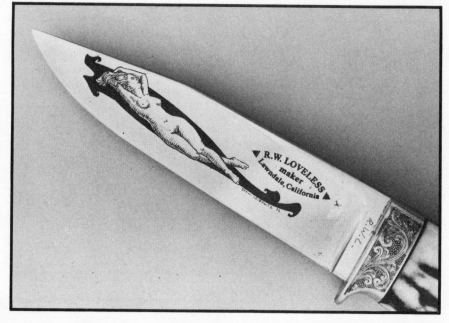

Another Bob Loveless knife, etched by Shaw-Leibowitz in 1972. Loveless has long since moved from Lawndale and knives so marked are sought by collectors for high prices!

steels such as 440C, he also works with sterling silver, gold, brass, bronze and aluminum. While some craftsmen want only the blade on which to work, Leibowitz often accepts finished knives on which to incorporate his art.

An outfit that has moved etching into what amounts to mass production is Aurum Etchings, 601 E. Walnut Circle, Garland, TX 75040.

Aurum Etchings was founded some fifteen years ago by Samuel Shortes and now is considered the largest organization in the country for commemorative etching.

Sam Shortes worked for Texas Instruments for seventeen years as a research scientist. During this period, he developed special technologies for using the age-old art of etching; these processes now are protected as Aurum's trade secrets. By using multi-layer techniques on a mass production basis, the firm has developed the etching art to the point that their work has the appearance, in many instances, of hand engraving.

Sam Shortes is the first to admit that, after he formed Aurum Etchings — Aurum being the Latin word for "gold" — he spent his first five years learning how to transfer the techniques he had developed in the electronics industry from soft metals such as copper to the hard steels of firearms and knives. Working on curved surfaces required techniques different from those he had encountered in printed circuit boards.

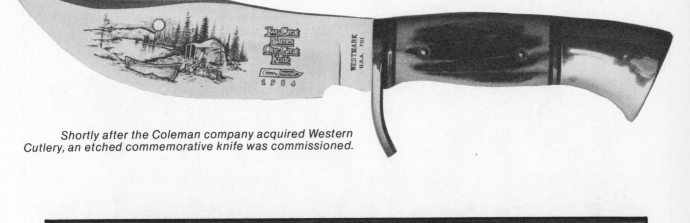

Shortly after the Coleman company acquired Western Cutlery, an etched commemorative knife was commissioned.

A close-up view of the etching on the Coleman/Western knife above reveals what might be a typical outdoor scene which, one presumes, shows Coleman products in use. Details show a canoe, tent, lantern, and wood ax.

While much of the Aurum technique is classified information, Shortes says any piece that is to be etched first is coated with a special light-sensitive material. A film pattern then is placed in contact with the metal and it is exposed to ultra-violet light. Exposure to this type of light changes the nature of the coating in such a manner that, after proper development, the metal will be etched in the acid bath only in the areas where the light did not strike.

With a great deal of experimentation and scientific know-how, Aurum has developed techniques that allow multiple layers of overlay patterns to be used, thus varying the depth of the etching when submitted to the acid bath. The technique also allows changing the color of the metal in the etched area, when that effect is wanted. Other means allow for selective plating certain parts of the pattern with gold or nickel.

The process, however, is a bit more involved than simply throwing several pieces of film on a knife blade, sticking it under an ultra-violet light for a specified time, then dropping it into the acid bath. The Aurm work areas look like a scientific laboratory — which it is, to a degree — with microscopes being used to superimpose the patterns over each other with surgical skills. Proper placement of the overlay films and application of the masking compounds is the secret of artistic success.

Aurum turns out special runs of knives for small groups

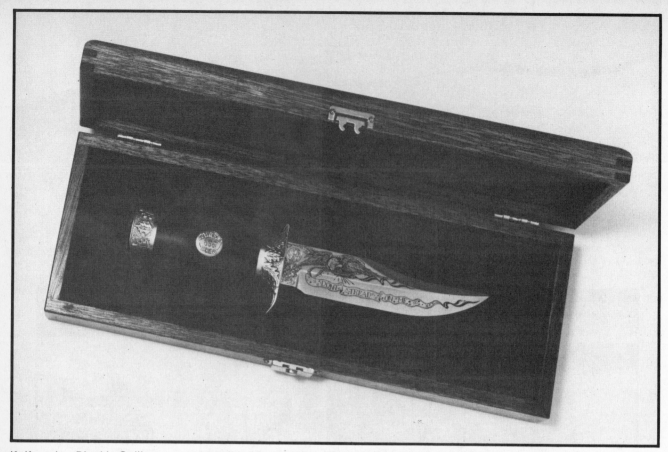

Knifemaker Blackie Collins was responsible for the decorations on the Smith & Wesson commemorative Bowie.

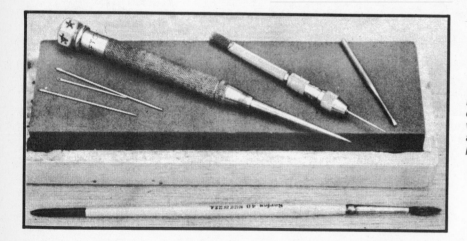

Necessary tools for the beginning etcher need not be elaborate. Pin vises will hold heavy sewing needles and a sharpening stone will restore points. A soft point brush is needed.

such as gun clubs, military reserve units and other groups that need a product that "is different" as an incentive reward or fund-raiser. But the firm also does big business, turning out hundreds — and even thousands — of special etched knives for Gerber, Buck and others.

After a group or company that is interested in an etching program has decided to go ahead, Aurum artists come up with a pencil sketch incorporating the theme suggested by the potential buyer and incorporating their own artistic ideas. These artists, of course, can work from photos,

rough drawings or almost any other type of source material. There is no charge for this work and the pencil art may be submitted several times for the sponsor to judge and make any changes.

Once the pencil sketch is approved, Aurum bills the buyer at cost for the finished work and a prototype. Both of these, however, become the property of the buyer. It is guaranteed that the artwork will not be used elsewhere.

The Texas firm has done a great deal of work with firearms companies as well as the knifemaking industries

Basic etching suppies may be purchased at local outlets. Ammonia is kept at hand to protect skin and clothing in case of a spill. See text for how to dilute shellac.

over the years and is constantly seeking new techniques that will cut down delivery cost and time.

However, none of this gets an etched pattern on the blade of that knife you've spent countless hours designing and making in your own workshop, does it?

In view of what you've already read here, you may still want to try your hand at etching. Truth is, the subject is not easily explained on paper; it is learned by doing. If you decide to give it a try, be sure to attempt your first efforts on bits of scrap metal, not on the blade of an expensive knife!

The tools for etching are rather basic, but you'll also require such items as acids, mordants and stopping-out varnishes.

The necessary tools for even fine etching — if you eventually find you have that talent and capability — usually can be found right in your home. For example, for scroll work, common sewing needles in larger sizes can be inserted into makeshift handles and used as your etcher. However, these needles should be shaped according to need by honing on an oil stone, then reshaped in the same manner as they are worn down through use. An excellent holder for

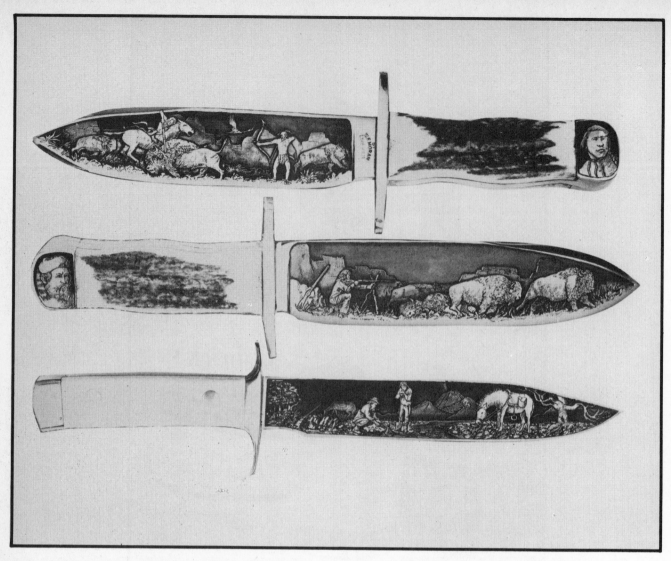

Elaborate etching work by Shaw-Leibowitz: Top knife is by W.F. Moran, with a depiction of an Indian buffalo hunt. The middle is the opposite side of the Bowie with a buffalo hunter in action. His portrait is on the butt cap. Arkansas knifemaker, Jimmy Lile, made the lower Bowie blade showing two prospectors panning for gold.

needles is the small scribe holder or pin vise manufactured by various tool manufacturers.

The etching needle should be perfectly round and blunt to prevent it from catching and skipping on the metal as it cuts through the varnish in tracing its design. This bluntness of the needle also allows the hand to travel in any direction without the likelihood of the needle snagging on the metal surface. Practice alone can lead to perfection in handling the etching needle.

Stopping-out varnishes are used to protect the steel parts that are not to be etched when the knife is placed in the necessary acid bath. Beeswax has been tried, but has been found pretty unsuccessful in etching due to the fact that, in the actual etching operation with the needle etchers, the wax has a tendency to flake off, leaving the exposed raw steel where etching is not desired. The stopping-out liquid should be applied with a brush, then allowed to dry thoroughly before actual etching begins. One of the proven formulae for this type of spirit varnish is as follows:

4 ounces of white shellac
8 ounces of pure grain alcohol
45 grains of methyl-violet dye

First, mix the alcohol with the shellac, allowing the shellac to dissolve completely, before adding the dye. This particular formula has been found to be ideal, as it provides the proper color necessary to correctly detail the etched designs. This mixture is painted over the entire metal surface to be etched and allowed to dry.

A well laid-out design should be drawn on paper first to give yourself a concise pattern to go by; too, it will help in deciding what type of ornamentation is best suited to the area to be covered. Floral designs, intricate scroll work,

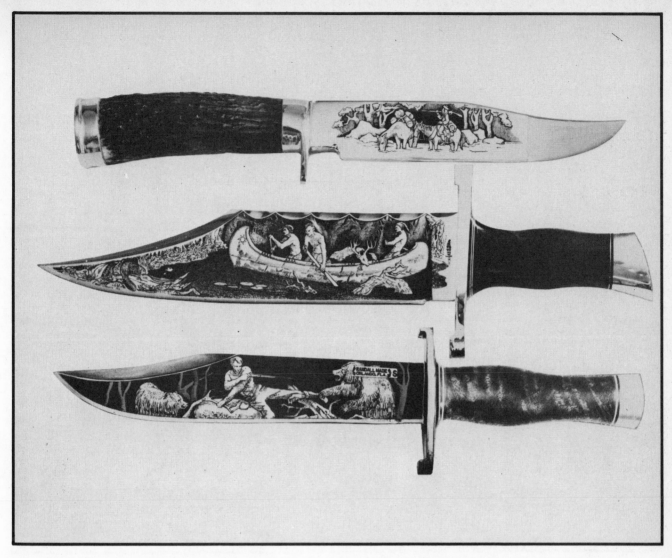

Walt Kneubuhler, who prefers to be known as W.K., made the knife on top. Shaw-Leibowitz etched the scene of the trapper. The same etchers decorated the center Bowie by Gil Hibben of Indians returning from the hunt and the Bo Randall Bowie showing a cowboy battling a bear. The best knifemakers realize the value of adding etching.

names and scenes are but a few of the recommended designs that can be applied by the artist.

Following the application of the stopping-out varnish and with a clear picture in mind of the design wanted, you can proceed to "cut" your design into the varnish, making certain that your etching needle completely penetrates the varnish coating down to the bare metal. This is an absolute must in order for the acid to bite into the metal during the later acid bath.

Great care must be taken in laying out the design on the varnish surface; any undue scratches or slips of the etching needles must be touched up with varnish and allowed to dry before that particular area is reworked. The design should be as intricate as possible and as beautiful as is the artist's ability to apply it, but for your early efforts, we suggest simplicity.

A word of caution is in order at this point to prevent one from receiving bad acid burns in his first attempt at etching. Always have close at hand a bottle of liquid ammonia to apply to acid spots on either your skin or clothing. Water is the next best thing to counteract acid should it be spilled or splattered. The use of rubber gloves is a must, while giving the metal parts their acid bath in the actual etching process. Use the greatest care in handling etching acids, as they can be dangerous. The fumes alone can turn bright, clean tools to rust in short order, so use the acid bath in a well ventilated room and the acid away from other metal objects.

The theory of etching lies in the ability to enhance the beauty of metal objects by the use of acids; to eat that metal immediately surrounding the design away, leaving a raised effect to the scroll, floral or other scenes used. The use of stopping-out varnishes is to prevent the acid from eating

The American Historical Foundation has offered a commemorative knife in what it terms its Vietnam Tribute Collection. This one, commemorating the U.S. Army, has a blade etched with scenes and dates of Vietnam fighting.

away metal that will comprise the design itself; it is well to keep in mind that, where there is not stopping-out varnish, the acid will eat; the longer the metal is in the acid bath, the deeper the metal is eaten away.

To prepare the metal to be etched, it first must be cleaned thoroughly, removing all grease, oil and fingerprints before applying the stopping-out varnish. If etching a firearm, plugs must be made of wood to be inserted in both ends of barrels to be given an acid bath. All threaded screw holes must be coated well with varnish inside and out and all wooden plugs liberally coated with varnish at the point where they enter the barrel or cylinder holes.

The agent used most often in etching is nitric acid. This is available at most drug stores at nominal cost. It is impossible to state just how soon the nitric acid's eating action will begin on the metal, as there are numerous fac-

tors involved. For example, the temperature of the acid will affect its power in etching.

The acid bath, itself, should be in a tray or vessel large enough to receive the knife blade or other metal being etched. This tray must be of some material that will not be affected by the eating action of the acid; baked enamel, porcelain or crockery make good acid bath trays.

Pour only enough acid into this tray to completely cover the metal being etched. As stated earlier, the length of time this metal remains in the bath will determine just how deeply it is etched by the acid; visual inspection is a good indication of this phase. All parts should be suspended in the bath by wires for easy removal. Never use string or cord for this purpose, as the acid will soon burn through, allowing the metal parts to drop to the bottom of the tank or tray. The resultant splash may be damaging to both your-

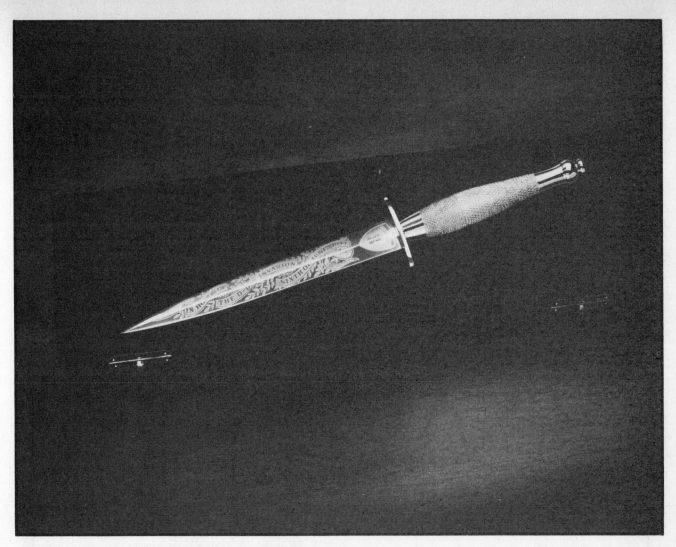

This etched-blade commemorative from the American Historical Foundation will be collected by World War II veterans.

self and to surrounding tools and materials.

As suggested earlier, the novice should select only the simplest designs to begin with, gradually working into the more complicated scroll and floral designs, as he develops his ability and understanding of the art. The worker must have considerable artistic ability, but regardless of this ability, it is best to begin with practice. A finely etched knife blade or other metal object is the result of having the etching needles properly honed at all times during the cutting phase of the design. Improperly sharpened needles result in coarse, rough lines which, in turn, result in a poor job.

Take your time, never try to cut corners in order to finish the job sooner. Etching is an art that requires utmost care and patience, but careful workmanship can easily increase the value of an arm many times both artistically and monetarily.

When we inspect some of the more complicated etchings done by professionals, it becomes obvious that this type of work has been accomplished in varying layers.

With enough practice and developed expertise, this type of work is not beyond the capabilities of the talented amateur. This is called multi-layer etching and is meant to make the design stand out in a type of relief that is almost sculptural in its appearance.

This type of work is accomplished by etching part of the design to specific depth, while stopping-out other areas with the earlier described shellac that have been etched to a lesser degree.

This is an advanced technique that takes some time to learn and, as stated earlier, your best custom knife is not the piece of metal on which to learn the process. Work with bits of scrap iron or steel until you learn what you can — and more specifically, can't — do in this type of effort.

ENGRAVING IS AN ART

Taking Years To Master — Here Are The Basics!

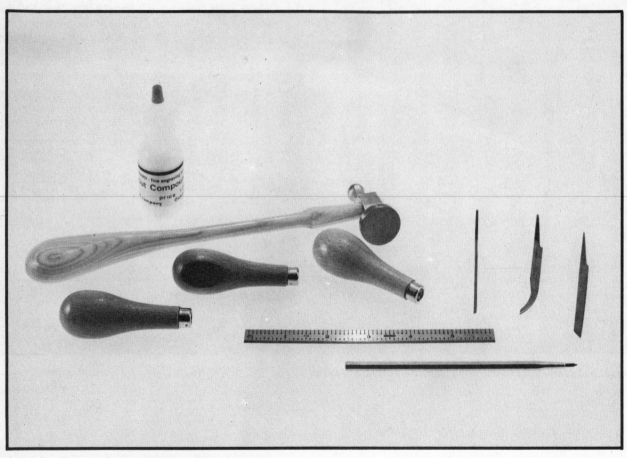

Learning the art of engraving is made a bit easier with the right tools. Brownells has assembled a set of basic tools for the beginner for about forty bucks.

OFFERING THE reader complete instructions on engraving within the confines of a sub-chapter is a bit like attempting to transfer the entire text of the Bible to the head of a pin. Total books have been written on engraving and are much more detailed than is allowed in the available space.

However, we can suggest some of the tools that will be needed by the beginning engraver, tell him where to learn more and offer some basic insights as to how to go about cutting a pattern in metal.

Undoubtedly the best source of engraving tools for the beginner is Brownells, Incorporated, Route 2, Box 1, Montezuma, IA 50171. Bob and Frank Brownell, father and son, have been supplying tools to gunsmiths for decades;

they work hard at developing tools for beginners in all facets of the gunsmithing trade, as well as supplying the needs of the professionals.

Neil Hartliep, a professional engraver who instructs a basic engraving course for the National Rifle Association's Gunsmithing Summer Schools, is one of those who helped the Brownells develop what he calls an "engraving school starter set." This is the set used at the NRA schools and includes a hands-on text by Hartliep.

There are twenty different tools included with this set, which sells for somewhere in the neighborhood of $125. If you aren't sure you have the talent for engraving and don't want to invest that much loot in the beginning, the Brownells have two other sets that are sufficient to allow one to

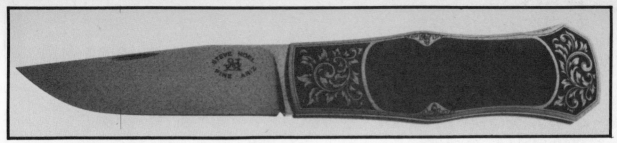

Steve Hoel made the folding Coke bottle knife and used desert big horn sheep horn for the handle scales. The engraving is by Lynton McKenzie who is among the best.

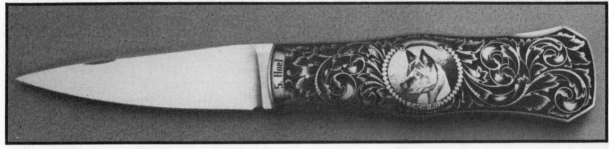

Another Steve Hoel folder with the handle scales engraved by Steve Lindsay. The dog is Sachi-Ko.

Custom knifemaker Jim Pugh knows how much work is required to learn engraving. The art is not for all.

try his hand and determine just where his talents lie. One is called the James B. Meek Beginner's Set. Meek, who authored the basic text, *The Art Of Engraving,* says, "This kit is for beginning engravers who are still in the process of finding out which tools they are most comfortable with." The kit contains nine different gravers and sells for $43.93 at this writing. Meek, incidentally, insists that as much as ninety percent of the scroll work in engraving can be accomplished with the kit.

For a few bucks less — $39.36, at the time this is written — Brownells also offers Neil Hartliep's Beginner Kit, which includes a chasing hammer, several gravers in varying sizes, a stainless steel rule, three hardwood handles for gravers and a bottle of layout fluid.

Should you determine that you can be an engraver and want to pursue the art, you'll find that several pages of the Brownell's catalog is devoted to more sophisticated engraving tools. While this is a catalog devoted primarily to gunsmithing tools, engraving is engraving, and the tools used are for all types of metal, whether a gun frame or the blade of a Bowie knife.

There are any number of basic patterns used by engravers — not to mention those they design for themselves — and Jim Meek's book, *The Art Of Engraving,* covers a host of these. The book also is available from Brownells at the Montezuma, Iowa, address.

The Iowa gunsmith suppliers also offer transparent patterns that can be laid on the metal to be engraved, the artist following the lines of the patterns with his gravers to achieve desired results.

Gravers come in a number of shapes and sizes, although James Meek insists the tools used most commonly are those called the onglette, the square or lozenge, and the flat

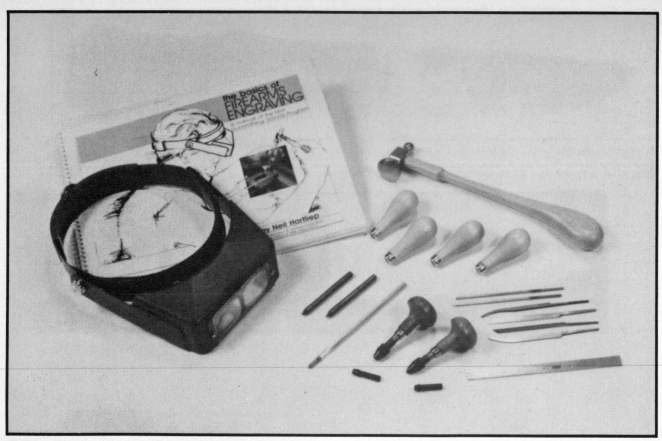

This basic engraving set is sold by Brownells. It is the same one used in the National Rifle Association's basic school conducted each year. Instruction book is included.

James Meek, the well known engraver and author, feels that this set of engravng tools is sufficient for the beginner, allowing him to learn which of the tools he likes to use best. The set is being sold by Brownells.

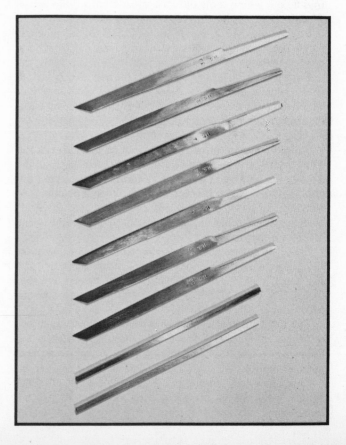

or chisel gravers. Many engravers also favor die sinker's chisels in their work.

At such time as you obtain your gravers, it is best to look them over carefully. In manufacture, the grinding wheels sometimes will cut deeper at the point, resulting in a rounded appearance. The tools must be ground until this forward rake has been eliminated, if it is to cut properly.

The gravers also will need handles, which are available in a variety of sizes and shapes. You'll have to try several to determine what fits your hand best and allows you to be most comfortable in your work.

Before one advances too far, he will require a vise for holding the metal that is to be engraved. Again, Brownells markets several of these or, with a bit of thought, one can build his own. We even know of one individual who used a bowling ball — splitting it in half — to build such a vise that met his personal needs. However, an ordinary swivel vise often will suffice so long as one uses blocks of wood to protect the metal on which he is working. One also should take care not to tighten the vise to the point that he will spring or bend the metal he wants to engrave.

When it comes to actually beginning to engrave, you

FIGURE 1

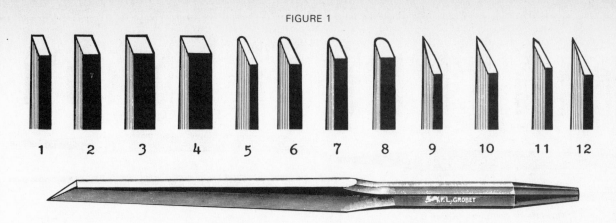

1 2 3 4 5 6 7 8 9 10 11 12

Die Sinkers Chisels, set of 12

(Illustrations courtesy of Brownells)

Many engravers prefer to use die sinker chisels, shown above. Shown slightly smaller than actual size, the largest chisels will measure about 7½ inches long.

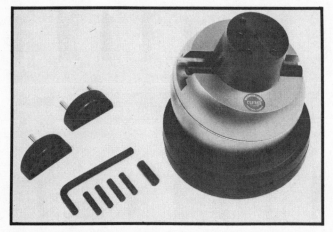

If one becomes serious about becoming an engraver, he or she will need an engraving block to hold the work that is in progress. This small block has thirty attachments.

A few short years ago, Michael Walker was still a probationary member of the Knifemakers Guild. These days, he is known for his engraving and his knifemaking.

may have noticed photos in major factories and shops that show the engravers standing over their work. Some companies require this approach apparently, especially in Europe. However, any number of professional engravers choose to use a stool that allows them the freedom they need, yet adds to personal comfort.

Traditionally, the scrollwork done by English engravers and the finer work by other Europeans has been accomplished with hand gravers. For the most part, these individuals were working on firearms that had not been heat-treated at that point. If one is attempting to engrave a knife blade, there should be no great problem, if it has not yet been heat-treated, but if it has, the going gets a bit tougher. A vast majority of the fine-line work is done with hand gravers. With tougher metals or when the fineness of the line is less critical, the hammer and chisel can be used to advantage...provided it's the right chisel for the job.

Most engravers have found their lives are simplified if they use some sort of lubricant on the tip of the cutting tools. It tends to make cutting an easier chore and there is less time taken out to resharpen the tools. Jim Meek, for example, uses a mixture of kerosene and the sulfur cutting

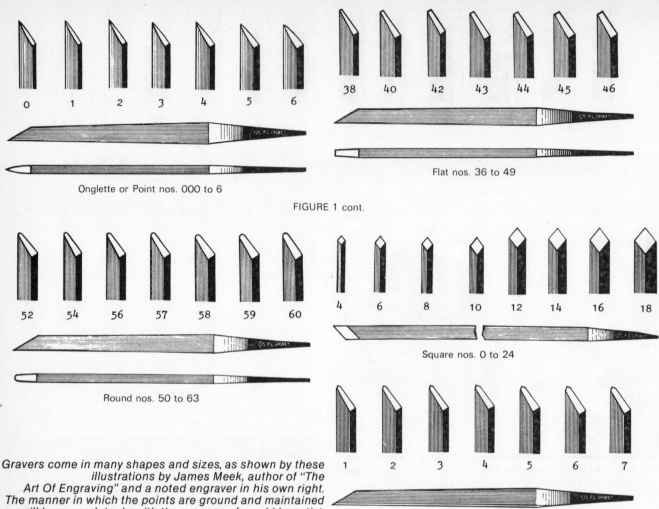

0 1 2 3 4 5 6

Onglette or Point nos. 000 to 6

38 40 42 43 44 45 46

Flat nos. 36 to 49

FIGURE 1 cont.

52 54 56 57 58 59 60

Round nos. 50 to 63

4 6 8 10 12 14 16 18

Square nos. 0 to 24

Gravers come in many shapes and sizes, as shown by these illustrations by James Meek, author of "The Art Of Engraving" and a noted engraver in his own right. The manner in which the points are ground and maintained will have much to do with the success of would-be artist.

1 2 3 4 5 6 7

Bevel nos. 1 to 7

oil favored by machinists. For tougher types of steel, he increases the amount of cutting oil in the mixture.

The beginning engraver often will find that he spends as much time sharpening his tools because of broken points as he does in cutting metal to a wanted design. This usually is because the would-be artisan has not learned to hold his tool correctly. The center line of the tool should be directed squarely into the cut throughout the operation.

The chaser's hammer and chisel, as indicated, can be used for the less delicate cuts, but when it comes to using the hand gravers for shading and modeling, the beginner all too often tends to try to cut too deep. For this delicate approach, one should attempt to perfect the ability to make uniform cuts, learning to control the tool.

An obvious question, of course, is what type of tool do you use for this? The hand graver may favor the onglette, but others have found the lozenge or square gravers do the work just as well; perhaps, for them, better. As mentioned before, success is largely a matter of personal comfort. Use the tools with which you are comfortable.

The chaser's hammer used for driving the chisel is rather light in weight when compared with mechanic's or ordinary household hammers. The face of the hammer, marketed by Brownells, is available in three different diameters: 1⅛-inch, 1¼- and 1 5/16-inch. In the beginning, one probably can get by with only one of these hammers and the lightest of the three — the one with the 1⅛-inch face — usually should be the initial choice. But as one develops his talents, he will find that, when heavier cuts are required, the work will go faster and more easily with one of the heavier models.

Before you start cutting on the blade of an expensive knife made by Corbett Sigman, Bob Loveless or another of the high-priced pros, it is suggested you try engraving on bits of scrap metal to learn the skills — and whether your potential is what you'd like it to be.

Atlanta Cutlery, Box 839, Conyers, GA 30207, markets sheet brass to knifemakers for liners and other purposes, but these sheets also make admirable practice aids for engraving. Brownells also sells sheets of practice metal.

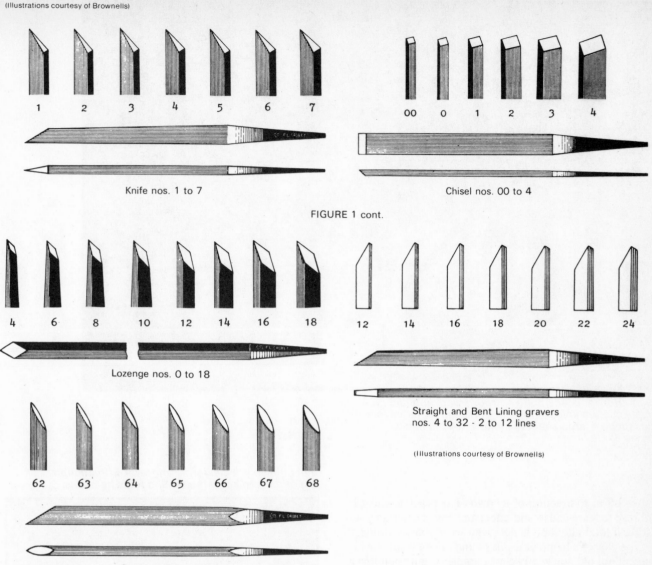

Knife nos. 1 to 7

Chisel nos. 00 to 4

FIGURE 1 cont.

Lozenge nos. 0 to 18

Straight and Bent Lining gravers
nos. 4 to 32 - 2 to 12 lines

Oval nos. 61 to 68

Each of these is a steel plate that measures two inches in width by 5½-inches in length and is .125-inch in thickness. The plates come in sets of five for a bit over $4 for the lot. They are of quality steel that is aluminum "killed" to prevent age hardening, according to Frank Brownell. Each sheet has a soft matte finish that can be worked easily with gravers.

Still another source is the Southwest Smelting & Refining Company, 10803 Composite Drive, Dallas, TX 75222. This outfit furnishes copper practice plates in several sizes.

The usual problem with the inexperienced engraver who is seeking his way is to attempt to practice on anything that's available. If you think engraving a length of steel rail from an abandoned railroad is silly, it probably is, but it's been tried. The result wasn't much to brag about, though.

As steel comes from the mill, it invariably suffers from a hard, scaled surface, if the metal has been hot rolled. Steel that has undergone the process known as cold rolling is smoother and suffers less from the rough, scale-like finish,

but it has a tough coating that is difficult for the beginning engraver to work. It's a lot easier to spend a few bucks for the practice plates offered by the organizations listed above and master the technique on softer metals. Take our word for that!

In working on the practice plate, one should choose a simple pattern, using the work to learn to control his tools. In most instances, a firm hold is all that is required, gripping the tool between the thumb and forefinger for the best control. When one has worked for a time, he will find that he can roll the edge of his cutting blade for specific cuts simply by rolling the tool between thumb and finger. This allows one to accomplish tight curves. All of this takes time and practice, of course.

When it comes to working with the hammer, the practice plate can help you learn what *not* to do. For example, it doesn't take long to learn that raising the back of the tool, increasing the angle of the bit, means that the cut is going to be deeper when the hammer strikes.

Such changes of angle also can cause the graving tool to

Gene Hoover is an engraver whose work appears on many custom knives. Here he works out an engraving design on a large sheet of metal at a knife show.

Jim English is a California engraver with enough experience to know the cutting tools he needs.

move off in a direction of its own. The practice sheet is utilized to learn cause-and-effect and how it can ruin your work, if total attention is not given what you are doing.

The chaser's hammer is not swung as one would swing his faithful old household claw hammer when pounding a nail into a stubborn two-by-four. The hammer used by the engraver is used with more of a tapping motion, causing the cutting tool to move a fraction at a time, cutting where the craftsman wants it to cut. But such short strokes also allow one to tap out a lot of strokes per minute, thus the engraving cuts will show real progress with a bit of practice in handling the hammer in conjuction with the cutting tools. Each engraver seems to develop his own technique for handling the hammer to achieve his goal. Like the other, you probably will use a hit-and-miss technique until you perfect a system that works, giving you the results you want.

While many truly experienced engravers make their own specialized tools for stippling, cutting outlines and other minute patterns, there are tools available that will simplify this sort of work and allow less potential for mistakes.

For example, there is a little device called the Micro-Scribber that features a solid carbide tip. It can be used to mark fine lines on hardened steel — even glass or jewels, if necessary — so that one can lay out a pattern on the surface before getting down to the serious business of cutting.

Brownells, for example, offers a carbide graver blank that is unshaped or one that has the end ground to a forty-five degree angle, ready for final shaping to your own

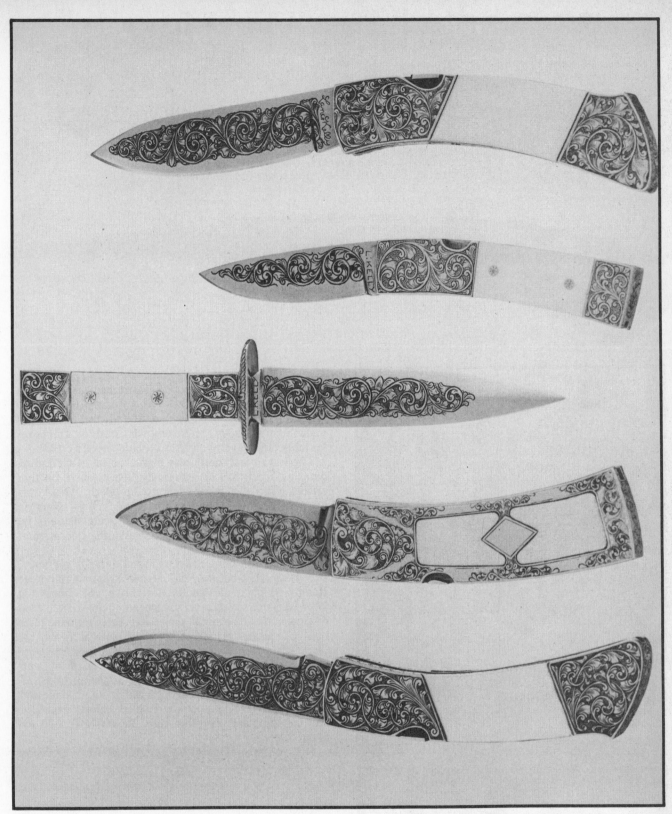

Lance Kelly is a full-time knifemaker and engraver who specializes in investor quality folding and fixed blade knives. Collectors will recognize the Florida resident's distinctive style of contemporary outlines.

Art Darakis of Ohio has been engraving for more than a dozen years and has developed his talent to this stage. Locking folders are his specialty. Darakis says he may spend up to 160 hours making and engraving his knives.

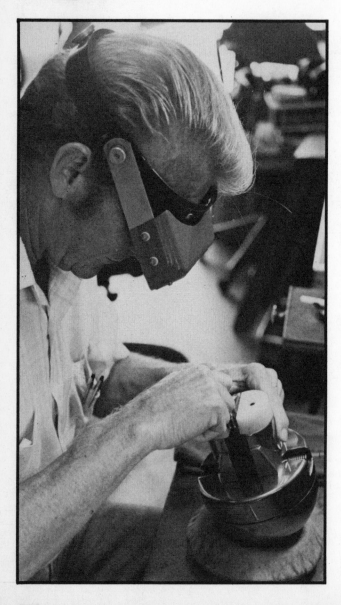

requirements. This particular instrument is designed specifically for engraving the tougher steels — those with a Rockwell hardness of more than 63C — that are used in making knife blades. Engravers who work on knives invariably have several of these carbide gravers on hand.

The Iowa-based outfit also markets a set of six dotting punches. Each has an extremely fine concave tip that creates a tiny raised dot when used properly. These dots usually are utilized in background detail. The #4 offers the largest dot and this is about the size of the shank of an ordinary straight pin. Other punches in the set are numbered as 00, 0, 1, 2, and 3.

When the day comes that you want to really get fancy, Brownells has what they call NgraveR inlay and border stamps, which are designed to simplify a time-consuming job. Using this set, one can use a center punch to make his original mark in the metal, then a star stamp from the set is used to create a star-shaped cut in the metal surface. This "hole" can be filled with silver or gold, if desired, using the tools included in the set. The kit is made up of four star stamps that range in size from one-sixteenth to three-sixteenths inch; a center punch, a punch/stamp guide and — probably most important — a detailed instruction booklet. Not including the silver and gold, the whole kit sells for about $45.

NgraveR also offers scroll stamps that are of precision

Left: Jim English works on a folder with the knife locked in his engraving vise. With experience, the vise quickly unlocks and the work is repositioned.

Above: A simple knife design is enhanced by Jim English's deep engraving. Using a different approach, knifemaker Don Karlin of Aztec, New Mexico, called upon Brown Engraving to engrave the lion bolster, below.

hardened steel for making border scrolls of the type that once were used on Winchester rifles. Since those rifles now are classified as antiques, this borders on a lost art...no pun intended.

In recent years, with the value of labor an increasingly important factor, a number of firms have introduced power engraving tools. GRS Corporation, Box 1157, Boulder, CO 10003, for example, introduced what is called the Gravermeister nearly twenty years ago.

"This is actually a miniature, self-contained jackhammer, with absolute and precise control of stroke power and speed," a company spokesman proclaims. "Since engraving is the process of selectively removing or altering a metal surface, the machine is designed to do just that."

In use, the speed of the hammer-like stroke — ranging from eight hundred to 1200 strokes per minute — and the maximum power level are set on the machine. The actual impact of each stroke then is controlled by a foot throttle. With a bit of practice, this affords a full range of strokes that will cut a hairline design or, with proper adjustment, remove greater amounts of metal as desired. The graver is chucked into a handpiece that will accept a wide range of tools. Depth of the cut is controlled, as indicated earlier, by the angle at which the handpiece is held — and the amount of throttle that is being applied.

The maker claims that "in just a few hours, even a begin-

A close-up of the engraved knife at right reveals the intricate scrollwork, obviously done by hand.

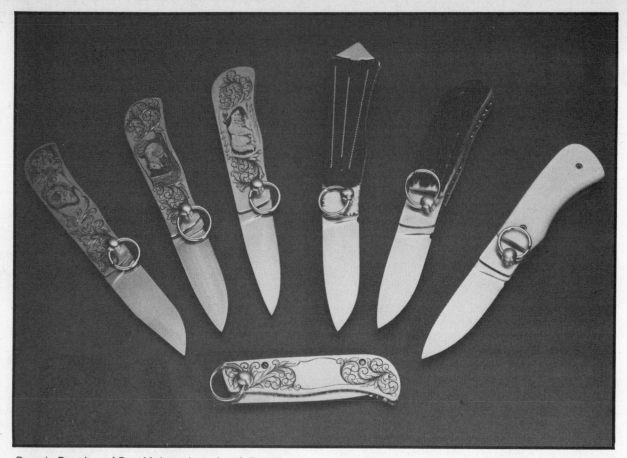

Dennis Brooker of Des Moines, Iowa is a full-time knifemaker and engraver who has not only unusual knife designs, but does fine engraving. He credits Bob and Frank Brownell for help and encouragement.

ner can be cutting clear, clean, sharp lines that would have taken months or even years to accomplish with the chasing hammer technique.''

That claim, of course, neglects to point out that more than a minor degree of artistic skill also is a requirement. The unit sells for under $1000, depending upon whether one wants a 115-volt or a 230-volt unit.

NgraveR also has an electric engraving tool that is meant to replace the hammer and chisel. It operates on the same jackhammer principle as the Gravermeister, but utilizes a flexible power shaft and a foot rheostat to create the hammering effect, rather than the air-powered approach of the Gravermeister. One can obtain one of these for as little as $300 from Brownells and several other sources.

What does all this mean? It comes down to time and money. If you are into knifemaking and doing your own decorative work as a hobby, to escape the daily worries and problems of life and career, you may tend to sneer at the idea of engraving with machinery. After all, this technique is less than twenty years old and it's a bit difficult to accept the idea that it might possibly replace centuries of careful crafting experience.

At the other extreme, if you are into serious engraving and hope to make a living at it, the only thing you really are selling is time. And the engraving tools *can* save time.

One point probably should be made, though. There are few multi-talented individuals in the world. Take a look at the motion picture business as an example. There are writers, there are actors, there are producers and there are directors. Some individuals manage to handle two of these jobs. In come cases, individuals have attempted to handle three jobs — usually failed miserably in at least one. But to the best of my knowledge, there are no hyphenates listed with the various craft guilds in Hollywood who list themselves as writer-producer-director-actor. At least, not on the same project!

You're asking, of course, what the hell Hollywood talent has to do with engraving. It's the same situation. There are knifemakers, there are scrimshanders, there are engravers. These diverse talents are all rolled up in one person's abilities only rarely. Bob Loveless, probably the daddy of modern custom knifemaking, sends out his engraving work. He admits he hasn't the talent and he'd be wasting valuable time at the bench, grinding blades, if he tried to engrave as well. Most of the other custom knifemakers feel the same: If you want an expert job done, get an expert.

So you may want to pass along that knife you've built from a scrap of steel and let an experienced engraver cut the decorative touches. After all, he's spent decades learning his craft.

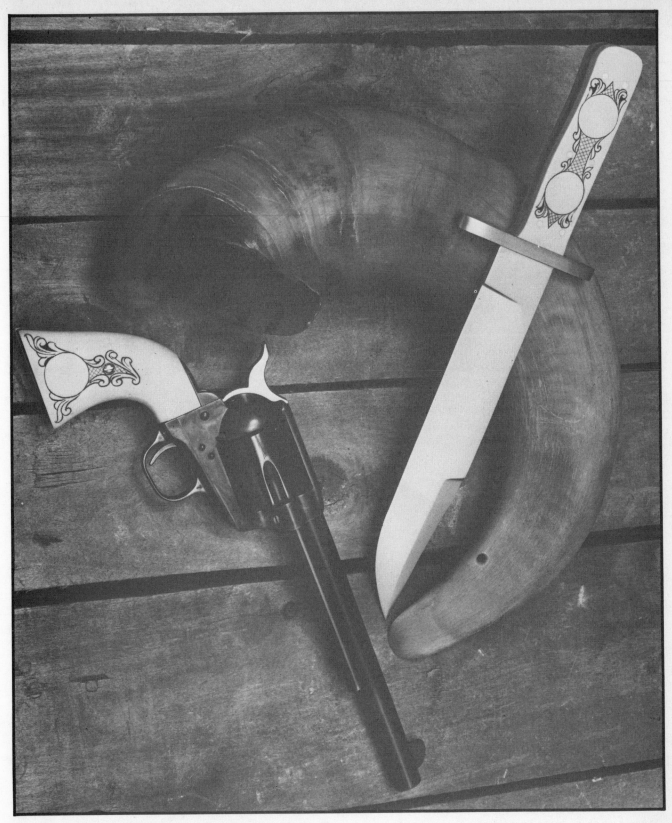

Brooker takes pride in his floral and decorative scroll work in both high and low relief. He prefers to do knife and gun presentation sets. Successful, he handles each assignment on an individual basis, first come first serve.

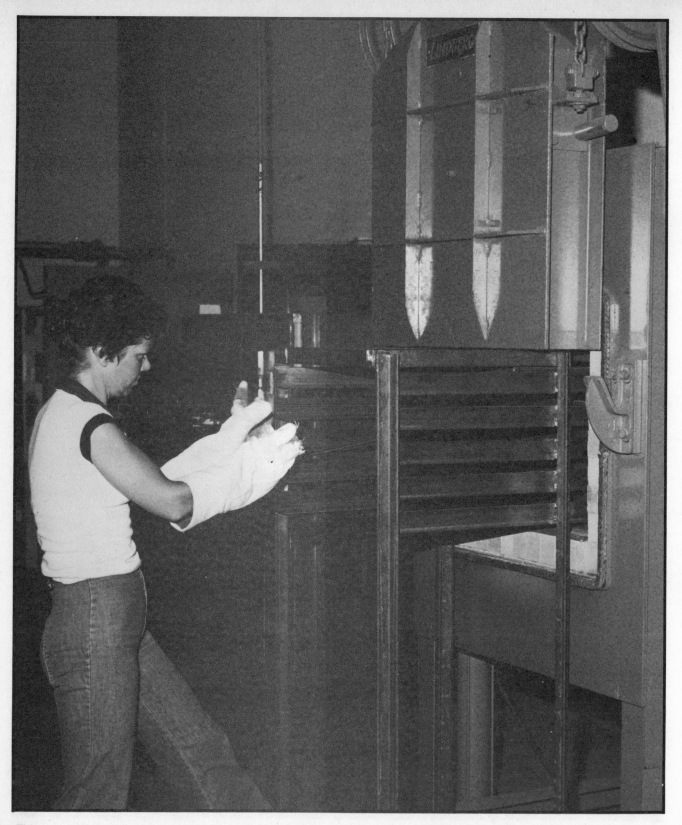

This is one of the huge heat treatment ovens at Buck Knives. The facility must handle thousands of blades per day to match the production line, far more than any custom maker. But the hardening steps are the same. These ovens are constructed at the Buck plant and provide for several shelves of blades to be loaded at a time.

Chapter 14

A TREAT FOR YOUR BLADE

Raw Steel Must Be Made Hard Enough For Knife Blades By Careful Heat Treating And Tempering

FRANKLY, the best advice we could give any knifemaker who values his time and sanity is to send out his knives to a professional heat-treater for tempering. There are a number of highly qualified and experienced heat-treating specialists around the country with plenty of background tempering custom knives. Some are, themselves, custom knifemakers.

The object of heat-treating a knife blade — or any other piece of metal — is to change its structure until it hardens; that is, reaches a specific tested hardness that is ideal for the particular steel alloy and its intended use. Some alloys can be heat-treated at home and others absolutely cannot. Some typical knifemaker steels may be tempered in your kitchen oven — if the wife doesn't mind — to a satisfactory hardness. Other complex stainless steel alloys require controlled temperatures up to 2000 degrees, followed by quenching in oil, then freezing in ice, going up and down this scale several times. Leave these processes to the professionals, is our advice.

But some blades can be heat-treated successfully at home. If you have gone to the trouble of obtaining a slab of steel, created your own unique blade design, cut it out and ground it to shape, you may want to carry out the next step yourself. After all that work, though, it might be a good idea to run a few practice sessions with metal scrap before risking your knife blank.

Steel producers publish heat-treating information and circulate it freely to industry. Professional heat-treating establishments thus have the information on hand for reference as steel comes in for hardening. The information also is printed in engineering texts and references that may be found in large public and university libraries.

If locating and wading through all the technical jargon seems too difficult or simply unintelligible for you, we recommend contacting the affable Bob Engnath at his House of Muzzleloading, 1019 East Palmer, Glendale CA 91205 and request his catalog of blades and knifemakers' supplies. Among the hundreds of useful items and knifemaking tips in the catalog, you will find heat-treating procedures for several specific knife steels. Most of what we and many other knifemakers know about heat-treating comes from Engnath and we are grateful to him for letting us share that knowledge.

Knife factories and professional heat-treating establishments have huge industrial ovens able to handle hundreds of knives per hour. They are electronically controlled, require trained personnel to operate them and are extremely expensive to build and operate. They are far beyond what we are attempting to accomplish here.

It is possible to heat-treat a blade in your garage or shop using three, or more blow torches, playing the hot flames on the steel. Heating is faster and more uniform if you build

a crude enclosure of oven brick to hold in the heat. From time to time, ceramic pottery ovens become available at swap meets or art shows; these offer a reasonable alternative which can be temperature controlled. The only drawback is that you won't be able to treat more than a few knives at a time.

Engnath went a step farther by constructing a crude, but effective heat treating oven behind his Glendale shop. The oven, itself, is not large, consisting of only a couple of layers of oven bricks placed in a frame without any mortar. The opening is at the top, covered by three slabs of brick material, hinged at one end.

The key to the set-up is a bottled gas pressure valve which he found in a surplus yard and a manifold distributor that he welded up himself. The gas feeds into an oblong distributor channel rigged with six outlets that open into as many burners inside the oven. This unit heats up rather rapidly and, after considerable experience and experimentation, Engnath can pretty much control the temperatures he needs.

If you were going to heat-treat several of your own blades or those of others, it might pay to construct something similar to what Bob Engnath has devised. You will have to be mechanically inclined and have, or know someone who has, real welding skills. Engnath swears by his machine and has heat-treated any number of blades in it.

Bob Engnath of the House of Muzzleloading, stands beside his heat tempering oven, constructed outside his Glendale, California shop. To give an idea of scale, Engnath stands more than six and a half feet tall in thin-soled boots.

Engnath points to the distributor manifold he constructed to feed gas to the five jet burners inside the oven. The gas inlet and control valve are located beneath the pipes.

Above: Paul Bos heat-treats blades for many of the top custom knifemakers from around the world. Bos, who has been in the business for more than thirty years, takes pride in furnishing his clients with warp-free blades.

Paul Bos (1900 Weld Boulevard, El Cajon, CA 92020) is a professional heat-treater with years of experience with custom knife blades. He currently contracts with Buck Knives to use their ovens and equipment on a non-interference basis, to treat his customers' blades.

Bos began his career as a heat-treater more than thirty years ago, just out of high school. Some of his first custom knives on which he worked were made by Al Buck, son of the founder and father of the current president of Buck Knives, Charles Buck. One thing lead to another and Bos was soon in the custom knife heat-treating business on a full-time basis.

Paul Bos believes that every knife blade should be stress-relieved before it is heat-treated. He says that several stresses may be established within a piece of steel, caused by cutting, grinding or forging the blades. These stresses should be relieved before treatment or the blade may warp. Not all blades of all types of steel will stress-warp, but Bos believes he should not take the chance; he stress-relieves each blade before starting the heat-treating process.

Bos uses the same ovens for stress relief. He heats the blade to 1200 degrees F. before actually beginning the heat-treating. He claims that, in most cases, the extra step will prevent the blades from warping.

If possible, blades to be heat-treated should be hung from wires within the oven so as to not touch the sides or top of the enclosure. If wiring is not possible, place the blades upon an extra oven brick or suspend the blade across an opening between two bricks. The point is that the metal of the blade should not touch anything else of metal — other than the suspension wire — while being heated.

One of the most sophisticated home blade treatment set-ups is that of custom knifemaker Jim Pugh. He has put his oven in an out-of-the-way corner of his shop.

Such contact will cause uneven heating and eventual warping.

Another way to end up with a warped blade is to immerse it in the quench material improperly. Different alloys require different quenches: water, oil, air, dry ice — or a combination of several. Blades should be quenched by carefully and evenly lowering the metal into the medium, tip first, then thrusting it downward without a pause. The blade should be lowered vertically with no side-to-side or tipping movement. Once cooled, the blade should be checked and, if necessary, re-heated, forged straight and re-quenched. Avoiding a warped blade is another area in which the experienced knife blade heat-treater more than earns his fee.

The first steel group under consideration is oil-quenched and hardened. The steels commonly used by knifemakers include: 0-1, 0-6, 1050 to 1095, W-1, W-2 and 5160. For 0-1 and 0-6, at least a half hour in an oven at 1450 degrees F. is recommended. The others on this first list may be heated by torch.

Before beginning heat-treating for any custom blade, Paul Bos insists the maker label it with the exact type of steel. Each alloy requires different treatment.

Ovens such as the one Chuck Buck is leaning on are far beyond any requirements of the home knifemaker, but heating and cooling steps are the same for any blade.

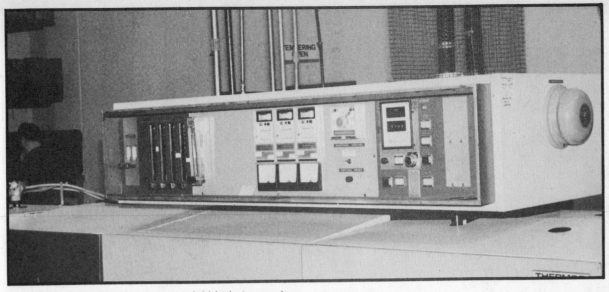

Electronic controls of a commercial blade tempering oven are sophisticated and highly accurate. This model is located at the El Cajon, California Buck factory.

The blades below are running through heat treatment at the Alcas Cutlery plant in Olean, New York. The oddly shaped blades are for a Solution Spirit Knife.

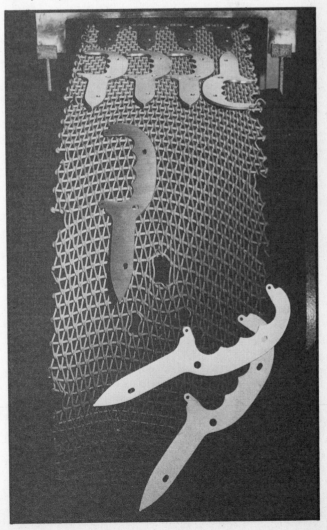

Bob Engnath says correct temperatures are difficult to determine by eye, even for the professional. He lists a simple test to determine when the steel is hot enough to harden: the use of a simple magnet. When a magnet no longer will be attracted to the blade, the steel is hot enough. Engnath urges frequent magnet testing, because the hardening temperature may be reached sooner than you expect. If the blade is overheated, it can shrink when quenched and thus be ruined.

These steels are quenched in oil that is heated to 100 degrees F. They can and should be tempered immediately after quench-cooling. Clean off the quench oil so it won't smell and the tempering may be done in the kitchen oven.

Tempering is done by temperature and color. Clean off a section of the blade — the tang is a good area to use — so the bright metal is visible. The following are draw temperatures for 0-1; the other steels may be a bit cooler. At 400 degrees, 0-1 steel will show a pale straw color and be at a Rockwell C-scale hardness reading of about 61; a bit hard. At 480 to 500 degrees F., the exposed metal will show deep straw yellow and be rated at RC 58-59 which is just about ideal for this steel. Tempered blades should be quenched again in oil for at least thirty minutes.

A-2 steel is fairly straightforward to heat-treat. It requires a double temper — an hour and a half each time — with a still-air quench after each heat cycle. The oven should be pre-heated first to 1250 degrees F., the blade loaded, then the heat increased to between 1725 and 1775 F. Each heat temperature is the same. After heating, a 400-degree F. draw will result in an RC of 61; 500 F., RC 59; 600 F., RC 58. A-2 steel resists warping and is ideal for thin or long blades such as those on a fish fillet knife.

D-2 steel requires slightly higher temperatures for successful heat-treating. The blade is placed directly in an

These blades and locking springs are being hardened through heat treatment at the Camillus Cutlery plant.

Five blades have been heated to glowing red for heat treatment at the Western Cutlery factory in Longmont, Colorado. The flame is gas-fired, carefully controlled.

oven at 1825 to 1875 F. and left for twenty minutes. It is quenched in still air. To temper, an oven at 450 F. will produce an RC of 59-60; 500 F., RC 56-57. Double tempering is recommended for D-2; one more hour at 1000 degrees F. when tempering should result in an RC 59-60 hardness.

Stainless steel alloys are more complicated and difficult because of the temperatures and procedures required. Stainless 440C steel requires an oven at 1875 F. to 1925 F. for thirty minutes. After heating, the blades may be quenched in air or in pre-heated oil at 225 F. to 275 F. Engnath urges extreme care when quenching and handling 440C, as it is prone to warp badly if not quenched properly. Temper 440C at 325 F. to reach RC 59-60; 400 F., RC 58; 500 F., RC 56; 600 F., RC 55. After an hour of tempering, the blades should be quenched again in air or warm oil.

After first quench, 440C will benefit from super cooling. It will result in two additional hardness points and better crystalline structure and toughness. The blade should be cooled to 100 F. below zero at the beginning of the process, then brought down to minus 325 F. Achieving that low a temperature is not easy; some people use dry ice and acetone, a process which is full of danger. The blade should be held at 325 F. for a half hour. This is really not a job for a beginner!

After the super cooling, 440C blades may be tempered in the normal manner. Hardness will be higher than normal and flexibility will be improved.

In this operation, Camillus knife blades are hardened by first immersing them in hot lead, followed by a quench in oil. Safety precautions are vitally important.

This is the famous Rockwell steel hardness testing machine. After treating the tempering, the blade is placed under point pressure to determine hardness.

If you have hammered your own soft Damascus steel, it, too, may be heat-treated. Use an open fire or forge to heat the blade; the same forge used to heat the Damascus in the first place. When the blade has reached a dull red color, take it out of the fire and try the magnet test. The magnet no longer will be attracted when the temperature is right. Test often through the heating process so as to not let the metal get too hot.

For most Damascus, an oil quench works best. If you know for a fact that the hard steel used in making the Damascus in the first place requires water quenching, then you will want to use that quench.

There are industry charts published for such stainless steels as 154CM and ATS-34, the latter imported from Japan. Both steels are extremely popular with many custom knifemakers. But the difficulties of reaching and maintaining the complicated steps of high temperatures, deep freezing and time demands by the home workman seem almost insurmountable.

For these and other special stainless steels, such as AEBL and Vasco Wear, we suggest the beginning knifemaker contact his nearest professional heat-treater. After you have gone to all that work, it would seem a shame to ruin your blade while attempting to heat-treat it yourself. Most of the successful custom knifemakers we know send all their work out. They spend their time and talents in making knives.

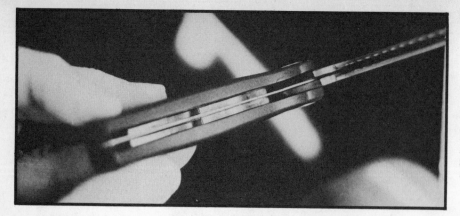

Pocketknives by nature live in pockets and purses. They present special care problems with the well into which the blade closes. This is the two blade Coleman/Western Model 952. Both blades lock open.

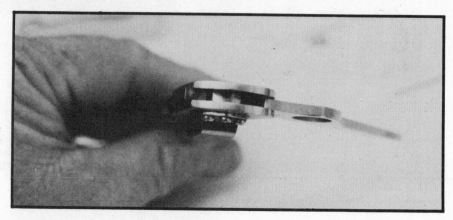

A folder has several moving parts which must be kept lubricated, as well as clean. This is the Spyderco serrated-edge folding knife.

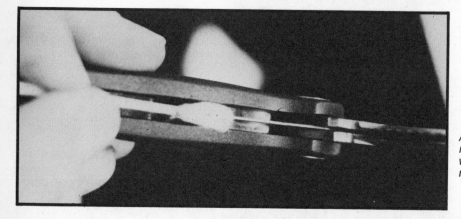

A cotton-tip stick soaked in alcohol may be used to get down into the well, left. Use the cotton after removing most clutter with forced air.

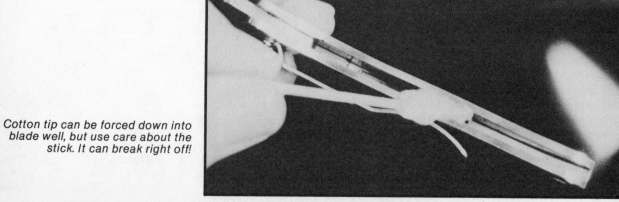

Cotton tip can be forced down into blade well, but use care about the stick. It can break right off!

Chapter 15

KNIFE CARE AND REPAIR

If Your Knife Is Damaged Through Use Or Abuse, Maybe It Can Be Fixed, Using These Techniques

KNIVES SOMETIMES do wear out. But most of the problems with knives stem from abuse and neglect. The best is, of course, to treat your knives kindly and don't let them become damaged. Prevention is the key word.

A knife is neither a screwdriver nor pry bar. It is not a chisel, a hole digger or a can opener. Yes, there are some folders with blades made for these purposes, but we're talking here about the regular cutting blade. Both authors of this book admit to abusing knives — military knives and bayonets — under unpleasant conditions: opening C-ration cans, cutting the metal straps around ammunition boxes and digging holes in the ground. For several reasons, we don't recommend it. The old Marine Corps drill instructors' adage of taking care of your rifle and it will take care of you also applies to knives.

The first rule of knife care is to keep the blade sharp at all times. A sharp blade is less likely to slip or hang up during a difficult cutting job. A sharp blade also is less likely to cause a nasty cut, because it is more easily controlled. It just makes good sense to keep the blade sharp. We have included a complete chapter of this book on the art and science of blade sharpening.

Any knife blade will break under enough pressure. Use it as a lever or pry bar and you are almost certain to snap it.

If the blade is one which you have spent numerous hours and lots of effort making, you certainly don't want to experience such a disaster.

One of the most common abuses of which we are aware is attempting to use a knife as a chisel or splitter. A good field knife may be used to cut kindling, but it must be done with care and without undue force. We have seen — perhaps you have, too — the uninformed hammering on the back of the blade with a hammer or rock, trying to cut through some tough substance or using the butt end of the handle as a hammer.

True, there are some knives which are designed with a hammer-like butt, but even these are not intended to drive nails or break rocks. There will be emergency situations when these tasks will have to be done with a knife, but they should not be routine activities.

Beware of foreign substances! The only substance not subject to corrosion damage is gold. Most of us do not carry gold knives into the field. Everything else is subject to varying degrees of corrosion, given enough time. Even stainless steel is not impervious to everything with which it might come in contact. Stainless still can stain.

Handle materials are even more likely to sustain damage from chemicals, blood, paint, extremes of hot and cold or from impact if dropped or struck. All natural materials

Cotton swab dipped in alcohol cleans the well, leaving no residual chemical to commence damaging corrosion.

If the knife, such as this Spyderco, has a locking mechanism, it must be kept clean. Use only the tiniest drop of oil and wipe off the excess after penetration.

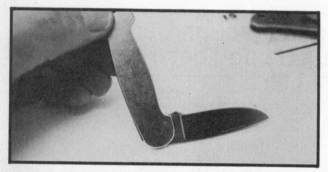

The little Jimmy Lile Gentleman's folder has been carried by one of the authors for years. It makes no bulge in the pocket and has a narrow profile.

Dirt and lint have accumulated in the hinge pin area. Folders should be cleaned and oiled on regular basis.

such as horn, wood and especially real ivory will crack and/or discolor in time if they become too dry or too wet or if exposed to temperature extremes. The naturals are beautiful to look at and feel, but are not the most reliable when working in the field under harsh conditions. Even our favorite Micarta handle material can be damaged by stress or impact. Micarta is great for knife handles, but cannot withstand every assault.

Heat is both the friend and the enemy of knife blades and handles. On a camping or hunting trip, while enjoying your campfire, be careful with your good knife. Most handle materials will melt or burn if in contact with a flame. Some epoxy cements will soften if heated enough; you don't want your handle slabs falling off in the middle of your camp dinner.

Keep your blade clean. Knives are intended to be used to cut things and they can be in contact with corrosive substances while cutting. What you must do is not allow that substance to stay in contact. Always wipe off your blade after use. Corrosion is insidious, taking place over months and years. By the time you notice it, it may be too late to prevent real damage.

Be especially careful when using a sheath knife in the field and replacing it in the sheath. Water, blood or many chemicals will do their dirty work quickly on a blade left inside the sheath. A blade of non-stainless tool steel can rust in a matter of hours, if stored warm and wet. It takes only seconds to wipe off the blade before it is inserted in the sheath. Those seconds may save you plenty!

Some risk is unavoidable. If you are working in the rain or snow, the knife and sheath will be wet. You may have to carry the knife wet for hours or days. But look after the blade as soon as you can and remember that under some circumstances, the knife may save your life, if it is kept in good condition.

Folding knives present special problems. All kinds of evil things can lurk down inside the blade liners, carrying out their subversive activities. Dirt, lint, bits of paper or anything which might hold moisture will accumulate inside the well, starting a rust attack. Keeping folders clean and dry takes special effort.

Aside from carefully examining the blade and the liner well from time to time, the well needs to be kept clean. The simple step of blowing out the well often is the answer for some, but remember that your warm breath also carries moisture. Depending upon the air temperature and humidity, you may be adding to the risk of damage to your folding knife. A simple expedient is to use a cotton-tipped stick or a toothpick with a bit of tissue wound around it to get down in the well to clean it out. Use whatever is handy, but don't neglect it.

A folding knife has moving parts that must be kept lubricated to prevent wear. The tiniest amount of oil is all any folder needs to keep it in top operating condition. Too much oil may actually trap moisture on the metal and probably will cause a stain on trousers or in a purse. Use less than a drop and wipe it off with a cloth or tissue. Too much oil also will attract lint from your pocket, so just the slightest bit of lube should be sufficient. Remember the locking system, if there is one. Let the oil penetrate, then wipe off any visible excess.

Every blade will benefit from a light coating of oil from time to time. The best time to apply is right after sharpening. Honing oil will fight corrosion, but a wipe of regular machine oil is a better idea.

When applying oil or when sharpening with honing oil, use care to not let any excess reach the handle. Natural materials will absorb oil and eventually become discolored or soft. Most man-made handle materials are impervious to petroleum products, but some may discolor.

The bottom line is that any knife should be treated with the same respect as any other precision tool. Keep the metal dry, clean and lightly oiled. Don't abuse your knives; use them only for what they were designed for. The knives you make should last for generations, with a little help from you.

We know a number of custom makers who got started knifemaking replacing the handle slabs on folding knives — as a matter of fact, they still do. The slabs may not be damaged or worn; perhaps the owner wants a new, customized look for the knife. New handle slabs will give the knife a whole new look.

Buck Knives of El Cajon, California, has produced millions of knives over the past several decades. Inevitably, some of their products have been damaged. Buck guarantees the company's knives against faulty workmanship or materials and will repair or replace any knife damaged by any means other than neglect or abuse. Most common complaints are from folder owners. Buck will take care of most damaged knives sent to the factory after an inspection to determine the extent and probable cause of the damage.

There are clear cases of abuse or damage which obviously are no fault of the manufacturer. In such cases, Buck will offer to repair the knife — if it can be repaired — at a nominal cost. The owner is so notified and a decision is made. Otherwise, the knife is returned to the sender. Infrequently, old Buck knives which may have been purchased at a swap meet or garage sale will be sent to the factory in hopeless condition. These are returned to the sender in the same condition.

Many of the knives sent back for repair have damaged blades. If there is enough metal left, the remaining steel can be ground down to approximately the original shape and the knife can continue a useful life.

Many times the broken blade is too short to be re-

Only the smallest amount of oil should be left on the blade. Too much will attract more dirt and may stain clothing. Wipe and soak up excess lubrication.

ground, so it must be replaced by one of the factory personnel. This usually can be accomplished with folders, but almost never for fixed-blade knives. Sometimes, in these cases, the owner will be offered a replacement knife in place of the repair.

If the blade — in the case of a folder — or handle slabs must be replaced, this is a relatively simple process for a skilled knifemaker. If the knife design is still in production by Buck, the repairs are simply a matter of disassembling the old knife and replacing the defective components. Knife designs which were made to special order or those no longer in the line require more extensive work.

At Buck, a cutler who has more than eighteen years service with the company does most of the repairs. Repair is not his full-time assignment, but he often has a dozen or more repairs to make a day.

His first step is to determine what the knife needs. He will examine the blade, check for loose rivets, pins and handle parts. In the case of folders, he checks the operation of the blade and the lock, if there is one, to determine that everything is tight and smooth or whether those parts need attention.

Most repairs are made to Buck folders. The pivot pin and the blade itself are the parts most commonly damaged. In either case, the first step is for the pivot pin to be drifted out of the knife. The Buck repairman has a special metal plate that has been drilled through with holes of various sizes for this purpose. He places the offending pin over the appropriate hole, sets a drift punch over the top of the pin and taps it out. The pin falls into a catch beneath his workbench.

Unless you are going into the knife repair business, you do not need anything so elaborate. If you have a bench vise, the jaws can be adjusted to allow the offending pin to fall between them when it is tapped out. In our case, you will probably want to save any pins thus removed so they can be re-used. If the pins or rivets are damaged beyond re-use, you will have to either contact the manufacturer for a replacement or fabricate a substitute.

The same pins or rivets will have to be driven out to replace damaged handle material. Your experience in building a couple of simple folding knives comes in handy now. Having a basic understanding of the construction and operation of folders, one usually can determine what must

A section of Buck Knives' factory is set aside for repair work. Most of the damaged or worn knives sent in are folders, as shown at left.

be done to repair them. The repairmen at Buck Knives have an advantage over most of us in that they have unlimited access to spare parts made expressly for the knife model under repair. But we can accomplish some simple repair work, when needed.

In some cases, the only damage to a folding knife's operation is a bent pivot pin. Once the pin has been drifted out of the knife, careful work with your ball peen hammer can straighten the pin for re-use. The pin metal is relatively soft, so care must be exercised while hammering. Too much pressure will flatten the pin out of round and it might be difficult or impossible to reinsert. Work slowly and carefully, rolling the pin frequently as you use light hammer blows to get it as straight as possible. The edge of the hammer should not be used for the same reason. Work only with the flat face.

To repair or replace handle slabs, the knife will have to be dismantled completely, whether folder or sheath knife. The slabs may be held only with pins or rivets or they may be held to the liners or the tang with epoxy cement. If this is the case, the work becomes a bit more complicated.

As we have learned, two-part epoxy cement will soften when heated to its liquid state. The difficulty is in determining what the melting point of a given cement might be. If the handle repair or replacement is for a knife you have made, the problem is considerably reduced. Presumably, you have retained the partly used containers of epoxy and the melting temperature is listed on the labels. Or you may simply remember the brand and type, so an unused package can be consulted to find the correct temperature.

If the type of cement and its specifications are unknown — and this can happen with a factory-made knife — you will have to do a bit of experimentation. Most commercially available two-part epoxy cement will liquify at about 400 degrees F. It can be done in a kitchen oven. Some cements will soften well below that temperature, which is the reason why some custom and factory knives are not "dishwasher-proof."

One amateur maker we know has used the following method with success: He starts by placing a sheet of aluminum foil on a cookie sheet or other shallow pan to be placed in the oven. The platform is placed in the oven as the oven pre-heats to 400 degrees. The offending knife is placed on the aluminum sheet and allowed to heat up. The foil helps the oven heat up faster and protects the oven if any heated cement should happen to drip off the knife.

Observe and test the knife frequently to determine if and when the epoxy softens. Test with a pair of pliers and another blade, wearing protective insulated gloves. The knife will be hot!

If the technique works, the broken handle parts can be pulled off the knife tang or liners with pliers. Before the residual cement hardens again, clean off as much as possible using a metal spatula, screwdriver or knife blade. The more that can be taken off at this point, the easier the final clean-up task will be.

Most likely, the broken handle parts eventually can be discarded, but don't toss them out just yet. If there is enough left of the broken slab, save it long enough to trace out a pattern for a new one or two. You can trace it onto a sheet of thin cardboard or heavy paper which can, in turn, be traced onto your selected handle material. Check out our earlier chapter on selecting handle materials and the chapter on handle repair for details on this part of the project.

If the knife needing repair is a factory-made knife and/or

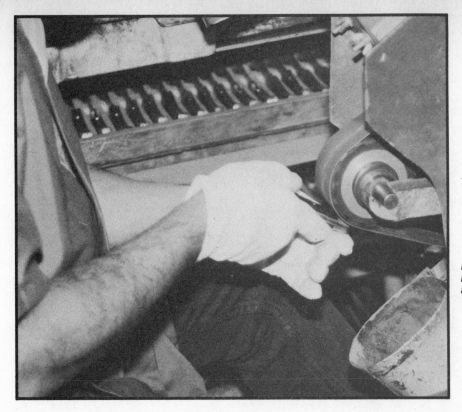

If seriously damaged, repairing a Buck knife is not unlike rebuilding a new one. Techniques are the same.

unless you are a rather skilled knifemaker, replacing a broken folding knife blade could be quite difficult. Producing a small, perfectly fitting new blade which will function as well as the original may be more than most of us want to attempt. On the other hand, if the knife is rather inexpensive or if you want to gain some valuable experience, you may wish to buy a second knife of the exact model as the damaged one and cannibalize the parts. This is an ideal way of gaining some valuable experience with small folders. In this case, all one need do is take both knives apart and repair the broken knife with the parts from the other.

The action of a folder is always checked for smooth operation and safety by the Buck factory repair staff. The locking mechanism can be broken or damaged, leaving the knife in an unsafe condition. Wearing gloves and using care learned during nearly two decades of experience, the Buck repairman always opens and closes the blade — or blades — several times to feel for uneven, rough action. Then he carefully tests the blade lock by forcing the open blade against the lock. This is done by pressing the back of the blade tip against the workbench. If the blade shows any movement at all, it is an indication that something serious may be wrong.

Another test consists of grasping the open blade from the back — there is always a danger of a slip and a serious wound, so be careful — and test it for side-to-side movement. If the blade pivots open and closes smoothly, there will be a slight amount of movement, but it should not be excessive. It is difficult to determine how much is too much movement; it should not feel sloppy or loose. The main pivot pin can be replaced, if the blade seems to give too much. If the folding blade is to be replaced anyway, it might be a good idea to replace the pivot pin at the same time. That is what the Buck people do.

Replacing the handle with new or repaired slabs means following the steps used when you were making your first simple folder. On larger folders, you may wish to follow the lead of many factories and not use cement for the handles. It will be your choice.

With your favorite knife back together and functioning like new, the last step is to buff it up and sharpen the blade.

Grind down the ends of pins and rivets flush with the new surfaces and smooth out any nicks and deep scratches. Work down the area near deep gouges, but not so far as to weaken a part or spoil design line.

A good buffing can make the knife look like new, as well as hide any minor dings and imperfections which still may be present. Simply cleaning up an old or neglected knife often is all the work necessary to make it look like new. This brings us to the care needed if we are to avoid repair.

One interesting way to learn about knives and knife construction, especially folders, is to disassemble several of them. An easy, inexpensive way is to visit a number of garage sales, swap meets and gun shows to take a look at old folding knives. There should be several around that are cheap enough — some with damage — that you can afford four or five. Remove the handle slabs and drift out or cut the various pins and rivets. If it proves too difficult to put them back together, you have gained considerable knowledge and will have a supply of spare parts for later repairs.

Some knives cannot be repaired. The Buck repair shop receives a number of knives from owners which are too far gone to be fixed. When every part has to be replaced, you end up with a new knife. If your broken knife turns out to be in this category, you should know already how to make a new one.

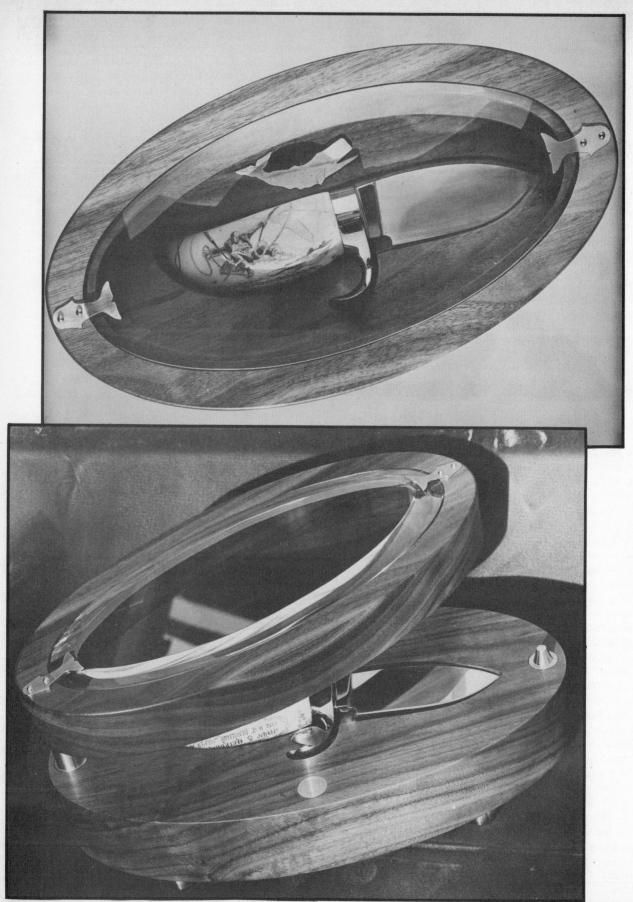

Here's a unique display case made by H.J. Schneider for a custom knife that used a whale tooth as its handle. In this example, the case is on a par with the knife in concept and execution, with intense attention to fine details such as the beveled oval plate glass cover held by clips shaped like stylized whales and the novel pilot system.

Chapter 16

KNIFE CASES

Display Cases Or Storage Cases Can
Be Produced In Several Variations
And Levels Of Excellence, As Outlined Here

EXCEPTIONAL KNIVES are objects of art in their own right and pride of ownership creates a natural urge to put them where others may see and admire them. Whether or not that is a good idea depends upon a number of factors. One of the primary considerations, from the viewpoint of the owner, is retention of ownership. If you put knives on display and they get ripped off, you've done something injudicious and it's too late for regrets.

That's to say the security of the display area is a key point. In the present marketplace, a small number of really choice knives — your own or another maker's — can represent an investment of several thousand dollars. That means their safekeeping warrants all the taut security you can bring to bear.

Display cases can be marvels of ingenuity and dazzling craftsmanship. Accompanying photos show details of one H.J. Schneider constructed for a unique knife he made several years ago. The handle of the knife was a whale's tooth, ornately scrimshawed with a picture of a luckless whaler with the harpoon line fouled around his peg leg.

The woodwork of the case is a choice grade of walnut, with a recess painstakingly inletted to accept the knife. In overall shape, the case is an oval and the lid carries a matching oval of plate glass, its edges exquisitely beveled and held in place by a pair of clips in the shape of stylized whales.

Schneider made that case himself, and he is a craftsman with abilities far beyond any we command. The pictures of the Schneider case are offered as examples of what can be done, but the exact details of its construction are not readily available for passing along.

We can, however, draw upon experience to offer some comments on the procedures for producing utilitarian cases that are not all that unpleasant to contemplate. The general process applies to making cases for the carrying, storage or display of knives and several related artifacts. We shall cover the bedrock basics, then list some approaches that will improve the end product to a useful extent.

As with many other projects and activities, your first product may not be a true masterpiece but, as you turn out further examples, you can expect to build skill and know-how to show substantial improvements. Perhaps, in time, you may be able to equal or even excel Schneider's whale-tooth knife case, but you're going to have to make a lot of that progress on your own steam and initiative.

For starters, we're going to construct a basic flat box, slit it about its perimeter, attach hinges at the rear and one or more catches at the front. Required equipment includes a table saw, with suitable blades, as noted, some gluing clamps, some glue, sandpaper and other minor stuff found about the shop of people who enjoy puttering with such projects. If you have already made a couple custom knives, you will have the tools on hand.

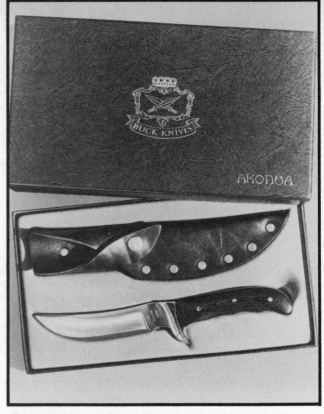

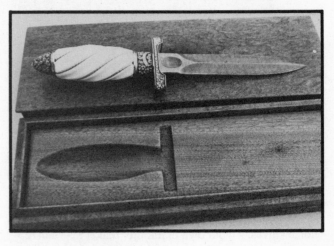

Cases can be relatively informal affairs, such as this box with interior padding in which Buck Knives ships their Akonua knife and its accompanying sheath.

Above, H.J. Schneider with a case for the Cobra custom knife, shown in greater detail on the facing page. Right, another Schneider case for a fancy dagger, with the wood inletted to accommodate the handle and hilt areas.

There are a great many hardwoods, many of them quite exotic and some of those offer great potential as the working material. If this is one of your early explorations into box-making, we suggest a more prosaic material, such as clear white pine or the like. We'll get back to the sensuous hardwoods after a little while.

Solid, whole wood — as opposed to plywood — is rarely available in thicknesses less than .75-inch: the nominal one-inch boards. If you build a case of such material, it is apt to come out rather gross and klutzy. What that means is that you have to set up and operate your own personal sawmill to obtain planks or slats of thinner dimensions.

Given a table saw with an eight- or ten-inch blade, it's possible to crank the blade as high as it will go and make cuts to depths of about 2.2 to 3.5 inches, thus producing planks of that width in the desired thickness. The planks, in turn, can be edge-glued to produce wider pieces at the selected thickness.

The edge-gluing jig can be made from a piece of particle board, with a strip of real wood glued along one edge to brace the workpiece against. Particle board serves well for the purpose, as it is relatively warp-free. Be sure to put a piece of waxed paper beneath the glued joint to keep the workpiece from adhering to the particle board.

Any of several glues can be used. We have found the

Plexiglas is an acrylic plastic that is well suited for use in knife displays, being unbreakable in normal use. It can be joined by this solvent adhesive.

A small applicator, of plastic resistant to the solvent, can be used to dispense solvent for joining pieces of Plexiglas.

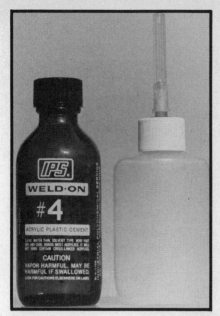

Together, the solvent and dispensing bottle make a handy means to "glue" pieces of Plexiglas for display cases.

Surely one of the most unfriendly looking knives ever made, this is H. J. Schneider's custom Cobra knife, used in the Sylvester Stallone film of the same name. Schneider built this case for storage or display.

aliphatic resin types, such as Titebond or Elmer's Carpenters' Glue (creamy yellow in color, rather than the white of plain Elmer's glue) to be satisfactory. Such glues, it should be noted, are not waterproof and, if exposed to moisture over a substantial span of time, will allow the glued joint to come apart. That is not a problem for customary uses of boxes such as we have in mind, as they are protected from the elements under most circumstances.

A good working thickness for planks used in constructing typical boxes is about 5/16-inch. You can get two such planks from a .75-inch piece of basic material, losing the width of the blade cut (kerf) in sawing. Depending upon the kerf width of the given saw blade, you may wish to slice

your planks a trifle thinner. If you cut the planks too thin, say under .25-inch or so, the resulting boxes will be rather flimsy. It's largely a matter of taste and proportion. If the box is quite small, you can do nicely with .25-inch stock, provided you do not anticipate it will be subjected to undue stresses in use.

After sawing the planks and before assembling, the stock should be sanded to remove any roughness left by the saw blade. You can use a belt sander or one of the palm sanders such as the admirable unit from Makita. The effective strategy is to use fine-cut papers, 80-grit or finer, and suitable patience to avoid removing too much stock. If

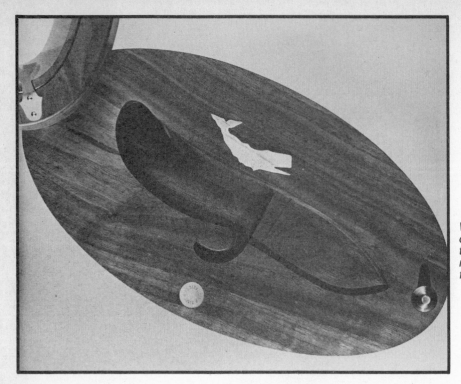

With its cover pivoted fully open, you can see how skillfully Schneider inletted the solid block of choice walnut that makes up the lower portion of the case for his whale-tooth knife, seen earlier.

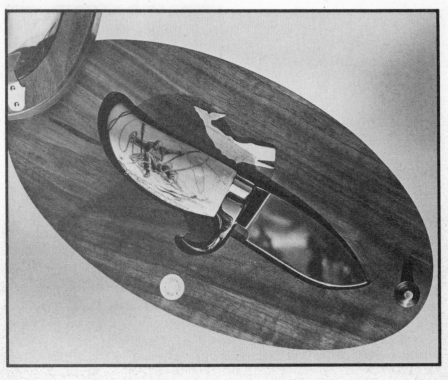

Note how neatly the knife nestles into its recess, with hardly too much room to get a good hold on it for removal.

you've edge-glued some plank to serve as the top and bottom of the box, it's quite important to sand those to a uniform thickness before assembly.

A box, in its most primitive form, can be made by butt-gluing the ends to the sides, or *vice versa,* then going on to glue the top and bottom to the basic frame. Quite probably, you will need to true the top and bottom to the framework by removing excess stock. That can be done by judicious use of the table saw, followed by powered or hand sanding.

Once the basic box has been completed to your satisfaction, you can adjust the rip fence on the table saw and slit it around the perimeter to separate the upper portion from the bottom. With that done, it remains a simple matter of installing hinges at the rear and a catch or catches at the front, plus adding such padding and lining as you may wish.

Both the working strength and eye-appeal of the ends

Note how neatly the knives nestle into their recesses, with sufficient room for lifting the knives from their recesses.

With a piece of glass or Plexiglas in the lid, cases such as this one are well suited to display the contents and, in the meantime, protect them from dirt.

and sides of the basic framework can be augmented by using mitered joints, rather than butt joints. In so doing, no end-grain remains exposed and the area of the glued joints is increased to a useful extent.

Apart from mitering the corners, further possibilities include box-lock and dovetailed corners, as well as the reinforced miter. Both the box-lock and dovetail joints require special equipment and know-how. The reinforced miter, on the other hand, is quite simple. All you need to do

is cut some strips of wood in triangular cross-section, at angles of ninety, forty-five and forty-five degrees, then cut them to suitable lengths and glue them into place on the inner corners of the perimeter framework. This results in a notably strong corner joint, with no more than minor encroachments into the box interior.

If you wish to produce a box with no exposed edges, you can cut both the top and bottom edges of the side pieces to a forty-five-degree angle, then go on to miter all the edges of

Hinges can be full-length, concealed affairs or as in this example, simple and inexpensive hinges from a local hardware store can be used, depending upon the preference of the maker and/or the final owner of case.

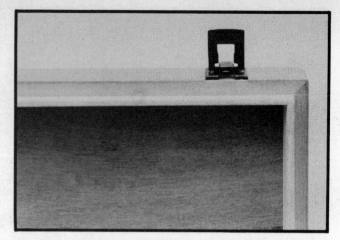

As discussed, an inner liner can be added to the lower portion of the homemade case, adding usefully to the strength and appearance of the finished product.

This case had the upper and lower edges of the basic framework mitered, with matching miters on the top and bottom pieces, leaving all edges neatly concealed.

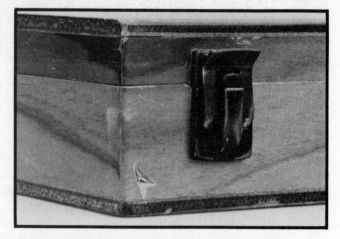

A case similar to the one at left, but with the upper and lower edges of the frame left square, resulting in the somewhat unsightly exposed edges of plywood covers.

the upper and lower covers in the same manner. Doing so demands a high degree of painstaking precision and we would suggest making your first box or two with exposed edges around the upper and lower covers, going on to the fully mitered approach after you've accumulated some experience.

The basic perimeter frame can be assembled with inexpensive corner clamps to hold the wood in alignment as the glue dries. Glue that oozes from the joint can be cleaned up with a putty knife and dampened paper towel. Glue should be applied sparingly to both mating surfaces and distributed evenly with a putty knife or similar tool. You'll find it a welcome convenience to have a small container of water and some paper towels handy for washing the glue off your fingertips.

The upper and lower covers can be glued to the framework

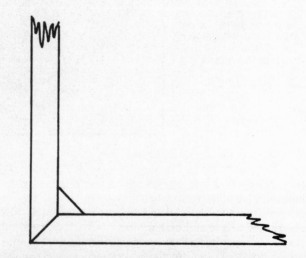

As discussed, the basic mitered joint can be reinforced by gluing a triangular filler strip in corners of joint.

A padded knife case with slide closure running around three sides, here in its closed condition. The same case appears in the lower photo here.

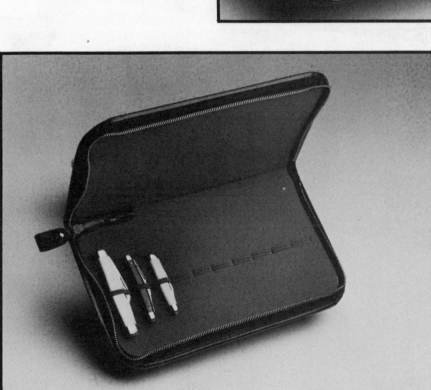

This case has elastic loops to prevent knives from shifting.

simultaneously, as there is little if anything to be gained in gluing them in place one at a time. Usually, C-clamps will hold the assembly in place, with strips of scrap wood to prevent the jaws of the C-clamps from inflicting unsightly dings in the wood of the case. We would counsel against trying to do this by weighting the assembly down on a flat surface. Unless the surface is dead-level, the pieces are apt to migrate before the glue sets up, leaving a sorry-looking mess.

If you don't wish to cut your own planks and edge-glue for the larger pieces, it works reasonably well to use plywood, in .25-inch thickness, provided you can find some surfaces with decent-looking wood. You will need a fine-toothed saw blade to cut the stuff, preferably hollow-ground, so as to obtain a clean, smooth surface, free of unsightly splinters.

When guiding the box along the blade, hold it by the front and rear upper corners, not by the sides. If you hold it

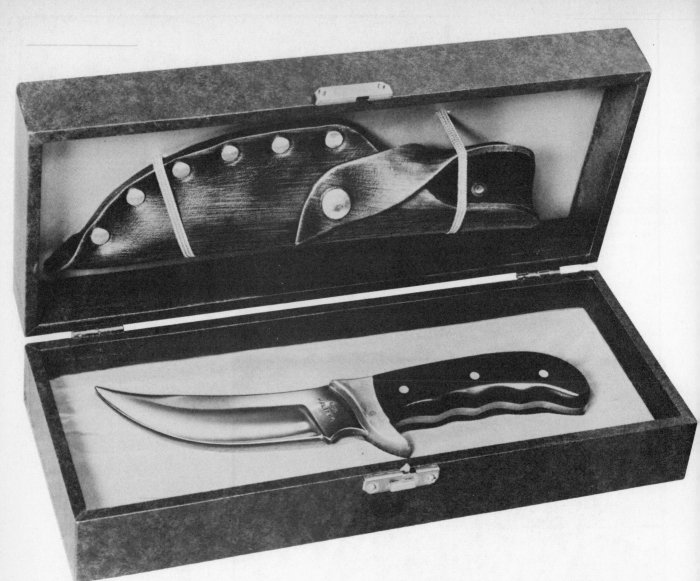

Another storage/display case supplied by Buck Knives for their Kalinga knife, with elastics to hold the sheath.

by the sides — particularly when making the final cut — you will force the pieces against the blade after the cut is completed and bite an unsightly gap out of the lower rear corner. If you make any of the mentioned mistakes, you will have to go back and start again. You don't need that extra frustration.

By this time, you should have a completed box, separated into a top and bottom. It remains to dress down the cut edges with sandpaper. Here is a useful trick of the cabinet-maker's trade: Take a standard sheet of sandpaper and fold it into thirds on the shorter dimension. This gives you a folded strip, one-third the size of the standard sheet, with

abrasive on the outer and inner surfaces. That simplifies hand-sanding to a remarkable extent, as it gives your finger-tips a lot more purchase than the usual slippery upper side of the sandpaper sheet.

With that done, we need to attach the hardware: hinges at the rear and snap catches at the front, perhaps a carrying handle, if you wish. Your local hardware store should have an assortment of such items on display, or they can be had from several specialty suppliers.

Alternatively, you may wish to apply the outer finish to the box, before attaching the hardware, as it complicates the finishing if the hardware is in place. In fact, you have

This padded storage/display case was furnished with a knife commemorating the sesquicentennial of the Texas Rangers, from 1823 to 1973, with Lone Star plaque.

the option of doing the bulk of the outside finishing before separating the upper and lower portions of the box. There are several attractive advantages to that approach.

In the area of wood-finishing, there are many interlocking factors to influence your final selection. If the wood is altogether gorgeous in color and grain, it remains but to apply some manner of protective coating to keep it from picking up unsightly stains from casual handling. If the surface is rather porous, even after sanding it down with the finest grits, you may wish to apply fillers to seal the pores. If the color does not please you to the proverbial sixteen decimals, you can improve it by staining.

We have used food coloring — sometimes diluted and other times swabbed on uncut — and we have brewed up stains by dissolving artist's oil pigments in lighter fluid or similar solvents. Avoid turpentine for the latter purpose, as it takes a long time in a warm environment for the smell to go away. Water-based stains will require further sandings to remove the roughness they raise.

Once the wooden surface has been brought into line with your personal taste, you may become rather partial to spray can Varathane, because of its convenience and long-term durability. They use the stuff to surface bowling alleys, which ought to provide credentials as to its suit-

With an integral insert of glass or transparent plastic in the cover, this padded display box holds knives securely.

ability. Apply it in thin coats, allowing ample time for the coat to set up and don't stint on the number of coats. It's available in both satin and gloss surfaces and feel free to take your choice.

After each coat sets up, it needs to be rubbed down lightly before applying the next one. The finer grades of wet-or-dry paper, such as 400- or 600-grit, can be used, initially. After the pores are fairly well filled, we like to shift over to a technique Dean Grennell stumbled upon, which he thinks of as solvent-polishing.

Varathane responds quite well to a latterday solvent usually marketed under the generic designation of *carbo-chlor* (1, 1, 1, trichloroethane); labeled as a replacement for carbon tetrachloride. In its day, good ol' "carbon-tet" was in wide use as a cleaning agent, but inhalation of its

fumes could really louse up your personal chemistry. It took a while before authorities became aware of that. As a result, carbo-chlor can be found in the paint departments of the better hardware stores but, even so, it is by no means innocuous. Use it with generous ventilation and avoid unnecessary skin contact.

With the most recent spray coating of Varathane set up nice and hard, clamp down the workpiece and apply a *small* amount of carbo-chlor to a folded swatch of paper towel or, better yet, to a small scrap of lintless cloth. Rub the moistened swab *lightly* but briskly over the finished surface. Properly done, that will remove all the inevitable little surface glitches and fair them down into the basic surface, giving you a dead-flat surface for the next spray application.

A custom storage/display box, with felt-padded slots to secure the blades, this unit can be used as a drawer in a custom cabinet.

Do this a number of times, with the skill acquired from practice and you may get the reaction from viewers that Grennell has had, on a few occasions. They will stroke fingertips across the surface, gaze wonderingly and ask, "Is that *plastic?*" Stifle your winces, as best you can manage — it isn't easy — and try to regard it as a tribute to your diabolical skill, which it certainly is.

With your basic box suitably finished, separated and fitted with hardware, there remains the matter of setting up the interior furnishings and that's an area where the builder's choice reigns supreme.

In the present state of the arts, we have a number of foam plastic padding materials readily available. In their own right, they're not all that aesthetically appealing, but they can be used and covered over with colored felts to provide a pleasing ambience.

There is nothing at all to stop you from providing a transparent insert in the cover of your case, so the contents can be viewed with the cover closed. The insert material can be glass or plastic. The plastics, such as *Plexiglas,* can be purchased from commerical outlets in larger cities and they offer interesting possibilities for the craftsman bent upon effective display. Available in an assortment of thicknesses, finishes and colors, the plastics can be cut and joined by means of solvents to provide an interesting assortment of further possiblilites.

MANUFACTURER'S DIRECTORY

KNIFEMAKING SUPPLIES

Anderson Cutlery & Supply Co., Shepard Hill, Box 383, Newtown, CT 06470
Art Jewel Enterprises, Ltd., Eagle Business Center, 460 Randy Rd., Carol Stream, IL 60188
Atlanta Cutlery Corporation, Box 839XW, Conyers, GA 30207
BDL Enterprises, dba Johannsen Industries, Inc., 68-487 E. Palm Canyon Dr., Suite 56, Cathedral City, CA 92234
Burr King Mfg. Co., 1875 Penn Mar Ave., So. El Monte, CA 91733
Belts for Burr King Machines, Tru-Grit, 11231 Thienes Avenue, So. El Monte, CA 91733
Boone Trading Co., Inc., 562 Coyote Rd., Brinnon, WA 98320
E. Christopher Firearms Co., Inc., Rt. #128 & Ferry St., Miamitown, OH 45041
Colorado Ceramic Abrasives, 9988 Fallen Rock Rd., Conifer, CO 80433
Custom Knifemaker's Supply, Bob Schrimsher, P.O. Box 308, Emory, TX 75440
Damascus U.S.A., P.O. Box 220, Howard, CO 81233
Dan's Whetstone Co., Inc., 207 Remington Dr., Hot Springs, AR 71913
Diamond Machining Tech., Inc., 85 Hayes Memorial Dr., Marlborough, MA 01752
Dixie Gun Works, Inc., P.O. Box 130, Union City, TN 38261
Eze-Lap Diamond Products, 15164 Weststate St., P.O. Box 2229, Westminster, CA 92683
Rick B. Fields, 330 No. Durango Ave., Ocoee, FL 32761
Flitz International, Ltd., 821 Mohr Ave., Waterford, WI 53185
Fortune Products, Inc, P.O. Box 1308, Friendswood, TX 77546
Gilmer Wood Co., 2211 N.W. St. Helens Rd., Portland, OR 97210
The Golfworks, the glanz woch, Ralph Maltby Enterprises, Inc., P.O. Box 3008, Newark, OH 43055-7199
Golden Age Arms Co., Box 283, 14 W. Winter St., Delaware, OH 43015
Hawkins Custom Knives & Supplies, P.O. Box 400, Red Oak, GA 30272
Bill R. Holt, 1253-F Birchwood Dr., Sunnyvale, CA 94089
House of Muzzleloading, 1019 East Palmer, P.O. Box 6217, Glendale, CA 91205
Johnson Wood Products, Route 1, Strawberry Point, IA 52076
Stanley A. Jones, 7702 E. Hopi, Mesa, AZ 85208
Knife & Cutlery Products, Inc., P.O. Box 54275, Tulsa, OK 74155
Knife and Gun Finishing Supplies, P.O. Box 13522, 624 E. Abram, Arlington, TX 76013
Knives, Etc., 2314 North Meridian, Oklahoma City, OK 73107
Koval Knives/IRT, P.O. Box 26155, Columbus, OH 43226
Kwik-Sharp, 350 N. Wheeler St., Ft. Gibson, OK 74434
Chris A. Lindsay, 16237 Dyke Rd., La Pine, OR 97739
Log Cabin Sports Shop, Inc., 8010 Lafayette Rd., P.O. Box 275, Lodi, OH 44254
Marks Forge, Rt. 2, Box 879-R, Breaux Bridge, LA 70517
Masecraft Supply Co., P.O. Box 423, 902 Old Colony Rd., Meriden, CT 06450
Daryl Meier, RR 4, Carbondale, IL 62901
Micro-Mesh MX, Micro-Surface Finishing Products, Inc., Box 818, Wilton, IA 52778
Mid-East Mfg., Inc., 2817 Cameron St., Melbourne, FL 32901
Mother of Pearl Co., P.O. Box 445, Franklin, NC 28734
Ozark Knife, 3165 So. Campbell, Suite A2, Springfield, MO 65807
James Poplin/Pop Knives & Supplies, 103 Oak St., Washington, GA 30673
Jim Pugh, P.O. Box 711, 917 Carpenter St., Azle, TX 76020
Purdy's, Inc., 2505 Canterbury Rd., Hays, KS 67601
R&R Sales, P.O. Box 498, Sycamore, IL 60178
Ramco, Box 175, Portage, MI 49081
Sandpaper, of Illinois, 838 Hill Ave., Glen Ellyn, IL 60137
Schep's Forge, Box 83, Chapman, NE 68827
Sheffield's Knifemaker's Supply, P.O. Box 141, Deland, FL 32720
Shining Wave Metals, P.O. Box 563, Snohomish, WA 98290
Smith Whitesmiths, Inc., 1500 Sleepy Valley Rd., Hot Springs, AR 71901
Texas Knifemakers Supply, 10649 Haddington, Suite 190, Houston, TX 77043
Tru-Grit, 11231 Thienes Ave., #A, So. El Monte, CA 91733
R.W. Wilson, P.O. Box 2012, Weirton, WV 26062
A World of Knives, 3376 Kietzke Lane, Reno, NV 89502
Yaun Forge, 31240 Highway 43, Albany, LA 70711

MAIL-ORDER SALES

A&J Enterprises, P.O. Box 1343 S.S.S., Springfield, MO 65805
American Historical Foundation, 1142 West Grace St., Richmond, VA 23220
Atlanta Cutlery, Box 839XW, Conyers, GA 30207
Atlantic Bladesmiths, c/o Peter Stebbins, 8 Hawthorne Village, Concord, MA 01742
Blue Ridge Knives, Rte. 6, Box 185, Marion, VA 24354
Boone Trading Co., Inc., 562 Coyote Rd., Brinnon, WA 98320
Carmel Cutlery, Dolores & 6th; P.O. Box 1346, Carmel, CA 93921
Casanova Guns, Inc., 1601 W. Greenfield Ave., Milwaukee, WI 53204
Catoctin Cutlery, P.O. Box 188, 17 Main St., Smithsburg, MD 21783
Crazy Crow Trading Post, P.O. Box 314, Denison, TX 75020
Creative Sales & Mfg., Box 556, Whitefish, MT 59937
Cutlery Shoppe, 5461 Kendall St., Boise, ID 83706
Ed's Engraving, 121 East Main St., Statesboro, GA 30458
Falcon Supply, 28 Halsey St., P.O. Box 1056, Trumansburg, NY 14886
Frost Cutlery Co., P.O. Box 21353, Chattanooga, TN 37421
International Cutlery Purveyors, P.O. Box 1525, Royal Oak, MI 48068
Ken's Finn Knives, P.O. Box 126, Republic, MI 49879
Doug Kenefik, 29 Leander St., Danielson, CT 06239
Knife & Cutlery Products, Inc., P.O. Box 54275, Tulsa, OK 74155
Knife Importers, Inc., P.O. Box 2122, Austin, TX 78768
Knife World, Inc., (Joe Davis), 5152 So. Broadway, Englewood, CO 80110
Log Cabin Sports Shop Inc., 8010 Lafyette, Lodi, OH 44254
Matthews Co., 4401 Sentry Dr., Tucker, GA 30084
Morty The Knife Man, 60 Otis St., West Babylon, NY 11704
Nordic Knives, 1634CZ Copenhagen Dr., Solvang, CA 93463
Ozark Knife, 3165 S.Campbell, Suite A2, Springfield, MO 65807
Parker Cutlery, 2837 Hickory Valley Road, P.O. Box 22668, Chattanooga, TN 37422
Plaza Cutlery Inc., 333 Bristol, South Coast Plaza, Costa Mesa, CA 92626
R&C Knives and Such, P.O. Box 1047, Mantera, CA 95336
R&R Sales, P.O. Box 498, Sycamore, IL 60178
A.G. Russell Co., 1705 Hiway 471N, Springdale, AR 72764
San Diego Knives, P.O. Box 326, 11280 Posthill Rd., Lakeside, CA 92040
San Francisco Collector Knives, 624 Stanyan St., San Francisco, CA 94117
Shofner's World of Knives, 2104 Prestonwood Ctr., Dallas, TX 75240

Smoky Mountain Knife Works, P.O. Box 4430, Sevierville, TN 37864
Sports Hut, 1311 Bell Ridge Dr., Kingsport, TX 37665
United States Cutlery, P.O. Box 418, Wyckoff, NJ 07481-0418
A World of Knives, 3376 Kietzke Lane, Reno, NV 89502

KNIFE SERVICES: ENGRAVERS

Sam Alfano, Rt. 1, Box 365, Pearl River, LA 70452
Gary Allard, Creek Side, Fishers Hill, VA 22626
Billy Bates, 2905 Lynnwood Circle S.W., Decatur, AL 35603
James P. Bina, P.O. Box 6532, Evanston, IL 60204
Lawrence T. Blakeslee, 1650 El Cerrito Court, San Luis Obispo, CA 93401
Gary Blanchard, 720 Holly Ave., P.O. Box 1123, Burney, CA 96013
C. Roger Bleile, 5040 Ralph Ave., Cincinnati, OH 45238
Benita Bonshire, 1121 Burlington, Munci, IN 47302
Bryan Bridges, 6350 E. Paseo San Andres, Tucson, AZ 85710
Dennis B. Brooker, Rte 1, Box 12A, Derby, IA 50068
Byron Burgess, 710 Bella Vista Dr., Morro Bay, CA 93442
Martin Butler, 162 Metcalfe St. West, Strathroy, Ontario, Canada N0L1W0
Frank Clark, 3714-27th St., Lubbock, TX 79410
Larry R. Cole, HC84, Box 10303, Broadbent, OR 97414
Jim Dashwood, 255 Barkham Road, Wokingham, Berkshire RG114BY, England
Bruce Dean, 13 Tressider Ave., Haberfield, N.S.W. 2045, Australia
Ed DeLorge, 2231 Hwy. 308, Thibodaux, LA 70301
Rod Dilling, 105 N. Ridgewood Dr., Sebring, FL 33870
Mark Drain, S.E. 3211 Kamilche Pt. Rd., Shelton, WA 98584
Rick Eaton, 1847 Walnut Grove Ct., Oakley, CA 94561
Ken Eyster, Heritage Gunsmiths Inc., 6441 Bishop Rd., Centerburg, OH 43011
Terry Flowers, P.O. Box 96, Midland, OR 97634
Fred A. Harrington, 2107 W. Frances Road, Mt. Morris, MI 48458
Fred D. Henderson, 569 Santa Barbara Dr., Forest Park, GA 30050
Benno Heune, 934 Jack London Dr., Santa Rosa, CA 95405
Ralph W. Ingle, #4 Missing Link, Rossville, GA 30741
Bill Johns, 1113 Nightingale, McAllen, TX 78504
Lance Kelly, 1824 Royal Palm Dr., Edgewater, FL 32032
Jim Kelso, RD 1, Box 5300, Worcester, VT 05682
Joe and Patty Kostelnik, RD #4, Box 323, Greensburg, PA 15601
John M. Kudlas, 622-14th St. S.E., Rochester, MN 55901
Ray Lee, 341 Alleghany Ave., Lynchburg, VA 24501
Franz Letsching, 620 Cathcart, Suite 422, Montreal, P.Que., Canada H3B1M1
Harry Limings, Jr., 5030 Patrick Rd., Sunbury, OH 43074
Steve Lindsay, RR2 Cedar Hills, Kearney, NE 68847
Simon M. Lytton, 19 Pinewood Gardens, Hemel Hempstead, Herts. HP11TN, England
Robert E. Maki, P.O. Box 947, Northbrook, IL 60065
George Marek, P.O. Box 213, Westfield, MA 01086
Lynton McKenzie, 6940 N. Alvernon Way, Tucson, AZ 85718
Harry E. Mendenhall, 1848 Everglades Dr., Milpitas, CA 95035
David A. Morton, 1110 W. 21st St., Lorain, OH 44052
Mitch Moschetti, P.O. Box 27065, Denver, CO 80227
Old Dominion Hand Engravers, Brett Irby, David Perdue, John Robyn, Lisa Tomlin, 10119 Timberlake Rd., Lynchburg, VA 24502
Scott Pilkington, P.O. Box 125, Dunlap, TN 37327
Jon Poulakis, Rt. 11, Box 260, Pinehaven Dr., Sevierville, TN 37862
Martin Rabeno, Box 37F, RD #1, Ellenville, NY 12428
Andrew Raftis, 2743 N. Sheffield, Chicago, IL 60614
Chris Reed, 4399 Bonny Mede Ct., Jackson, MI 49201
J.J. Roberts, 166 Manassas Dr., Manassas Park, VA 22111
Bob Rosser, 142 Ramsey Dr., Albertville, AL 35950
Lewis B. Sanchez, 11711 Gillette St., Tampa, FL 33617
Bruce Shaw, P.O. Box 545, Pacific Grove, CA 93950
George Sherwood, Box 735, Winchester, OR 97495
Ben Shostle, 1121 Burlington, Muncie, IN 47302
W.P. Sinclair, 46 Westbury Road, Edington, Wiltsh. BA134PG, England
R.E. Skaggs, P.O. Box 34, 114 Miles Court, Princeton, IL 61356
Ron Smith, 3601 West 7th St., Ft. Worth, TX 76107
Robert D. Swartley, 2800 Pine St., Napa, CA 94558
Terry Theis, P.O. Box 252, Harper, TX 78631
Robert Valade, 931 - 3rd Ave., Seaside, OR 97138
George A. Walker, Star Route, Alpine, WY 83128
Patricia Walker, P.O. Box 2343, Taos, NM 87571
Terry Wallace, 385 San Marino, Vallejo, CA 94589
Kenneth Warren, c/o Mountain States Engraving, 8333 E. San Sebastian Dr., Scottsdale, AZ 85258
Claus Willig, Siedlerweg 17, 8720 Schweinfurt, West Germany
Mel Wood, P.O. Box 1255, Sierra Vista, AZ 85636

KNIFE SERVICES: SCRIMSHANDERS

John Alward, 879 Watkins Road, Allen, MI 49227
Terry Jack Anderson, 430 E. 1st North, Richfield, UT 84701
Duane Baker, 1656 Vilardo Lane, Columbus, OH 43227
C.M. Barringer, 244 Lakeview Terr., Palm Harbor, FL 33563
Miles Barrows, 524 Parsons Ave., Chilcothe, OH 45601
Connie Bellet, P.O. Box 111, Ringling, MT 59642
Benita Bonshire, 1121 Burlington, Muncie, IN 47302
Boone Trading Co., Inc., 562 Coyote Rd., Brinnon, WA 98320
Judy Bouchard, 1808 W. Pleasant Ridge Rd., Hammond, LA 70403
Sandra Brady, 9608 Monclova Rd., P.O. Box 104, Monclova, OH 43542
Bob Burdette, 4908 Maplewood Dr., Greenville, SC 29615
Mary Gregg Byrne, P.O. Box 2394, Bellingham, WA 98227
Jerry Cable, 332 Main St., Mt. Pleasant, PA 15666
Lynda Capocci-Christman, RR 4, Box 289A, Wabash, IN 46992
Lyle Caudill, 720 W. Walnut St., Felicity, OH 45120
Michael Collins, Rte. 4, Batesville Rd., Woodstock, GA 30188
Raymond A. Cover, Jr., Rt. 1, Box 194, Mineral Point, MO 63660
Barbara Cricchio, P.O. Box 656, Ringwood, NJ 07456
Jean E. Curtis, 2809 Midwood, Lansing, MI 48910
Guy M. Dahl, Box 308, Horsefly, BC, Canada V0L1L0
Mary E. Davidson, 2419-25th St., Lubbock, TX 79411
Jean E. DeSavage, 9168 Redwood, Fontana, CA 92335
Richard DiMarzo, 2357 Center Place, Birmingham, AL 35205
Kyle Duncan, 2034 Sidney, St. Louis, MO 63104
Joni Elbourn, P.O. Box 404, Hudson P.O., Hudson, Que. Canada J0P1H0
Bob Engnath, 1217 Apt. B Crescent Dr., Glendale, CA 91205
Rick M. Evans, 2717 Arrowhead Dr., Abilene, TX 79606
Rick B. Fields, 330 No. Durango Ave., Ocoee, FL 32761
B.J. Fischer, P.O. Box 310, Nixon, TX 78140
Dale Fisk, Box 252, Council, ID 83612

W.C. Frazier, 1029 Kavanaugh St., Mansfield, LA 71052
Gigi, P.O. Box 624, Clovis, CA 93613
Vicki and Darrel W. Goff, 5725 New Holme, Baltimore, MD 21206
Jim Gullette, Rte. 8, Box 265, Greer, SC 29651
Charles Hargraves, Sr., 1839 Kingston Rd., Scarborough, Ont., Canada M1N1T3
Star Harless, P.O. Box 5913, Lake Worth, FL 33466-5913
Stan Hawkins, 2230 El Capitan, Arcadia, CA 91006
Bob Hergert, 12120 S.W. 9th, Beaverton, OR 97005
Tom High, 5474 S. 112.8 Rd., Alamosa, CO 81101
David R. Himmelheber, 6841 Southern Blvd., West Palm Beach, FL 33413
Dennis K. Holland, 4908-17th Place, Lubbock, TX 79416
Harvey Hoover, 1263 Nunneley Rd., Paradise, CA 95969
Howard L. Imboden, II, 4216 Barth Lane, Kettering, OH 45429
Alan Jiranek, 9065 Van Emmon Rd., Yorkville, IL 60560
Linda K. Karst, P.O. Box 171, Coppell, TX 75019
Susan B. Kirk, 1019 Poseyville Rd. Midland, MI 58640
John W. Land, P.O. Box 917, Wadesboro, NC 28170
Erik Lovestrand, 325 Rolfe Dr., Apopka, FL 32703
Larry E. McCullough, Rte. 4, Box 556, Mocksville, NC 27028
Berni McFadden, 2524 N. 16th., Coeur d'Alene, ID 83814
Frank McGowan, 12629 Howard Lodge Dr., Sykesville, MD 21784
Gayle McGrath, 904 S.E. 24th Ave., Cape Coral, FL 33904
Lou McLaran, 603 Powers St., Waco, TX 76705
Carole McWilliams, 4334 C.R. 509, Bayfield, CO 81122
Anita Miller, 450 S. 1st., Seward, NE 68434
Petria Mitchell, R.D. 1, Box 244, Brattleboro, VT 05301
Mary Mueller, 3124 W. 64th, Anchorage, AK 99502
Michelle Ochonicky, 4059 Toenges Ave., St. Louis, MO 63116
Belle Ochs, 124 Emerald Lane, Largo, FL 34641
Vaughn Parish, 103 Cross St., Monaca, PA 15061
Larry H. Peck, 14 Patricia Lane, Hannibal, MO 63401
Lou Peterson, 514 S. Jackson St., Gardner. IL 60424
Linda A. Petree, Rte. 14, Box 2364A, Kennewick, WA 99337
Trena Polk, 3526 Eller St. Fort Smith, AR 72904
Bob Purdy, 2505 Canterbury Rd., Hays, KS 67601
Nancy Quinn, P.O. Box 692, Julian, CA 92036
Charles V. Rece, Wildwood Studios, P.O. Box 1465, Albemarle, NC 28002
Joe Rundell, 6198 Frances Rd., Clio, MI 48420
Robert Satre, 518-3rd Ave., N.W. Weyburn, Sask Canada S4H1R1
Robert Schaber, 3710 No. Palm, Sebastian, FL 32958
Patricia Schwallie, 217 Parliament Rd., Greenville, SC 29615
Lura Schwarz, 8033 Sunset Blvd., Suite 233, Hollywood, CA 90046
Peggy Smith, Rt. 1, Box 119A Glades Rd., Gatlinburg, TN 37738
John Stahl, 2049 Windsor Rd., Baldwin, NY 11510
Harry L. Stalter, 2509 Trivoli Rd., Trivoli, IL 61569
Mary Austin Talley, 2499 Countrywood Parkway, Cordova, TN 38018
Larry Thompson, 23040 Ave. 197, Strathmore, CA 93267
Gerald Tisdale, 6 Aurora St., Laredo, TX 78041
Gil Velasquez, 7120 Madera Dr., Goleta, CA 93117
Karen Walker, Star Route, Alpine, WY 83128
Gary Williams, 221 Autumn Way, Elizabethtown, KY 42701
Becky Wilson, 8080 Greenwood Ct., Denver, CO 80221
Mary Young, 4826 Storeyland Dr., Alton, IL 62002
Russell Zima, 4725 Raleigh St., Denver, CO 80212

KNIFE SERVICES: HEAT TREATERS

Jim Barbee, P.O. Box 1090, Sabinal, TX 78881
Bay State Metal Treating Co., 6 Jefferson Ave., Woburn, MA 01801
Paul Bos, 1900 Weld Blvd., El Cajon, CA 92020
Richard Bridwell, 801 Miford Ch. Rd., Taylors, SC 29687
John E. Chase, 217 Walnut, P.O. Drawer H, Aledo, TX 76008
El Monte Steel, 355 S.E. End Ave., Pomona, CA 91766
Hauni Richmond Inc., 2800 Charles City Rd., Richmond, VA 23231
Bill R. Holt, 1253-F Birchwood Dr., Sunnyvale, CA 94089
Metal Treating, Inc., 710 Burns St., Cincinnati, OH 45204
Texas Knifemakers Supply, 10649 Haddington, Suite 190, Houston, TX 77043
The Tinker Shop, 1120 Helen, Deer Park, TX 77536
R.W. Wilson, P.O. Box 2012, Weirton, WV 26062

KNIFE SERVICES: MISCELLANEOUS

Etching
Aurum Etchings, 601 E. Walnut Circle, Garland, TX 75040
Baron Technology, Inc., 62 Spring Hill Rd., Trumbull, CT 06611
Fountain Products, 492 Prospect Ave., West Springfield, MA 01089
Leonard Leibowitz, 1202 Palto Alto St., Pittsburg, PA 15212
Shaw-Cullen, Inc., 212 East 47th St., New York, NY 10017
Custom Handle Artisans
James M. Cooper, 2148 Cook Place, Ramona, CA 92065
Richard Di Marzo, 2357 Center Pl. So., Birmingham, AL 35205
Ed Harrison, 10125 Palestine, Houston, TX 77029
Russell S. Hill, 2384 Second Ave., Grand Island, NY 14072
Jim Kelso, Rt. 1, Box 5300, Worcester, VT 05682
Mel Kemp, c/o Scottsdale Casting Inc., 3949 N. Buckboard Trail, Scottsdale, AZ 85251
Pete and Alice Semich, Rt. 4, Box 502, Murfreesboro, TN 37130
Glenn L. Smith, 1037 Custer Ave., Billings, MT 59102
Gary Vann Ausdle, R.R. 1, Box 50, Wingina, VA 24599
Other
Bill's Custom Cases, Wm. C. Mittelman, P.O. Box 555, Boyes Hot Springs, CA 95416 (knife cases)
Nelson Gimbert, P.O. Box 787, Clemmons, NC 27012 (custom display cases)
The Long Island Sutlers, 2836 Grand Ave., Bellmore, NY 11710 (display boxes)
Charles R. (Dick) McDonald, 1918 Leavenworth, Manhattan, KS 66502 (custom made display cases)
Frances Oliver, 3832 W. Desert Park Lane, Phoenix, AZ 85021 (pouches for folding knives)
Custom Grinders
R&S Sharpening School, Inc., 604 Phyllis Ct., Conroe, TX 77303 (knifemaking, sharpening, correspondence courses)
Bob Engnath, 1217 Crescent Dr. Apt. B, Glendale, CA 91205
Kelgin Knives, Ken Largin, 110 W. Pearl, Batesville, IN 47006
Knife Appraisers
Chas. Clements, 1741 Dallas St., Aurora, CO 80010
Bernard Levine, P.O. Box 2404, Eugene, OR 97402
A.G. Russell, 1705 Hwy. 471 N., Springdale, AR 72764